11:

MAKING BASEBALL HISTORY

Jim Crosby

Copyright © 2021 Jim Crosby
ISBN: 978-1-0880-0476-0
Library of Congress Control Number: 2021923366
Published in the United States of America

All rights reserved as permitted under the U. S. Copyright Act of 1976. No part of this publication may be reproduced, distributed, or transmitted in any form or by any means, or stored in a database or retrieval system, without the expressed written permission of the author and publisher.

Cover Photo by FSU Sports Information

DEDICATION

11: *Making Baseball History* is dedicated to all the loyal Seminole baseball fans who have supported Florida State and Mike Martin through the years. You were always there through the rain and lightning delays, cold weather, and sweltering heat. You hung with the team while experiencing all of the exhilarating wins and depressing defeats. It takes everyone—fans, batgirls, and grounds crew included—to make FSU baseball games a unique experience.

Special thanks are extended to the Animals of Section B, the ultimate, creative cheering section who can always be counted on to be there, be loud, and be supportive. Their presence transforms Seminole baseball into an entertaining, one-of-a-kind place befitting college baseball's most elite program.

N-O-L-E-S! Noles!

ACKNOWLEDGMENTS

40 years is a long time. That's how long I have known and been privileged to call Mike Martin my friend. Obviously, 11, as he is universally called, is the first person who is owed major thanks in acknowledging those who helped this story get written. He lived it, and his faith, family, and achievements inspired every page of 11: Making Baseball History.

My wife, the Lovely Susette, is the rock that kept this story rolling with her love and her commonsense observations and editorial suggestions.

The Florida State Sports information department is, without a doubt, the best in all of the college sports; just ask any media person who has worked with them. They have provided endless information that translated into putting this story together.

Charlie Ward is owed my unfailing gratitude for supporting this project and providing the foreword. His popularity in Seminole Territory is immense, and when he endorses something, it is golden.

Tim Taylor of Burkart Books has been a Godsend. He is ultimately responsible for the way this book looks and reads. Hardworking, technically knowledgeable, and always available, Tim made publishing this book a pleasure.

Those are some of the major players who helped make this book a reality. There are many more who had a role in this story getting told. For these, please look inside the back of the book under "Unsung Heroes."

PREFACE

How many people are known by their number? You know you have it made when they don't even have to say your first name. Just say "11" and everybody knows who it is.

-Rod Meadows-
VP, Sales & Marketing
Minor League Baseball

A MESSAGE FROM 11

On my first day on the job as FSU baseball's head coach, I was a guest on Jim Crosby's sportscast on WECATV (now WTXL), the local ABC affiliate. Since then, we have shared many exciting times and innumerable conversations about baseball, the sport we both love. In 11: Making Baseball History, he has captured the true essence of how Seminole Baseball transcends wins and losses and speaks to victories in daily life as well.

Mike Martin, #11

CONTENTS

Dedication
Acknowledgments

Preface	7
A Message from 11	9
Foreword by Charlie Ward	17
The Lineup	19
Pre-Game	19
On-Deck Circle	21
1980: The Martin Era Begins	23
Play Ball: A Magical Beginning	23
The Stars Speak	25
Craig Patterson (1978-79)	25
Mike Fuentes (1978-81)	28
Don Deloach (1978-81)	29
Building an Elite Program	31
Danny Litwhiler (1955-63)	31
Fred Hatfield (1964-68)	32
Jack Stallings (1969-74)	32
Then Along Came Woody	33
Woody Woodward (1975-78)	33
The Short Memorable Reign of Dick Howser	34
Dick Howser (1979)	34
A Man of Faith	35
Becoming 11	37
Describing 11	38
Collecting Martinisms	39
Martinism #1	40
The Animals of Section B	41
Always A Seminole Fan	43
Martinism #2	44
The Big Shooter Arrives	44
Chip Baker (1985-present)	44
Prime Time Plays Baseball	45
Deion Sanders (1986-1988 BB) (1985-88 FB)	45
Setting the Record	48
Martin Gets 500th Win in Less than a Decade	48

Martinism #3	49
The Stars Speak	49
J. D. Drew (1995-97)	49
Buster Posey (2006-08)	52
Adding Meat to the Menu	54
Mike Martin Jr.	54
#1000 Comes … Finally	56
Martinism #4	57
The Stars Speak	57
MattE Diaz (1998-99)	57
Mike Loynd (1983-86)	59
Mike Loynd Tradition Room	62
2008: Winning #1,500	63
2008: A Very Good Year for #1,500	63
Martinism #5	64
The Stars Speak	64
Luis Alicea (1984-86)	64
Barry Blackwell (1985-88)	66
2018: A Good Year for Record-Setting	68
Season Opener—2018	68
Martinism #6	71
Chris Chavez (1995-98)	71
Zach Diaz (1996-99)	73
Bulletin: February 21, 2018	75
Martinism #7	76
Bulletin from Florida State Baseball	77
Relentless Pursuit of the Record	78
76 Days Later …	78
A Historic Evening—Win # 1,976	78
Clemson—Tough Place to Set a Record	78
Martinism #8	81
The Stars Speak	81
Jonathan Johnson (1993-95)	81
The Stars Speak	83
Jeff Ledbetter (1979-82)	83
The Last Roundup:	86
2,000 Wins & Beyond	86
The Decision	86
The Final Team	87

2019 Florida State Seminoles	88
The Roster	88
The Record-Setting Staff-2019	89
Martinism #9	90
Getting Started	90
Lots of Baseball, Lots of Fans	92
Martinism #10	94
There Were Some Losses Too	94
The Stars Speak	94
Jose Zabala (1995-98)	96
Youngstown State Penguins	98
Martin Named ACC Player of the Week	100
Martin Marches On	101
Mercer Pays a Visit	101
Next up: North Florida on Wednesday, March 6	103
History-Making Weekend	104
The Historic Weekend	104
Mike Martin Was One Win Away from 2,000	105
Let the Celebration Begin!	106
The Stars Speak	107
A Game for the Ages	109
How Would they Rebound from This? Or Would They?	111
Martinism #11	120
11 Talks About the Importance of Goal Setting	120
The Stars Speak	120
Ricky Kimball (1988-91)	120
John-Ford Griffin (1999-01)	122
The Griffin Family Clubhouse	125
Jeremy Salazar (1995-98)	125
Brooks Badeaux (1995-98)	127
The Mad Hatters Return	136
Wake: Another ACC Weekend	137
Mike Martin Chalked Up His 2015th Win.	139
Photo Gallery	141
Martinism #12	163
11 Talks about People:	163
The Stars Speak	163
Randy Choate (1995-96)	163
Paul Sorrento (1984-86)	165
The Bell Rings Again	167
Mendoza Named ACC Player of the Week	170
Playing Two with the Dolphins	170
Road Game with the Hatters	171

Back Home to Close the Season	172
A Night with 11 and His Friends, May 11, 2019	174
A Celebration and Roast	174
Buster Posey's Video Message to Mike Martin	175
May 11, 2019, at "An Evening with 11 and Friends"	175
The Stars Speak	176
The Last .400 Hitter	176
Tyler Holt(2008-10)	176
Link Jarrett (1991-94)	178
Martinism #13	180
11 Talks About Decisions in Life hat People Must Make	180
Closing on the Road	181
The Stars Speak	182
James Ramsey (2009-12)	182
Craig Ramsey (1978-81)	184
Martinism #14	187
11 Told a Sales Group	187
The Stars Speak	187
Blair Varnes (1999-2002)	187
Jody Reed (1983-84)	189
ACC Tournament	191
The Stars Speak	192
Ryan Barthelemy (1999-2002)	192
Frank Fazzini (1983-85)	194
Martinism #15	196
NCAA Tournament	196
The Stars Speak	200
Paul Wilson (1992-94)	200
Richie Lewis (1985-87)	202
Super Regional	203
The Stars Speak	206
Doug Mientkiewicz (1993-95)	206
Kevin Cash (1997-99)	208
Martinism #16	211
Seen in Omaha	211
Game Two-College World Series	213
Game Three-College World Series	214
11's Final Post Game	215
Martinism #17	216
11's Challenge to Us All	216
The Stars Speak	216
Eduardo Perez (1989-91)	216
Copy of The Letter to Mike Martin from National Hall of Fame	218

Eduardo Perez Essay on Coach Mike Martin	219
Pedro Grifol (1989-91)	219
The Day After	221
A Sterling Finish	221
The Stars Speak	222
Tim Davis (1991-92)	222
Stephen Drew (2002-04)	223
The National Championship	225
Eduardo Perez (1989-91, 13 years in MLB)	225
Mike Bianchi (Orlando Sentinel) on Not Winning the CWS	225
Florida State President John Thrasher	226
Blair Varnes (1999-2002):	226
Doug Mientkiewicz (1993-95, 12 yrs. MLB, Olympics Gold Medal	226
Andy Lopez, Florida Coach (1995-2001)	226
Ricky Kimball (1988-1991)	227
Paul Mainieri LSU Coach (2007-20)	227
Walking Off a Winner	228
Regional Walk-offs	229
College World Series Walk-off Wins	229
Martin's Final 2 seasons: Walk-Off Bonanza	230
The Cast of Characters	233
All in the Family	245
Seminole Football Players who played Baseball	245
Heisman Trophy Winner Plays Baseball	247
Jameis Winston (2012-14)	247
Assistant Coaches Under Mike Martin	249
The Coaches	250
Dave Fannin Coach (1981-83)	250
Mike McLeod (1982-90)	251
Randy Gailey (1982-84)	252
Rod Delmonico (1984-89, 2008)	253
Steve Winterling (1986-91)	253
Jamey Shouppe (1990-2011)	254
The Palm Ball Artist	255
Clyde Keller (1988-89)	255
Mike Bell (2012-18)	256
Jack Niles (1993-97)	257
Martinism #18	258
11's Winning Philosophy	258
CJ Van Eyk (2018-2020)	258
The Stars Speak	259
John Bentley (1997-2001)	259
Scooby Morgan (1993-96)	261
Martinism #19	264

Major League Success Story	265
The Stars Speak	266
Bryan Henry (2005-07)	266
Charlie Cruz (1992-95)	268
From the Field to the Press Box	269
Rod Meadows (Radio-1980-89)	269
Lee Bowen (1990-2004)	270
The Lee Bowen Radio Booth	272
Jim Crosby (1981-2004)	273
Steve Melewski (2005-06)	273
Eric Luallen (2007-2021)	274
FSU Baseball on Television	276
Tom Block (1995-2021)	276
Gene Deckerhoff (1979-2021)	276
A Final Martinism #20	278
Next Up for the Noles	279
Mike Martin Immortalized	281
Mike Martin Inducted into College Baseball Hall of Fame	283
Unsung Heroes	284
Abbreviations	290
Sources	291
About the Author	

FOREWORD

Growing up in a sports-loving family, I can appreciate what it takes to excel in athletics.

My Dad, Charlie Sr., was a talented football player at Florida A&M under legendary coach Jake Gaither. My grandparents were exceptional athletes, too. Both of my grandfathers excelled in baseball, and my grandmother was a terrific tennis player. Going way back, my great-grandmother was a good basketball player. Playing sports came naturally to me.

My hometown of Thomasville, GA, was a sports haven so to speak. As a kid, I played football, basketball, and baseball. I enjoyed and did well in all three sports and wanted to play them for as long as I could.

I was recruited to play football at Florida State under Coach Bobby Bowden, with the promise that I could also play basketball. Playing those two sports full time, and staying on top of my academics, left no time to continue playing baseball, even though I was drafted by the Milwaukee Brewers in 1993 and the New York Yankees in 1994.

In my family, our faith was very important. Playing under a Christian coach like Bobby Bowden was a factor in my choosing to attend Florida State University. I knew that I could depend on him to honor any promise he made. When he promised that I could play basketball, too, even though I would be on a football scholarship, that sealed the deal.

While at Florida State and over the years since, I have been able to observe what was happening in Florida State baseball as well. What was happening in baseball was Mike Martin, known by fans and players as 11, a coach who was also grounded in the faith.

The way Martin shaped FSU baseball into an elite program was in direct proportion to hard work and a faith-based approach. In the book: 11: Making Baseball History, author Jim Crosby, who has covered Seminole Sports for 40-plus years, captured the highs and lows of 11's historic career. Martin followed two Major Leaguers, Woody Woodward and Dick Howser, as FSU's head coach and took Seminole Baseball to unmatched heights of greatness. When his 40-year coaching career ended, he had won more games than any college coach in any sport ever had. He did it the right way and has made all of us Seminoles proud of his accomplishments.

11: Making Baseball History is not only a book about the fun and excitement of baseball, but it shows us how a principled approach to life and work excels even beyond wins and losses on the playing field.

Charlie Ward
Heisman Trophy, 1993

THE LINEUP

PRE-GAME

Mike Martin was born on February 12th—Abraham Lincoln's birthday. And like the man who rose to the highest position in America, President of the United States, Martin also reached the top of his profession—Baseball.

Referred to by his players, coaches, and fans simply as "11", the number Martin wore on his garnet-and-gold Seminole uniform for 40 years as the head baseball coach, he now stands alone atop the record books. This is the story of the history-making career of a colorful, highly competitive coach who strives as hard to beat you in a game of horseshoes or a round of golf as he would to win a baseball game for the Seminoles.

Those who have been around 11 for any length of time have learned not to tell him he can't do something, or he darn sure will. This dates to his boyhood when his dad told him to forget about baseball. He said that in the long run, it was just a game, and Mike would never amount to anything sticking to it. In 2019, as Martin began the 40th season of a historic career, he said: "I'm still trying to prove him wrong."

11: Making Baseball History follows this legendary coach through his 40th and final season (2019) as he leaves his indelible imprint on the game of college baseball. The author, Jim Crosby, in his 45th year of covering Seminole baseball, also delves into Martin's past achievements revealing how he led his Seminole teams to unmatched heights in the NCAA record books—a story that was 40 years in the making.

Jim Crosby

ON-DECK CIRCLE

Mike Martin's baseball career had its beginning at Wingate Junior College, some 30 miles east of his hometown of Charlotte, NC. The lanky 6-0, 180 lb. center-fielder drew attention to his talents by making the All-Conference team in 1963 and '64 and adding National Junior College All-American honors in 1964.

Martin came to Florida State for his junior and senior seasons to play for former Major Leaguer Fred Hatfield. Nicknamed "scrap iron" for his willingness to "take one for the team," Hatfield led the majors in being hit by the pitch in four different seasons and played for five different teams. Hatfield brought that "scrap-iron-mentality" into his coaching, and the hyper-competitive Martin fit right in.

A rangy long-striding center-fielder with good baseball instincts, Martin got to a lot of fly balls that had base hit written all over them. He was leading the team in hitting with a .325 average, and having an All-American type of season when playing the scrap-iron role backfired.

On April 26th, 1965, in a tight game at Clemson, Martin "took-one-for-the-team" a fastball on his left arm in the eighth inning. He shook it off and trotted down to first base. When the next batter, RF Tom Thomas, hit a ground ball Martin was out, sliding into second for the third out.

When they threw him his glove, and he got ready to go to center-field for the bottom of the ninth, he couldn't get his glove on because of the swelling and the pain. In fact, he wouldn't put that glove back on for about six months due to a broken arm. Fifty-four years later, on May 5th, 2018, at this same place, Clemson SC, Mike Martin would be involved in another historic game as he set the record for the most games won by a head coach in college baseball.

The injury also cost him to miss the first Major League Draft of amateur players held in 1965, and he returned to Florida State for his senior season. Reflecting back on that situation in a 2018 interview with Unconquered Magazine, 11 said: "I honestly feel that God had other plans for me. Because had I gone professional (at that time), who knows what would have happened."

When Martin came in as a junior in 1965, the Seminole Media guide showed two names under the "Noles in the Pros" listing: Dick Howser with the Cleveland Indians and Woody Woodward with the Milwaukee Braves. Both of these men would play a key role in Mike Martin's future in Seminole Territory.

1980: THE MARTIN ERA BEGINS

PLAY BALL: A MAGICAL BEGINNING

February 24, 1980—There's magic in the air in New York.
Lake Placid, NY (AP)—The United States hockey team won its first Olympic hockey gold medal since 1960, scoring three third period goals to beat Finland, 4-2, and complete a storybook journey into the hearts of the nation.

The Soviet Union team that the United States had dramatically defeated on Friday evening in the match called the "Miracle on Ice"—viewed on TV by 34.2 million people—settled for the Silver medal by defeating Sweden.

February 24, 1980—There's magic in the air in Miami.
FSU rally Clips UM in 9th
by Henry Seiden, Knight-Ridder news service.

Miami—It was a familiar scene Yastrzemski hitting a ninth-inning home run to win the game. Only Sunday, the homer was by Mike Yastrzemski, a freshman right fielder for Florida State. His three-run blast gave the Seminoles a 9-8 victory over the University of Miami. When the ball streaked over the right-field fence at Mark Light Stadium, Mike's father Carl stood up from his right field bleacher seat, put his arms over his head, and cheered.

Nine years later, Carl Yastrzemski was inducted into the Major League Hall of Fame after a career with the Red Sox in which he hit 452 homers. Mike Yastrzemski would go on to play in 294 games for Florida State and was drafted by Texas. Sadly, he passed away at the age of 43.

After replacing Dick Howser, who became the Yankees new skipper, Mike Martin got off to a rocky start by losing his first two games in Coral Gables, a place that would witness some titanic battles over the next 40 years.

On Friday evening, the Noles were shutout 10-0. Saturday's game was tighter as FSU lost a 4-3 pitcher's battle.

On Sunday, Miami was looking for a sweep and jumped out to an 8-2 lead through six innings. But in the top of the 7th, UM Coach Ron Fraser, who had played baseball at Florida State, took starting pitcher Jeff Morrison out. Fraser later explained that Morrison had a sore arm. He replaced him with freshman Danny Smith.

Smith retired the first two batters but then lost his control and walked the bases loaded. Seminole SS Don Deloach then walked, and the Miami lead was 8-3. Fraser replaced Smith with another freshman George Reyes who walked FSU pinch hitter Dick Wiggins to make the score 8-4 before retiring the side.

In the 8th Reyes walked pitcher John Gagnon. Mike Yastrzemski singled, and catcher Craig Ramsey walked. Fraser replaced Reyes with Senior Gary Rose, who promptly walked Roy Alvarez and George Tebbetts, bringing in two more runs and cutting the Canes lead to 8 to 6. Having seen enough of that, Coach Fraser went to the bullpen for his ace even though Heaton had pitched just two days ago in the Friday night win. Heaton retired the side.

Then came the fateful ninth, which would be one for the record books and a lasting memory for Seminole baseball fans. With Heaton still blazing fastballs in and trying to close out a sweep for Miami, Center fielder Mike Fuentes walked. Then left fielder Jeff Ledbetter (holder of the current HR record at Florida State) doubled. Those two would become a history-making one-two punch for the Seminoles. The stage was set for the dramatic finish. Freshman right-fielder Mike Yastrzemski came to the plate. As his 3-run-game-winning blast sailed out of the park and into the tropical South Florida sunshine, history was being made. It was Mike Martin's first win as Seminole Head Coach. It set the stage for a career that would not end until he became the all-time winningest coach in college baseball.

After the game, Carl Yastrzemski, The Red Sox Hall of Fame player, said: "There is more pressure on me sitting here watching him (son-Mike) play than if I was playing in the World Series or any place."

When questioned the next day about what his Major League Dad said to him after the game, Mike Yastrzemski recalled: "He told me I was playing too deep for right-hand hitters." He explained that his dad was not a guy who would say that he did good because he didn't want it to go to his head. He wanted him to keep working hard and getting better. Mike Yastrzemski would go on to play in 279 games as a Seminole (1980-83), a record that still stands 40 years later (tied by Barry Blackwell (1985-88).

Looking back, Martin recalls how that first win played out. "Being the smart guy, I am I had taken a lot of players out of the game. When we cut their lead to 8-4, I'm fussing at myself, looking at the bench and the players I couldn't use. Then they go get that future Major Leaguer Neal Heaton, who had already beat us on Friday. So, with two men on, Mike Yastrzemski runs into a fastball and lifts it up into the wind and over the fence for a three-run homer that wins the game, 9-8."

That's how Mike Martin got his first of the 2,000 plus wins in a stellar 40-year head-coaching career—a record that is sure to last through the ages.

In that initial season, the 1980 Seminoles finished 51-12, with a winning percentage of .809. The Martin era had begun, and his teams would win 50 plus games a season for the next 12 years, and 40 plus wins every year. The magical journey was off to a rousing start.

The Stars Speak

CRAIG PATTERSON (1978-79)
Played for all 3 FSU Hall of Fame Coaches

- LaGrange Park, Illinois
- Pensacola JC
- 123 games; 464 AB; .373 Avg

How a Chicago Boy Played Ball in Florida

Patterson wanted to go where it was warm to play ball. He sent letters to 20 junior colleges in California, Arizona, and Florida. The western schools said he could walk-on, but they didn't give scholarships. But Pensacola JC (now Pensacola State College) offered him a scholarship to play shortstop. Patterson calls that "the biggest break of my life." He had two stellar seasons there.

Seminoles Grab Patterson Away from LSU, Auburn, Florida, & Mississippi State

Patterson recalls: "I always played second base in high school but was recruited by PJC to play shortstop. I really wanted to get back to second base. When I met Coach Martin at the state junior tournament, I remember he had on this powder blue leisure suit. I think he had a light green one and a beige one too, but he said: "We want you to come to Florida State and play second base for us. All those other schools were recruiting me to play shortstop. So that's how I became a Seminole."

Patterson Was One of the Few Players Who Could Claim They Played for Three Hall of Fame Coaches

11 was an assistant under Woody Woodward when he recruited Patterson, and he was also the Head Coach and 3rd baseman of the Federals Summer League team that Patterson played on.

Patterson Remembers When Woodward Left for the Reds

"The Federals were in Lenoir, NC, playing a game, and we learned that Woody would be leaving to become the General Manager of the Cincinnati Reds. We all knew that Coach Martin would love to have the job. So, we actually called President (Bernie) Sliger long-distance and told him we thought Coach Martin would be a great choice for the head coach. He said: 'I totally agree.' But then Howser applied for the job and got it.

One year later, when Dick left to manage the Yankees, and 11 got the job, we were ecstatic."

11: Then and now

"When he was playing 3rd base and was coach of FSU's summer league team, The Federals, 11 was a fiery guy. He was intense. Always ready to get after it. As time went on and you see him in the dugout interviewed on ESPN and others, he was like this grandfatherly guy, more laid back. We all get more laid back as we get older, but when he was playing, he was a fiery, fiery player."

11's long term influence

"He was always a hard worker, so he instilled that in all his players. He would get out there on the field for three hours and give it his all, and he modeled that for the players. So that's what we all did. He kept encouraging us after we left and played pro ball. He encouraged us with whatever we were going to do in our life to give it our all.

Whenever we would come back and play a round of golf, he was always concerned with what we were doing. 'Is everything going well with your family?' He did that with all of us.

He was a great influence." But he didn't give you any strokes in golf.

Patterson Off to a Rocking Start in the Garnet and Gold Uniform

March 3, 1978, was Patterson's first game day as a Seminole. He made the most of it, going 5-for-7 with two RBI. He has a vivid memory of that day: "It was surprising to me. First time up, I hit a triple off the CF wall. It wasn't even a very nice day. Was rainy and muddy. But what a great way to start a career."

So, Craig Patterson was officially a Seminole. Must have been that powder blue leisure suit that nailed him.

What Patterson Liked Most About Playing College Baseball

"My teammates. Most of them are friends for life. I liked just about everything about Tallahassee. Friendly town. Loved the ballpark because I was a right-hand hitter, and I hit the ball the opposite way a lot. The right-field fence was accessible. You walk in, and the infield is perfect. Never had a bad hop. Just a lot of fun."

Summing Up What Playing for 11 Means

"Everybody who played for him or was part of the program is just so proud of him. The winningest coach in baseball history. That's remarkable. It just shows what 11 is all about. He worked hard and was after it all the time. He was so much fun to be around and play for. Just everything is great for him. Everybody takes pride in being able to say they played for him."

In his two seasons at FSU, Craig Patterson was a major contributor to the team's success. Including walks, he came to the plate over 500 times and had an OBP of .441 with only 26 Ks, banging out 173 hits for an AVG of .373 as an All-American player. He still lives in Chicago, where he always wears his Garnet-and-Gold in an area where there are lots of Notre Dame and Michigan fans.

Mike Fuentes (1978-81)

- Coral Gables, FL
- FSU's first Golden Spikes Award winner
- 208 games; .373 Avg.; 64 HR

How Martin Was Able to Impact Players in All Eras

"When 11 got the job, it was like a smooth transition, and the rest is history with Florida State sports. We played in the early '80s, and the kids nowadays are just completely different from those back in the day!

The sign of a quality coach, quality manager, or a quality person is the ability to change with the times. He was able to keep that in mind and to learn from each year and continue to grow with it. He has been able to relate to these kids."

Remembering Martin's First Win

At Miami, we had lost the first two games and fell behind in Martin's 3rd games as head coach. Neal Heaton, one of the top pitchers in the country, came in to close out the game. The pressure was on because we did not want to get swept by Miami in Martin's first series as head coach. I remember the guys got up for it and pulled the game out. Who would have known that 39 years later Mike Martin would still be winning games at Florida State?"

Fuentes only played eight games in 1978 and was expected to be back up CF in 1979, but ...

"So, Florida State was stuck with me to open the season. But, in a season-opening doubleheader vs. Troy State, I hit two home runs in both games, four HRs for the weekend. I don't think I missed a game after that." Fuentes said with a smile.

11 on Fuentes

"I saw him as a guy who could bust the game open with a stolen base, a double, a great catch. Just glided when he ran—a beautiful baseball player."

Teammate Don Deloach on Mike Fuentes

"Mike Fuentes had the best opposite-field power of any batter I've ever seen. He was a right-handed batter, and he could hit the ball to right-center-field a long way."

Mike Fuentes Inducted into the FSU Hall of Fame in 1987

One of the most celebrated walk-ons in Florida State history, Mike Fuentes, went from the humble beginnings of being cut from the Seminole team to winning the Golden Spikes Award in 1981, symbolizing college baseball's best player.

After making the Seminole team in 1978 on his second try, Fuentes went to bat just five times. But before his career was over, he would leave a trail of honors after his name in Florida State record books.

He was twice named the Metro Conference Tournament's MVP, and twice he was named to college baseball's All-America team. The Coral Gables native, nicknamed "Tito" by his teammates, became the fourth Seminole to hit .400 in a season when he hit .408 as a junior while leading Florida State into the 1980 College World Series. He capped a brilliant career with a senior season that included 27 homeruns, 81 RBIs, and a .360 average. During that storybook season, he broke Arizona State Slugger Bob Horner's NCAA career homerun mark, finishing with 64. Fuentes also hit .377 and drove in 182 runs over his four-year career.

One of Florida State's top student-athletes, Fuentes was a second-round draft choice of the Montreal Expos in 1981 (Nolefan.org).

Don Deloach (1978-81)

- Tallahassee, FL, Leon HS
- 221 games; .331 avg; 35 sb
- Homerun vs. Tulane 1981 in Metro Championship

Before Florida State

Don DeLoach was a stellar athlete at Leon High. He played Quarterback before Wally Woodham and Jimmy Jordan, who would later become famous as Bobby Bowden's two-headed QB(s) alternating roles behind center and leading the Seminoles gridiron group to elite status. Additionally, he played QB ahead of Blair Williams, who also became a Seminole QB. DeLoach attracted Seminole baseball as both a pitcher and an infielder.

About DeLoach at Florida State

Donnie Deloach was a dependable everyday player who was the shortstop and other half of the double play combination with Craig Patterson as they both played for the Seminoles under three coaches. DeLoach played a year each under Woody Woodward and Dick Howser, then played his final two seasons under Mike Martin.

In his initial season (1978), DeLoach proved to be a valuable addition as he split time between pitching (8games) and playing a utility role, DH, 2B & 3B in 19 others.

In his second season, he took control of the shortstop position playing in all 61 games. He batted .325 with nine homers, including a grand slam against the Gators.

For his career, Deloach batted over .300 each year and totaled 818 at-bats while recording a .403 on-base percentage and slugging at a .467 clip. Forty years later, he remains 4th on the list of most doubles in a season with 29. Deloach was a fierce competitor. The 1981 media called Deloach "Pigpen" for his diving attempts to catch balls.

How Martin was received as Head Coach:

"All the players at that time were really comfortable with Coach Martin getting the job.

When you are a player, of course, you want the assistant coach to get the job because he knows you."

Lessons DeLoach Learned under Martin that Stayed with Him

"I think the number one thing Coach Martin always taught us was—compete. He always talked about it—even today. You are not going to quit. You got 27 outs, and you are going to give it your all 'til it's over with.".

11: MAKING BASEBALL HISTORY

BUILDING AN ELITE PROGRAM

The first Seminole baseball team set the stage for a winning tradition when they took the field on March 29, 1948, against the visiting Mississippi College Choctaws. The field that they played on was Centennial Field, with 963 fans in attendance.

Tallahassee Democrat Sports Editor Fred Pettijohn described the outcome thusly: "Backed by Howard "Howdy" Calhoun's fancy three-hit flinging that set 19 Mississippi Choctaws down on strikes, Florida State University opened their initial diamond campaign here last night with a 6-0 victory before 963 fans in Centennial Field."

Coached by Charlie Armstrong, the Seminoles finished their 17-game season 9-8. It would be the closest to a losing season ever in the history of the program. In 2019 Florida State started its 71st year of baseball, never having lost more games in a season than they have won.

Along the way, the baseball program attracted lots of attention, especially when they hired former Major League players as head coach.

Danny Litwhiler (1955-63)

1955-1963 (9 years) at FSU. MLB 1940-1951 (12 years) (Braves, Cardinals, Phillies, Reds)

Danny Litwhiler signed on as Seminole head baseball coach on January 21, 1955. FSU Athletic Director Howard Danford introduced Litwhiler just before Danford left for Europe and a U. S. Army assignment as a special instructor at volleyball clinics.

Litwhiler, 33, said: "I am happy to be in Tallahassee. College coaching is something I have always wanted to do. I like to teach, and I hope to do some graduate work here."

During his nine years at the helm of Florida State Baseball, Danny Litwhiler's teams racked up 189 wins against 63 losses. Among his notable players were Dick Howser, Lee Corso and a pitcher by the name of Tony Avitable, who still holds the record for the most strikeouts in a game. On March 16, 1956, he struck out 24 batters in a 1-hit, 6-1 season-opening win over Furman.

Fred Hatfield (1964-68)
1964-1968: (5 years) at FSU. MLB 1950-58 (9 years) (Red Sox, Tigers, White Sox, Indians, Reds)

On December 8, 1963, the Seminoles reached into the Major League ranks again and hired Fred Hatfield to replace Danny Litwhiler, who left to coach Michigan State. A 39-year old Alabama native, Hatfield, was hired by another Alabama native, FSU AD Vaughn Mancha.

Hatfield said: "I realize the great job Danny Litwhiler did at Florida State, and only hope I can fill his shoes. I think Florida State is one of the finest universities in the South, and I'm happy to become a part of such an organization."

In his five years at the helm, Hatfield's FSU teams won 74% of their games, going 161-57-1. They played in the 1965 World Series in Omaha.

Ken Suarez and Jim Lyttle were first-team All-Americans. Although the true significance of it was not noted at the time, Hatfield signed a junior college All-American outfielder by the name of Mike Martin to a scholarship in 1965. Martin was still there in 2019.

Jack Stallings (1969-74)
Coached Wake Forest (his alma mater) from 1959-68, where he was 152-109-2. He signed a pro contract with the Red Sox out of college.

Fred Hatfield said that "pro baseball was still in his blood" when he tendered his resignation to Florida State AD Vaughn Mancha on November 5, 1968. Then on Christmas Eve, 1968, Mancha handed the keys to the Seminoles baseball locker room to Jack Stallings. "I talked with some very capable baseball people, and I think Stallings is a wise choice," he said.

Stallings was a second baseman for Wake Forest, where he roomed with future golfing legend Arnold Palmer. Drafted by the Red Sox, he played minor league ball before returning to his alma mater as head coach (1960-68).

Stallings would coach the Seminoles for five years, winning 248-losing 108 with three ties. It was the general feeling that the baseball fortunes had slipped a little at the end of Stallings regime as they fell under 60% in wins, going 37-25-1 in 1974. That was the most games that an FSU baseball team had ever lost in a season.

After leaving, Stallings would go on to coach for 23 years at Georgia Southern, where he won 859 against 583 losses. His career total of 1,259 wins placed him 28th in all-time wins among Division 1 coaches. His #1 jersey was retired by the program. Jack Stallings passed away in 2018 at the age of 87.

Then Along Came Woody

Woody Woodward (1975-78)
Woody Woodward's MLB career (Braves, Reds & GM of Mariners)

A popular player and coach everywhere he went, Woody Woodward came back home. On August 1, 1974, Woody signed a contract to become the Seminoles 6th head coach and third former Major Leaguer. He played in the Majors for nine seasons with Atlanta and Cincinnati.

Woody said: "I realize that Florida State has had an honorable past under such outstanding coaches as Danny Litwhiler, Fred Hatfield, and Jack Stallings, and I intend to continue that tradition. I'm glad to be back in baseball, especially at the university level."

Woody was an All-American in the two years he played at Florida State. In 76 games, he batted .337, playing in the College World Series in both seasons (1962-63). In the four years that he was head coach, he won 170 games, and with only 57 losses, he established the highest winning percentage of any Seminole coach, at 75 percent, which still stands as a record winning percentage at Florida State. In 1981 he was inducted into the Seminole Hall of Fame.

Woodward retained Mike Martin as assistant coach and four years later would recommend him to be head coach when he left to return to the Reds as assistant general manager.

JIM CROSBY

THE SHORT MEMORABLE REIGN OF DICK HOWSER

Dick Howser (1979)
1979: (1 year) MLB (8 years) Player: A's, Indians, Yankees. (10-years) 3rd base coach Yankees' (8 years) Mgr. Yankees & Royals

When Woody Woodward resigned, on August 15, 1978, to return to the front office of the Cincinnati Reds, he said: "I was hoping something might work out at FSU that would make it a tougher decision. As it was, it was a simple decision. Cincinnati showed me a little brighter future than FSU."

Woodward continued: "I would hope that Mike Martin would be given top consideration. He knows the players; he has headed the summer program for the last four years. I think he would be received well in all areas."

Nevertheless, Dick Howser, another very popular former Seminole player with Major League experience (10 years as NY Yankee third base coach), was hired. Howser was FSU's first All-American, an honor that he won two years in a row. Playing in 83 games, he had an average of .361. In 1977 he was voted into the FSU Hall of Fame. In 2008 he was further honored by being inducted into the National Collegiate Hall of Fame.

He bought the first house he had ever owned here in Tallahassee with hopes that he would have a long and productive career at Florida State. It was not to be.

A very persuasive Yankee owner George Steinbrenner hired him to be the New York manager. It was one-and-done for Dick Howser after 42 wins and 17 losses. His recommendation was Mike Martin. Now Martin was in for the long haul.

11: MAKING BASEBALL HISTORY

A MAN OF FAITH

In a 2009 article I wrote for the Tallahassee Democrat, Mike Martin recalled: "My mother wanted me to be a preacher. The only thing I wanted to do was to play sports. My daddy told me I would never make anything of my life in baseball. I'm still trying to prove him wrong."

After 40 years in which he has won more games than any college baseball coach, Martin attributes his success to his faith and the plan that God had for his life. He became a Christian during a Billy Graham crusade in his hometown of Charlotte, NC, at the age of 16. Like most people, his faith journey was a roller coaster ride.

Always a highly competitive person, Martin struggled to overcome a temper that would flare up when his own plans went awry. His wife Carol Martin remembers: "People used to laugh and call him, wild man. He wanted to win so badly. Some people would think that he went to extremes to obtain that end."

Carol's easy-going manner and unwavering support have been one of the main factors in the dramatic turnaround Mike's life has taken over the years.

Reverend Bob Tindale, his pastor at Killearn United Methodist church and friend for many years, says, "Mike attributes most of his success to Carol for her love and support. Carol is the rock in this family, and Mike is a great example of a family man."

Martin's faith has been an important factor in attracting key players over the years. Zach Diaz, who pitched in 116 games as a Seminole, said the coach's faith influenced him: "Coach Martin is definitely a man of faith. I wanted to be in an atmosphere where being a strong Christian was encouraged." Zach pitched for four years, and his brother Matt came along for two years at Florida State, then played in the Majors for ten years. Their father, Ed, was the Spring Training chaplain for the Detroit Tigers. So, Martin's faith was a strong attraction for the Diaz family

Martin has always made himself available to speak at churches whenever he is invited. He feels as comfortable in the pulpit as he does in the dugout. His talks are sermons in which he shares Biblical stories that have modern applications.

On May 19, 2018, before Game Three against N. C. State, the Seminoles had a huge celebration honoring Mike Martin for becoming the all-time winningest coach in college baseball.

Florida State President John Thrasher said of Martin's success: "His faith has something to do with it. His beliefs serve him well in baseball and life. He knows that sometimes you're going to strikeout, but you've got to keep stepping up to the plate. He accepts losses with dignity and celebrates wins with grace."

BECOMING 11

When a person's uniform number becomes the name that everybody in baseball and many people outside of the Seminole program know you by, there has to be some deep, intriguing story as to how this came about, right? Wrong!

When Mike Martin played for Florida State (1965-66), his uniform number was 15. His friend Woody Woodward, upon being hired as head coach in 1975, contacted him to come along as an assistant. Martin rejoined the baseball program where he had played ten years earlier and asked for #15. It was already taken by Bob Mayer, a sophomore pitcher from Somerset, PA. So, Martin settled for #11, which was the only uniform left that would fit him.

One day at practice, outfielder Jim Busby hollered across the outfield to Martin; "Hey 11, when is batting practice?" From that one simple information request, a name was born, and so was part of a legend surrounding Florida State baseball. Thereafter folks simply called Mike Martin—"11."

JIM CROSBY

DESCRIBING 11

Orlando Sentinel sportswriter Mike Bianchi has covered sports in the Sunshine State for over 20 years. Here's how he described Mike Martin in a column on May 12, 2018:

"If you ask me, hockey's "Miracle on Ice" isn't nearly as impressive as college baseball's "Miracle of Nice." You see, Mike Martin isn't just the winningest baseball coach in his sport's history, he is also one of the nicest guys and greatest ambassadors in his sport's history. He is truly the Bobby Bowden of college baseball.

His down-home humor, slow-talking storytelling, and countrified fish-and-grits charm have helped make him one of college sport's most enduring and endearing treasures."

11: MAKING BASEBALL HISTORY

COLLECTING MARTINISMS

An ism, when attached to the end of a word, indicates that there is something unique about that word. Looking at the many informative and colorful statements made over the years by Coach Martin, the idea was born to collect and use them in this book. To draw attention to them, we have labeled them "Martinisms."

These even reached the Major League Level when two Seminoles traded their remembrances of them during a game at Fenway Park.

Former Seminole Hall-of-Fame First Baseman Doug Mientkiewicz (1993-95) shared this story:

"When I was playing first base in Minnesota, and Luis Alicea (1984-86) was the first base coach with the Red Sox we literally sat there, nine innings for four straight days and talked to each other in Martin's voice saying his 'isms' for the entire nine innings. That voice and the things he used to say to us were absolutely priceless."

So, look for the "Martinisms" as you read this story. They will inform, enlighten, and entertain you.

MARTINISM #1

Mike Martin Talks about Autographing Baseballs

"I am in the habit of putting a scripture verse on a baseball when I am asked for an autograph. So, no matter where it comes from, I must have the verse memorized. One day a lady, standing by the fence asked me to sign a baseball for her son. So, I did, and I wrote Colossians 3:17 on it. The verse says, "Whatever you do in word or deed, do it all in the name of the Lord Jesus, giving thanks to God the Father through Him."

The next day I saw the woman again, and she had a really angry look on her face. I started wondering if I put down Colossians 3:18 in error. So, I went and looked it up, and it said: 'Wives submit to your husbands."

11: MAKING BASEBALL HISTORY

THE ANIMALS OF SECTION B

In 1978, the late Sol Carroll, a Seminole Super Fan, was in the habit of bringing day-old semi-stale do-nuts to the baseball games and throwing them out to fans. When he got to Section B, an uh rowdy, well, maybe boisterous or lively group, would better describe them; they threw the stale do-nuts back at him with accompanying jeers. Sol fired back: "You are nothing but a bunch of Animals." The name stuck.

So, the group, which dates its beginnings back to 1997 when a bunch of students started sitting together in Section B and cheering loudly for the Seminoles while razzing the opponents mercilessly, became known as the Animals.

At one early game, a student named Warren Dropkin, on an impulse led what would become the Noles cheer. Urging the fans to join him, he would accompany each letter of the cheer by forming that letter with his body. N-O-L-E-S became a standard cheer initiated by the Animals who would get the entire stadium, section-by-section, to join in.

Years later, Steven Budnick, known as Mongo, became an expert at leading the Noles cheer and getting the entire crowd, all the way out to the farthest seats in the bleachers involved. The sheer loudness of the cheer was intimidating to the opponents and inspiring for their beloved Seminole team.

As the years passed, the Animals became even more creative at intimidating the opponents while still displaying good sportsmanship. They even developed an "Animals Songbook" with the more popular cheers/songs in it. Many of the songs were written by animal Dayton Owens.

As their role became more and more integral in the playing of a baseball game at Dick Howser Stadium, they needed a leader to coordinate it. Drew Hankin stepped forward to be the "Zookeeper." Drew became well-known for his total commitment to the Animals and Seminole baseball until his untimely demise in 2011 at the age of 38.

The Animals have continued to instill new, innovative ways to force the opponents into making mistakes that could contribute to a Seminole win. "K-Time" is chanted when a Noles pitcher gets 2-strikes on a hitter. "Walk- him-on-rag-arm" is chanted when an opposing pitcher gets 3-balls on a Nole batter." They are very creative when it comes to playing off of different player's names.

In the 5th inning, they sing the Canadian National Anthem- "O Canada." That's a tradition formed because they learned it while watching the Olympics held in Canada, then sang it in the 5th inning of a game. The Noles put on a big rally after that to win the game. So, the 5th inning became the "O Canada Inning" forever.

During the 7th inning stretch, the Animals accompany "Neil Diamond's version of Sweet Caroline," played over the intercom with the entire crowd singing it.

In a letter that Coach Mike Martin wrote to the Animals, he expressed the importance of their role in Seminole baseball. "Florida State baseball is built on tradition and pride. Our goal is to do our best to continue the tradition that was started in 1948. The Animals of Section B help create an atmosphere that is second to none in college baseball."

The Animals and their contribution to baseball have been recognized on television, radio and written up in newspaper and magazine articles. Their fame has spread far and wide.

They make Seminole baseball even more fun!

11: MAKING BASEBALL HISTORY

Always A Seminole

Jose Zabala, FSU 1995-98

"People ask me: Weren't you a Seminole?
I answer No! I wasn't—I AM a Seminole!"

JIM CROSBY

MARTINISM #2

On the Job Training:

"I have found if you put a bad fielder in the game, the ball will find him."

(Something Mike Martin learned that stayed with him through 40 years of coaching)

The Big Shooter Arrives
CHIP BAKER (1985-PRESENT)
Director of Baseball Operations
Catcher, High Point University,
1979 NAIA World Series Runner-up,
Assistant Coach at Virginia Tech and Georgia Tech

It may have slipped by without any fanfare at the time. In 1985 Mike Martin hired Chip Baker as an assistant coach. The "short coach" would turn out to be one of the most popular coaches/administrators in the proud history of Seminole baseball.

At the time, Martin had 273 wins and ranked 9th among active coaches in winning percentage. Upon retirement, 35 years later, he had become a legend with 2,029 wins, most ever by a college coach. Right there with him, all the way was the one referred to as "The Big Shooter," Chip Baker. The Shooter logged in 18 years as an assistant coach and 17 in the important Director of Baseball Operations post. Baker was with #11 through 1,756 victories.

As a coach, Baker excelled in developing catchers. He created a record-selling video entitled: "Expanding the Strike Zone." It was because of his knowledge of catching that Mike Martin Jr. decided to come back to Florida State (1983-85), after a year at Manatee Community College, to play for his dad and learn the catching position from Baker.

All-American catcher Barry Blackwell (1985-88) said: "I was a football player who wound up playing baseball. Chip Baker took a football player and helped him achieve All-American status and play in two World Series. I promise you none of that would have taken place without his expertise and coaching."

When Baker was promoted to Director of Baseball Operations in 2003, his role in Seminole Baseball enlarged even further to include overseeing all aspects of the program, including the important areas of budgeting and travel. Mike Martin summed up the Big Shooter's importance to the entire Seminole baseball program when he said: "Chip Baker is invaluable to our program."

A Play to Forget

Shortly after Chip Baker was hired, Coach Martin decided to move from the third-base coaching box that he had always occupied to the dugout. He felt like this would give him more freedom to manage all team aspects.

He chose Baker to take on the third-base coaching responsibility. The Big Shooter recalls a play, in his first game there, he feared might cost him that third base coaching job. Years later, the memory was still crystal clear in his mind as he explained what happened to Unconquered Magazine:

"Luis Alicea was at bat with slow-running catcher Ed Fulton on second and Steve Taddeo, who could run on first. When Alicea hit a long fly ball to right field, Fulton tagged up, but Taddeo, who was on his heels, didn't slow up."

Much to Baker's dismay, not only was Fulton out at home on a perfect throw from right field, but the catcher then tagged Taddeo, who was sliding in behind him, out at the plate as well.

Umpire Bruce Ravan threw up his right hand, calling Fulton out, then called Taddeo out with his left hand.

Obviously, the only way the Big Shooter's career could go from there was up.

Prime Time Plays Baseball
Deion Sanders (1986-1988 BB) (1985-88 FB)

- Fort Myers, FL
- 76 GP, 270 AB, .281 Avg. 306 OB%; .407 SLG%
- FSU Hall of Fame 2009, College and NFL Hall of Fame 2011

Deion Sanders was the most extraordinary athlete to wear the garnet-and-gold because he proudly wore those colors in three different sports; baseball, football, and track.

The following story told by Mike Martin to www.seminoles.com on Dec. 15, 2003, shows just what a unique talent the one called "Prime Time" was for his ability to show up big-time when the spotlight was on him:

"It was 1987; we were at South Carolina (Metro Conference tournament), and track coach Dick Roberts had come to me and said, 'Deion can help us win the 440 relay. Will you allow him to come over one afternoon and practice the hand-off and run with Sammie Smith and those guys.'"

I said, "Dick, we may not even be playing then. The baseball tournament starts on a Wednesday or Thursday, and (with no guarantee) there was going to be a Saturday (game). So sure enough, we played the afternoon game on Saturday, and it just so happened that the relay was scheduled right between games.

The players gathered around Deion, and he took off his baseball uniform and put on those track shorts right in the dugout. He goes over to the track. I left the baseball field and rode over in a golf cart, and asked somebody where he was going to get in. I sat there and watched.

I don't think I've ever been as thrilled watching athletes run like I was that day. They were flying and won the relay. Deion went back over, put his uniform back on in the dugout, and won the Metro Conference Tournament Championship that night.

I remember Dick thanking me and saying he'd see me at the ball game that night. The track team came over to the game and was just going nuts yelling for us. They really helped pull us through."

Thus, the Seminoles and their University partners in athletics remain Unconquered. While Deion Sanders had many highlight moments in football, giving him the title of "Neon Deion," he was not just a flashy Seminole baseball player. He had his solid moments. When Mike Martin won his 400th game on February 18, 1987 (vs. Samford), Deion played CF, was the lead-off batter, went 2 for 3, had a walk, scored two runs, and stole 2 bases.

When he turned pro, Prime Time became the only player ever to hit a home run in MLB and score a TD in the NFL in the same week; only player ever to play in a World Series and a Super Bowl. He also played in an MLB World Series game and an NFL game on the same day

He played for the Braves against the Pirates in Pittsburgh in Game 4 of the WS, then flew to Miami to play for the Falcons against the Dolphins, then flew back to Pittsburgh for Game 5 of the WS.

11: MAKING BASEBALL HISTORY

Here's how his FSU Hall of Fame induction reads:

Deion Sanders Elected to the FSU Hall of Fame in 1994

If there was a quintessential athlete, a guy everybody wants, someone who is so unique that he is nearly indescribable, then that athlete would be Deion Sanders.

Deion proved from the start at Florida State he would be something special. As a freshman, Sanders started in the Seminoles' secondary, played outfield on the baseball team, which finished 5th in the nation, and led the track team to its 10th conference championship.

A two-time All-American at cornerback, Sanders was the 1988 Thorpe Award winner as the nation's finest defensive back. He led the Seminoles to some of their most memorable wins, including picking off an Auburn pass with seconds left to preserve a win over the Tigers in the 1988 Sugar Bowl.

Deion was drafted as a professional by both the Atlanta Falcons of the NFL and the New York Yankees in Major League Baseball. Sanders continued to play two sports earning him All-Pro honors with the Falcons and becoming a superstar in center-field for the Braves. He also played for the Reds, Yankees, and Giants. An extraordinary athlete when Deion Sanders is around, it's always "Prime Time" (Nolefan.org).

JIM CROSBY

SETTING THE RECORD
Martin Gets 500th Win in Less than a Decade

In his first nine seasons at the helm, #11 had never failed to win at least 50 games a season. In fact, in 1986, his Seminoles put up a record high 61-win season.

Now entering season #10, the Noles were ranked #3 by Collegiate Baseball. Instead of scheduling a parade of "cupcakes" upfront, they invited the 5th ranked Arizona State Sun Devils to Tallahassee.

Mike Martin needed just two wins to become the first Seminole coach to win 500 games. In fact, his total would top the combined totals of the ten years and three coaches prior to him.

The Noles got the season underway on February 4th with a come-from-behind win in an afternoon contest. Trailing 6-2 in the 6th, they put a four-spot on the board and followed it in the seventh with three more to secure a 9-6 victory—Martin's 499th win.

With ESPN covering the second & final game of the series, once again, the Seminoles came from behind. ASU jumped on top—in the second. They held the FSU bats to a couple of lone runs in the fifth and seventh innings.

But in the 8th, a six-run outburst highlighted by catcher Marc Ronan's bases-loaded triple basically put the game away. Just two games into the season, Mike Martin had his 500th win, and the Seminoles would finish ranked 3rd that season—just where they began.

In the post-game recognition of his feat, #11 was quick to credit his players for all they did and acknowledged his crack coaching staff—Rod Delmonico, Mike McLeod, Steve Winterling, and Chip Baker (who worked with Martin for 35 of his 40 years as head coach.)

11: MAKING BASEBALL HISTORY

MARTINISM #3

Mike Martin decided early in his coaching career that he needed to be a role model for his players. In a talk to the Killearn United Methodist Singles Sunday School Class he shared something he did along those lines:

"I decided that since my players look to me to set an example, there were some things I needed to do. I concluded that my drinking beer was not setting the right example. So, I stopped drinking beer. I really liked beer. If there is beer in heaven when I get there, I'm going to have me one."

The Stars Speak

J. D. Drew (1995-97)
FSU Hall of Fame 2003

- Hahira, GA
- 200 gp, 683 ab, .391avg, 69 hr
- NCAA record 30 for 30—HRs + SBs in a season

JD Drew, 23 years after playing at Florida State, is still considered by many to be the best player ever to don the garnet-and-gold. In 2017, Drew became only the second player to have his jersey number 39 retired. The other retired number (#34) belonged to Dick Howser.

J. D.'s Thoughts on Mike Martin's Success

"Longevity. Being able to do what he has done for so long at a high level. I was a raw talent as a baseball player, but one of the best things he ever did was not mess with my swing. Taught me how to do everything else. He saw that my swing was OK, and I had worked and worked on my swing."

11's Impact on Drew's Career

"He developed me from a raw talent into a mentally prepared baseball player that knew how to play the game. Defensively—offensively—all aspects of the game. When I left after three years, I knew what I needed to know at a professional level."

JIM CROSBY

One Year After FSU Drew Was in MLB

"J. D. made it very quickly, and he stuck. We are all just very proud of him and his accomplishments," said Coach Martin.

JD Drew went to MLB the year after he left FSU and played in the Big Leagues for 14 years. Drew played in 1,566 games; had 5,173 ABs; 1,437 hits; 242 HRs; 795 RBI. One of his best seasons was with the Atlanta Braves (2004). He batted .305 in 145 games with 31 HR and 93 RBI.

J. D. Drew Elected to FSU Hall of Fame in 2003

JD Drew was an outfielder from the small town of Hahira, Ga., near Valdosta. He wasn't a heralded player being recruited by colleges from all over, but it didn't take long for coach Martin to realize that this kid from Hahira was destined for greatness. Drew had picked up the game of baseball at age 13, playing with his brothers and neighbors in the cow pastures across from his family home. He joined the Boys Club team in Valdosta, and from there, baseball became his focus. Drew went on to be named the Vikings' best offensive player all four years, all-regional MVP, and a member of the Team Georgia All-Star squad his senior year.

Drew's college career was impressive. He rewrote history as he established himself as one of the best hitters in college baseball. He was a consensus first-team All-American after becoming the only player in Division I baseball history to hit 30 home runs and steal 30 bases. He was named Player of the Year by Baseball America, Collegiate Baseball, The Sporting News, and the ACC. He received the Dick Howser Award given by the American Baseball Coaches Association. Drew was also a member of Team USA and crowned the Golden Spikes Award winner, given by USA Baseball to the best amateur baseball player.

Drew batted an FSU-record .455 in 1997 while becoming one of just three players in Division I history to record a triple-triple—100 hits, 100 runs, 100 RBI. He broke a total of 17 Florida State and ACC records, including the FSU season batting average, FSU and ACC career slugging percentage, and ACC season and career home runs. Drew completed his third and final season being named to the College World Series All-Decade team and eighth in Baseball America's collegiate "Player of the Century" poll.

The left-handed-hitting outfielder was a first-round draft pick by the St. Louis Cardinals (Nolefan.org).

11: MAKING BASEBALL HISTORY

FSU's Drew Enshrined in National College Baseball Hall of Fame

July 7, 2016, LUBBOCK, TX – Florida State's JD Drew, who is arguably one of the best hitters in collegiate baseball history, was one of seven individuals inducted into the National College Baseball Hall of Fame this evening in Lubbock, Texas.

The 2016 class, the 11th in the history of the National College Baseball Hall of Fame, also included Augie Garrido (Texas), Bob Braddy (Jackson State), Matt DeSalvo (Marietta College), Rick Monday (Arizona State), Tom Paciorek (Houston) and Tommy Thomas (Valdosta State).

Drew, who was elected to the FSU Hall of Fame in 2003, joined former Seminoles head coach and shortstop Dick Howser as the second inductee in National College Baseball Hall of Fame in the storied history of the Florida State program.

Among the many accolades in his career, Drew became the only player in NCAA Division I history to hit 30 home runs and steal 30 bases as he posted a .455 batting average as a junior in 1997. He was the third player in NCAA history to record a triple-triple (100 hits, 100 runs, 100 RBI) after closing his Seminole career with 267 hits, 254 runs, and 257 RBI.

"It's an awesome honor," said Drew. "It's not your intention when you come here as an 18-year-old. You don't comprehend or reflect on anything like that. I learned a lot about how to play the game here, and it translated a lot over into my junior season. Really, my whole time here. It carried over into those organizations I played with in the big leagues for sure."

After being named player of the year by Baseball America, Collegiate Baseball, The Sporting News, and the ACC, Drew was drafted fifth overall in 1998 by the Cardinals and completed a 14-year major league career in 2011. In 1999, he was listed eighth in Baseball America's collegiate "Player of the Century" poll (www.seminoles.com).

Buster Posey (2006-08)

- Leesburg, GA
- Won 9 Awards including 4 Player of the Year Awards
- 195 GP; .398 avg; 33hr; 206 rbi; .626 slg.

Buster says:

"Mike Martin is a great example of mental toughness. To do as well as he has for as long as he has—he had to be strong-minded. Whether it was directly or indirectly, I took a lot of good lessons from the way he went about his business." (See more comments from Buster in "An Evening with 11: The Martin Roast.")

Posey was elected to the FSU Hall of Fame, 2018

Buster Posey earned All-America honors as a shortstop for the Seminoles as a freshman in 2006, then switched to catcher and became arguably the greatest player in FSU history.

As a sophomore in 2007, Posey was a first-team All-American (Collegiate Baseball), earned a spot on the All-ACC first team, and was a finalist for the Johnny Bench Award, presented to the nation's top collegiate catcher. He would blow away those achievements his next year.

Buster's junior season saw him win virtually every award in baseball, including the Golden Spikes Award, Dick Howser Trophy, Brooks Wallace, Johnny Bench, and Player of the Year honors by Baseball America Collegiate Baseball and Rivals.com. A consensus first-team All-American, he led the nation in six offensive categories, including batting average (.463), hits (119), RBI (93), total bases (226), on-base percentage (.566), and slugging percentage (.879). His batting average was the highest recorded in a single season in Seminole baseball history. He led FSU to the College World Series in 2008, the Seminoles' first trip to Omaha since 2000.

He also led the ACC in eight categories en route to being named 2008 Player of the Year and became just the fourth player in ACC history to capture the triple crown as he led the league in batting average, home runs (26), and RBI.

A five-time All-Star with the San Francisco Giants, Posey was the 2010 Rookie of the Year, the 2012 NL MVP, a three-time Silver Slugger winner, and the 2016 Gold Glove, winner. The Giants won World Series titles with Posey behind the plate in 2010, 2012, and 2014.

11: MAKING BASEBALL HISTORY

Posey gives Mike Martin lots of credit for his development as a player and person (Nolefan.org).

Buster's Big-League Achievements

Buster Posey became an instant fan favorite with the San Francisco Giants after signing with them in 2009. A list of his accomplishments makes it clear as to why:

- World Series 2010
- World Series 2012
- World Series 2014
- Gold Glove Award (2016)
- NL Hank Aaron Award (2012)
- All-Star (2012, 2013, 2015–2018)
- NL MVP (2012)
- NL Rookie of the Year (2010)
- 4× Silver Slugger Award (2012, 2014, 2015, 2017)
- Golden Spikes Award (2008)
- Dick Howser Trophy (2008)
- World Baseball Classic 2017
- National League Comeback Player of the Year, 2021

JIM CROSBY

Adding Meat to the Menu
Mike Martin Jr.
Tallahassee, Maclay High School
Catcher FSU 1993-95
Assistant Coach 1998-2019, head coach 2020

It is not really clear when people started calling Mike Martin Jr. "Meat." The best explanation and the one we will go with for the purposes of this book is that he has always been thin, and when he was a kid, people would say that he needed to get some "meat on his bones." In backyard baseball games, his dad would pitch to him and say: "Come on, Meat, you can't hit me." Somehow the meat-moniker stuck. Then, when he became a good player, he often batted cleanup—the "meat" of the batting order.

When it came to baseball, obviously, Meat had a good teacher. He became a star player at Tallahassee's Maclay High school, where he captained the 1991 state championship team, and his #10 jersey was later retired.

Martin Jr. literally grew up at the ballpark. He said his family environment was that of a "live, love and laugh" family. Although he spent many hours at Dick Howser Stadium as a kid, he did not start out playing for the Seminoles despite his stellar high school exploits.

His college career started at Manatee Community College. He had considered playing for his Dad at Florida State but didn't, at first. That choice would become a reality in his second year after he had earned All-Conference honors at Manatee. The deciding factor was the addition of Chip Baker to the FSU staff. Meat figured he could become a better catcher while learning from the Big Shooter. So, he wore the Seminole uniform as a player from 1993-95.

In his playing days, Meat went to the College World Series in back-to-back seasons ('94-95), was a member of Team USA in 1993, and was drafted by the San Diego Padres in 1995. He had many big moments for the Noles. See "Walking Off a Winner" section. After his minor league career ended, Meat returned to Florida State as an assistant coach for the next 22 years.

Over his first 21 seasons as a hitting coach Martin Jr. led the Seminoles to a .302 team batting average, including a school-record .355 in 2008. His charges had 17 seasons with at least a .4000 slugging percentage while averaging 7.8 runs per game. His reputation as an exceptional recruiter also grew over the years as he became a familiar figure at high school games around the Sunshine State.

11: MAKING BASEBALL HISTORY

One of his major achievements as an assistant was convincing Buster Posey to switch positions. Posey came in as a shortstop, and his switch to catcher, where he was a natural, has led to mega-baseball success.

At the end of the 2019 season, upon the retirement of #11, Mike Martin Jr was rewarded for his devotion to Florida State University and stellar accomplishments as a player and long-time assistant coach by being named the Seminoles ninth head baseball coach.

JIM CROSBY

#1000 COMES ... FINALLY

On April 8, 1998, Martin's Seminoles notched the 1,000th win of his career ... finally. Coming into the season with 970 wins, it was expected that he would reach the coveted 1,000-win mark during the season. But, when?

Starting the season with the ACC Baseball Blast at Disney World in Orlando. The Seminoles dropped two of three. Losing 10-1 to Notre Dame. Beating Ohio State 6-4. Then dropping a 5-3 game to Tennessee, coached by Martin's former assistant Rod Delmonico.

The Seminoles jumped out to a 3-0 lead and stayed there, garnering only 2-hits in the game.

FSU soon righted that start and ran off 15-wins in a row in March. The countdown was on with arch-rival Miami coming to Tallahassee for a weekend series on April 3rd and Martin's win total sitting at 999; it seemed the proper time to get the record.

But, as fate would have it, the Seminoles pulled off a rare feat. They dropped all three games at Howser Stadium, and the Canes left town with FSU's head coach still one-win shy. They would get it in a hunt-and-peck 4-3 win vs. Jacksonville, three days later at home.

Tallahassee Democrat Sportswriter John Nogowski would write after the game: "You would think God had better things to do on a muggy Wednesday night. But there was something awfully suspicious about Florida State's 4-3 win of Jacksonville University for FSU coach Mike Martin's 1,000th career win."

Basically, FSU stole the win. In the bottom of the 8th with runners on first and third, Brian Cox walked off first and got caught in a rundown while Jose Zabala, carrying #11's 1,000th win with him, raced home from third base with the go-ahead and eventual winning run and shocking the Jaguars. Then Zach Diaz completed the win by tossing a scoreless ninth inning in relief.

Rod Delmonico pretty much summed things up: "I think the thing he (Martin) does extremely well is he prepares the team to win (every game) throughout the season. That he does as good as anybody, I've ever seen."

"The other thing is his competitive spirit and commitment to excellence. He hates to lose. He's competitive in everything he does, and that filters down to his ball club." Only 54 years old at this point, there was no telling what Mike Martin could still accomplish.

11: MAKING BASEBALL HISTORY

MARTINISM #4

In 1998 Mike Martin was invited to talk to the sales staff at Clear Channel Communications, a group of five radio stations that included the flagship station for Seminole baseball, WNLS. He was asked to share his keys to winning at work and in life.

Martin said:

"I could look at my job as having some things in it that are impossible to do. But when you think about things that are impossible:

1) "It is impossible to get chewing gum out of an angora sweater."
2) "It is impossible to dribble a football."
3) "And it is impossible to get off of Jerry Falwell's mailing list."

"Other than that, nothing is impossible, really. You can do whatever you set your mind to do."

The Stars Speak

Matte Diaz (1998-99)
FSU Hall of Fame 2013

- Lakeland, FL
- 142 games; .384 avg; 570 ab; 43 hr; 178 RBI
- Hit 6 hrs. in regional while batting .750 with 4 hrs. in a game vs Oklahoma

Why FSU?

"My freshman year, I came in pretty much unheralded. They took a look at me because my older brother, Zach, asked them to take a look at me. I had a good game. I had a pro contract in hand, and 12 days before class started, I decided to go to Florida State. To be honest, I wanted to go anywhere else but Florida State. My older brother had been all-everything all my life, and I wanted to blaze my own trail. God had different plans, and I am so thankful He did because He got me to Tallahassee to play for Coach Martin."

11's Influence

"Coach Martin influenced me in many ways, more than just baseball, obviously. On the field, he taught me how to win. I had a relatively successful high school career in terms of winning championships. But I had a different idea of what it took to win. Walking in that first day at Florida State, I learned how to expect to win … didn't hope to win; didn't just think I could win. I learned how to be on a team that expected to win."

Learning Not to Believe All You Read

"I remember my freshman year the first article I read in the Tallahassee Democrat with my name in it had the headline: 'No Drew, No Morris, No Omaha for FSU.' That belief never crept into the locker room."

Observing Coach Martin in All Aspects

"Mike Martin definitely takes baseball very seriously, obviously. But you never thought of him as a one-dimensional human being. You knew he loved his wife and his family adored him. Even though he and Meat would argue in the dugout once in a while, you knew they loved each other. It wasn't just baseball with him, yet he was so successful in baseball."

The Name Thing

Diaz came to be known as MattE because, in grammar school, there were five kids named Matt in his class. To keep from having all five of them answer when she called out "Matt," she attached Matt Diaz's middle initial "E" to the end of his first name. In the Majors, he was able to drop the "E" from his name and simply be Matt. But the media still mispronounced his last name as "Dee-az" instead of correctly calling him "Dye-az."

Matt Diaz Elected into the FSU Hall of Fame in 2013

Lakeland native Matt Diaz burst on the college baseball scene virtually from his first at-bat in 1998 and finished his freshman season as The Sporting News Freshman of the Year. He earned first-team Freshman All-America honors and was a third-team outright All-American as a rookie. He also earned a spot on both the AFCA and NCBWA first-team All-America squads as a sophomore.

FSU's star outfielder posted impressive career numbers over just two seasons, including finishing sixth in both batting average (.384) and all-time slugging percentage (.700). His 43 career home runs ranked him among FSU's all-time Top 10, and he finished 22nd in both RBIs (178) and total bases. Diaz also appears on a number of FSU's single-season Top 25 lists, including Top 10 finishes in home runs with 22 in 1998 that ranked 11th all-time and 21 in 1999, which ranked 13th. His 94 RBI as a sophomore ranked eighth all-time and his .390 batting average in 1998 was the 21st best in Seminole history.

After his sophomore year, the Tampa Bay Devil Rays drafted Diaz in the 17th round. He went on to lead the Rays in the minor leagues in hits and extra bases. His professional career led him to Kansas City, Braves, Pirates, Yankees, and the Marlins (Nolefan.org). Matt Diaz played 11 years in MLB: 736 GP; 2,052 AB; 546 H; 45 HR; 226 RBI, .290 Avg.

Mike Loynd (1983-86)
FSU Hall of Fame 1993
Golden Spikes Award Winner 1986

- Millburn, New Jersey
- 74 app; 395.2 ip; 417 ks
- Only FSU pitcher with 20 wins in a season ('86) 45 total wins

Coach Martin's Achievements

"The main thing that stands out over time with me with Coach Martin is he obviously loves Florida State. He is a Florida State guy through and through and as time goes by. He has done a great job here. When he left Florida State, a big piece of the puzzle disappeared. He won at least 40 games every year he was there. He's a Florida State guy."

Loynd Climbed the Ladder

"When I showed up on the Florida State campus, I was number 16 out of 16 on the pitching staff. They said I was not going to make it. I guess I proved them wrong. As time went by, I was told I was a power, breaking ball pitcher. I guess that is what I did and utilized to my advantage."

How Loynd Got 11's Attention

"Just my time at Florida State, I learned so much. I was so green when I showed up. So basically, I learned almost everything, and thank God I knew I needed to learn everything. I showed up, listened. I ran. I did whatever I could and just kept plugging along.

One day when Jody Reed came out of the batting cage complaining that he couldn't hit my stuff ... nothing I was throwing was going straight---the light bulb went on in Coach Martin's head. That's how I became one of his pitchers at Florida State."

Winning the Golden Spikes Award

"Even today, you tell some people you won the Golden Spikes, and it doesn't resonate. Not like the Heisman Trophy does. What I remember is when I played at Florida State, I played specifically for the love of the game, love of the season, love of my teammates. Awards were not something that was on my mind."

Mike Loynd Elected into the FSU Hall of Fame in 1993

An imposing 6-5, 215-pound right-hander from Short Hills, N.J., Loynd was blessed with an elusive curveball and a very lethal slider. Most will remember Loynd as a fiery, self-assured hurler for the Seminoles. A day at the park for Loynd usually meant stalking around the mound, gritting his teeth, fists clenched, and giving opposing batters glowering stares.

As a freshman, Loynd led all Seminole pitchers in victories with 12 while striking out 79 batters. Showing the poise to excel at the collegiate level, Loynd possessed ferocious intensity and concentration on the mound.

After a 13-4 sophomore season and 113 strikeouts, the young Loynd was selected as an alternate on the U.S. Olympic baseball team.

During his junior season with the Noles, Loynd went on a school-record tear. By the time the season's final out was completed, Loynd had set school records for wins in a season (20) and career (45) and strikeouts in a season (183) and career (377). His 20 wins tied an NCAA record and made him the winningest pitcher in all of college baseball for 1986.

Loynd became the 10th recipient of the Golden Spikes Award, considered the "Heisman Trophy" of college baseball. He was named "Pitcher of the Year" by Baseball America for 1986 and won MVP honors in the Metro Conference Tournament. He was named to the all-tournament

11: MAKING BASEBALL HISTORY

and All-South II Region teams en route to the College World Series, where his FSU team finished #2 in the nation.

He left FSU after his junior year with a career record of 45-10 (.880 avg.) and 377 strikeouts in less than 396 innings of work. He is remembered as the pitcher who, after striking out his 16th batter in one game, yelled to the team's dugout, "Next!"

It took Loynd only six weeks once he departed Tallahassee to continue his winning ways for the Texas Rangers. In his first major league game, Loynd ended a Rangers seven-game losing streak by beating the Cleveland Indians and future Hall of Famer Phil Niekro (Nolefan.org).

JIM CROSBY

MIKE LOYND TRADITION ROOM

Florida State's baseball program has had many outstanding players and has enjoyed much success throughout the decades. To commemorate their storied baseball program, they have built a large tradition room to honor players, coaches, and the University program as a whole. The Mike Loynd Tradition Room is located next to the Griffin Family Clubhouse under the first base stands. The trophy room, as stated above, showcases the stories of the great players in Florida State baseball history, telling of their stories and successes. The room holds awards, plaques, championships, and more.

Inside the tradition room is a lounge area with multiple televisions that continually broadcast historic moments that have occurred within the baseball program throughout the years. On the walls of the tradition room, there are tributes to the Seminole teams that made twenty-three appearances in the College World Series and appeared in seventeen conference championship games.

In addition to team awards, certain individuals were signaled out and awarded for their excellence. The individual awards are showcased in glass cases; they include the four Golden Spikes Awards (an award given to the best NCAA division one player in the country) won by Mike Loynd, Mike Fuentes, J. D. Drew, and Buster Posey.

Additionally, other individual awards on display include the coveted Gold Glove Award, an award that honors the best defensive player in the country at their given position. Buster Posey most notably won both the Golden Spikes Award and the Golden Glove Award. He was the first Seminole baseball player to be presented with the award in only its second year of being given as an award.

The Mike Loynd Tradition Room was built as a part of the nearly twelve-million-dollar two-year renovation project that ended in 2004, giving rise to the Dick Howser Stadium we see today. The room was built in large part because of a generous donation by former Golden Spikes Award winner Mike Loynd (www.wikipedia.org).

11: MAKING BASEBALL HISTORY

2008: WINNING #1,500
2008: A Very Good Year for #1,500

The Seminoles were hot. They sported a 13-1 record when ACC opponent GA Tech came to town. In game one, they got a walk-off win when left-fielder Ohmed Danesh delivered a two-out, two-run single up the middle for an 8-7 win.

On Saturday, second baseman Jason Stidham's 3-run homer highlighted an 11-2 Seminole blowout leaving Mike Martin one-win shy of the 1500 mark, a spot previously occupied by only two coaches: Augie Garrido (Texas) and Gene Stephenson (Wichita State).

On Sunday afternoon, the Seminoles left no doubts that Mike Martin would pick up win #1,500. They pounded out 19 hits and scored 17 runs to sweep GA. Tech, 17-8 and to run their season record to 16-1.

Afterward, Martin said: "The memories have been wonderful. I am a blessed individual to have worked here at this great university. I am proud to be a part of it, and yeah, it does mean something to me, but it is also a thank you to every individual that has put on a Seminole uniform."

Florida State would go on to win 54 and lose only 14 advancing but losing two straight in the College World Series.

Buster Posey's role in the 2008 season, his final one as a Seminole, was just short of phenomenal. Posey's .463 average tops the record for 200+ at-bats. He also had 26 HRs and 93 RBI. The catcher from Leesburg, GA, won every individual honor available. These included: ACC Player of the Year; Dick Howser Player of the Year; Johnny Bench Award; Rawlings Gold Glove Award-Catcher; Brooks Wallace Player of the Year; and the biggie, The Golden Spikes Award.

So, #11 established a great FSU mark for wins, but he was only too happy to share the limelight with Buster Posey, one of Florida State's all-time greats.

MARTINISM #5

Martin Explains his Job at a Media & Client's Luncheon

"My job is selling an 18-year-old kid on what is best for him—come to school and play baseball and turn down a million dollars from a major league team or sign to play pro ball and skip college baseball.

I had a young player, and his mother convinced the boy to come to school and turn down $1.6 million from Minnesota. The night before classes would begin and the boy would be in college, Minnesota raised their offer to $1.85 million, and he signed with them.

I would have signed for the $1.6 million. But you see the challenge I face in my job selling baseball."

The Stars Speak

Luis Alicea (1984-86)
FSU Hall of Fame 1993

- Guaynabo, Puerto Rico
- 238 games, 970 ab, .341 avg, 71 sb
- Started DP in '86 CWS still talked about (beat Miami)

11 from Alicea's Perspective

"You have got to understand all the guys that 11 has helped in his career as a coach. All the people he has been able to touch and the consistency he has done it with throughout the years.

People don't understand a job like Mike Martin has, to be able to every single year start a cycle of teaching the freshmen and going through the amount of time he spends teaching and developing the system to be able to maintain it for that long. That's impressive!"

Personal Attention

"I didn't speak a word of English when I came here … He took me under his wing and made sure I was taken care of. He treated me just like family. I could have easily packed up and said I don't understand. So many things with Mike Martin resonated with me in my life and were steppingstones for my career for my life."

How Alicea was Attracted to Florida State

"When I was 16 and 17 years old, I had an opportunity to sign a contract with the Yankees, then the Padres. My parents said: 'Why don't we try to get Luis into a school?' They organized a tryout in Puerto Rico and invited eight different schools. When I looked at the Florida State brochure, it looked classy, beautiful on glossy paper. I am a horse lover, so I loved the picture (Renegade) on the cover. There was nothing held back."

Playing at Howser

"I look back now, and it was a privilege to be a part of that. To have the Animals with Mongo leading cheers to intimidate the other team. And they created songs for the players. Having your own song. When I came to bat singing, 'Louie, Louie' by The Kingsmen. It was amazing. It was something that you will always take with you and make you remember FSU baseball."

Alicea Elected into the FSU Hall of Fame in 1993

Alicea arrived at Florida State University in the summer of 1983 from Guaynabo, Puerto Rico. His first conquest came not on the playing field but against an English-speaking environment to which his Latin ears and tongue were not accustomed. He took on intense lingual courses, spending nights in his room learning the English language.

Once inside the confines of Dick Howser Stadium, however, the all-star second baseman/shortstop was "home" again. As a freshman, Alicea set a school record with a 27-game hitting streak and led the team in triples. His Seminole team won a Metro Conference Championship while Alicea won a spot on Baseball America's Freshman All-American team.

Alicea quickly became a crowd favorite at Florida State. Throughout his career, Seminole fans always greeted Luis Alicea's every at-bat with their personal rendition of "Louie, Louie."

The switch-hitting sophomore continued to blossom throughout his second season. He averaged .325, had 116 hits, and crossed home plate 100 times. His swift speed-of-foot allowed him 26 stolen bases.

In 1986 the quiet confidence behind Alicea's ever-present smile spoke loudly: "All-American." Batting .392 and bringing home 73 base runners, Alicea's eight-home-run junior season was his finest. Pro scouts hailed him as the nation's premier collegiate 2nd baseman. His speed, style, and hand/foot quickness rated high on scouting evaluations.

Alicea won the South II Regional MVP award en route to FSU's appearance in the '86 College World Series. While the Seminoles fell one game short of a national championship, Alicea was named to the CWS All-Tournament team.

He was the only CWS player chosen during the first round of the '86 draft. The St. Louis Cardinals made him their #1 choice and 23rd overall selection (Nolefan.org).

Alicea played 13 years in MLB for five teams (Royals, Rangers, Angels, Cardinals, and Red Sox). Was in 1,341 games, with 4,614 plate apps.; 1,031 hits; 551 runs, and 422 RBI.

Barry Blackwell (1985-88)
- New Providence, New Jersey
- 259 games, 800 ab; .328 avg, 31 hr.
- Co-inventor of Chest Bump

11's Impact on Barry

"It is a very interesting point. You know, as 18- to 22-year-olds under 11's tutelage, you don't realize what he is teaching you is going to do for you the rest of your life. How to play the game correctly at 18, 19, 20, yea, that's all great. Being a Seminole and wearing the Garnet and Gold in games are all the things that sadly are the only things right in front of you at that age.

It isn't until you move on in a career and the next phase of your life starts that you realize the service he has done for you. Great, he made me an OK baseball player, and I owe him for that. But I am forever indebted to him for making me a man and teaching me to do the right things."

Persuading Barry to Play Third Base

"We didn't have a third baseman. We had two catchers—Ed Fulton and me. 11 called me in. Basically, he said, 'Here's the deal, fat boy. I need both of you in the lineup. Fulton can't play third base. You have to play third base. True story. I was fighting back the tears. I was a catcher; third base was not my spot. As I was walking out, I could hear him laughing, and I thought, you son-of-a-gun, you talked me into it. But truthfully, it wasn't that bad. With Fulton catching Jose Marzan at first, Luis Alicea at 2B, Bien Figueroa at SS, and Mike Loynd on the mound, all I had to do was not mess up, and we were going to win" (Blackwell moved back to C in his final two seasons).

The Big Shooter's influence: "It is hard to explain. I will just tell you the stars and moon lined up for Chip Baker to come into my life. He was more than just my coach. He kept an eye on me. He kicked my butt when I needed it. He patted me on my back when I needed it. He had all the right answers for every situation. When I got to pro ball, everything Chip had taught me was pertinent. He took an athlete, that's what I was, and made me into a reasonably good catcher."

Recalling Two Out HR in 9th vs LSU in CWS to Go to Extra Innings

"We were down 1-0 in the bottom of 9th, 2-outs, nobody on. The LHP Gregg Patterson was good. He was throwing a gem. 11 turned me loose on a 2-0 pitch, and I literally took a pitch right down the middle of the plate, and to this day, I still don't know why I didn't swing at it. I stepped back from the plate, and I thought never again in my life am I going to be hesitant in anything. Next pitch, he threw me elevated just a tiny bit, and I think the ball just landed recently. I think, after I hit it, it was orbiting the moon."

11's Influence

"The truth is I love what he did for me from ages 18 to 22. I am truly indebted to him for what he did from ages 22 to 52. He taught me that there are no shortcuts. You do the very best you can every day with the faculties you have at hand. No excuses."

Barry Blackwell was a solid player at third base and catcher for four seasons. He went on to play in 259 games which ties him with Mike Yastrzemski for most games played in by any Seminole. In four seasons, he had a batting average of .328 in 800 official at-bats with 262 hits, 31 home runs, scored 194 runs, and drove in 188. In a 1985 game against Jacksonville, he went 5-for-5 with three home runs and seven RBI, attracting the kind of attention that led to his becoming a first-team All-American as a freshman.

JIM CROSBY

2018: A GOOD YEAR FOR RECORD-SETTING

Season Opener–2018

It was with high expectations that the baseball season got underway at Dick Howser Stadium on February 16th. The Florida State Seminoles took the field as the pre-season consensus number five ranked team in the nation and the odds-on pick to successfully defend their Atlantic Coast Conference championship with hopes to return to the College World Series for the 17th time under Coach Martin.

Approaching his 39th opening day as Seminole Coach Martin said: "There is nothing more exciting than opening day. It builds up to where everybody is anxiously awaiting that first pitch."

The Opponent: Xavier Musketeers. Coming off a 34-27 record in 2017. Winners of the Big East Championship. Invited to Louisville regional. Have never played Florida State in baseball.

The first pitch of the game came at 4:06 on a sunny Friday afternoon but preceding it, the crowd of 5,036 gave a warm welcome to two stars of the past. Former left fielder Jeremy Morris (1994-97), who still holds the season record for doubles, 20 years later with 36, threw out the ceremonial first pitch.

It was caught by his teammate Hall of Famer JD Drew (95-'97), whose #39 was retired in 2017. He still has five records at FSU and has completed a 14-year Major League career.

Jr. LHP Tyler Holton, the ace of the staff and local favorite from Lincoln High School, seemed in mid-season form as he shook off an error by 3B Drew Mendoza on the first batter and retired twelve in a row. To start the 5th, he was touched for a double, then struck out the next two batters before giving up his first walk of the game.

That prompted Coach Martin and team trainer Brandon Stone to head to the mound. After a long consultation, Holton left the game. Fans were wondering, but the only news forthcoming was that Holton had suffered some tightness in his arm and would receive an MRI on Monday or Tuesday.

11: MAKING BASEBALL HISTORY

By the time Holton departed, the Seminoles had a 5-0 lead with the big blow coming from Sophomore DH Nick Derr (Sarasota), who led off the 3rd inning with an HR over the right-field fence.

The Seminoles would bang out 13 hits on the way to an 11-1 opening victory. Mike Martin fondly remembered it as "much better than last year"—a 3-0 shutout by Virginia Commonwealth University (the first time the two teams had met).

Pitching was exceptional in the opener. Andrew Karp (Jr RHP from Winter Garden) got the win with 1.1 ip and allowing 1 hit and 0 runs.

Clayton Kwiatkowski (So LHP, Tampa) threw a scoreless inning, whiffing two. But the most impressive performance was that of Cobi Johnson (Jr, RHP, Holiday, FL), who struck out 4 in two innings with a fastball topping out at 96 mph. Back from Tommy John surgery, Johnson expressed his thanks to all those who supported him in his return.

Game Two—Saturday, 1:00 pm

Another local product, Cole Sands (Jr, RHP, N. Fl. Christian), was named the starter for game two. He had 12 wins in 36 games ('16-'17), recording 122 ks in 153 ip. Yet, the feeling was that he had barely scratched the surface of his potential.

Pitching in the Cape Cod, summer league Sands worked hard on developing his two-seam fastball. The results were startling. There he struck out 21 in 17 innings. Then in FSU's fall practices, no one could hit him

"Electric" is the way Tyler Holton described Sands' redesigned pitch. Coach Martin said, "He has jumped as much in one year if not more than any pitcher I have ever coached."

The Xavier batters found that out. After a shaky start—3 hits and two runs—caused by, in his words, "Kinda had some nerves at first. Pitching the top of the zone." That soon changed.

With a fastball topping out at 96 mph and a changeup in the 80's Sands set a career-high with 9 Ks in 5 innings, and those 3 hits were all he surrendered. He retired 15 of the final 16 he faced (one reached on an error).

Another local product (that's 3 in two games), Austin Pollock (Fr, LHP, Leon HS), finished off the final four innings. In his first collegiate appearance, Pollock struck out 5 and surrendered no runs.

The big hit for FSU came from a Seminole legacy … Raphael Bournigal, a Senior graduate transfer from Belmont University whose dad played at FSU and in the Majors. With the score 3-2 FSU in the 5th and the bases loaded, Bournigal blasted a fastball high over the right-field screen scoring three runs to make it 6-2. That's all Florida State needed as they went on to win 7-2.

Game Three—Sunday, 1:00 pm

Looking for the sweep, Coach Martin named LHP Drew Parrish from Rockledge to pitch the finale. Parrish had settled into the number three role as a freshman, winning six in 19 app. With 93 Ks in 91.2 innings.

Parrish kept up the weekend pitching excellence with six solid innings of 3-hit, 1-run (an HR) ball. He added 9 Ks to pick up the win in the 5-1 contest. Fr. Conor Grady (RHP, Tampa) struck out 5 in two scoreless innings. Then another Fr. Jonah Scolaro from Valrico finished off the victory with a scoreless 9th.

Veteran catcher Cal Raleigh (Jr, Cullowhee, NC) had the big hit, a two-run double.

Weekend pitching stats are impressive. FSU pitchers struck out 43 batters and only walked two. The Seminole staff leads the country in strikeout-to-walk ratio and has a WHIP (0.59). FSU struck out at least one hitter in 26 of the 27-innings played.

The Seminoles used nine of their 14 newcomers, with four of them getting a start—a very satisfying season-opening series for Florida State.

Mike Martin's Magic Number (total wins needed for the all-time record) moved to 29.

11: MAKING BASEBALL HISTORY

MARTINISM #6

Addressing an Advertising Sales Group, Mike Martin Said ...

"Life is 10% what happens to you and 90% how you react. I look at y'all, and I know that trying to sell someone advertising when there is doubt in your mind is like me having a young man approaching a ground ball and wondering if he is going to catch it. You can't approach the day that way."

Chris Chavez (1995-98)

- Pensacola/Tallahassee
- 109 app; 296 ip; 312 ks; 24w; 3.55 era.
- 1st team All-American; last complete-game no-hitter.

11's Influence on Chavez

"Under 11, I became not only a better player but a more well-rounded player. Just his approach to the game. He taught us that it was more important to be a great teammate than it was to be a great player. That has translated to me even to this day when I coach my son Noah's travel ball team. Stressing the importance of being a team player."

Why FSU?

"I always loved FSU. Even when we moved from Tallahassee to Pensacola, FSU was the team I loved most. When I became a decent player, I came over to camp and received a lot of attention from Coach Martin, Coach Shouppe, and Coach Baker. When Coach Shouppe gave me an offer, I was happy, but I wanted to take other visits. But I didn't wait long. I thought, 'Wait a minute, what am I doing. FSU is the place I want to be no matter what any other school offers.'"

Remembering Your No-Hitter, February 18, 1998

"I think it was about the 6th inning I realized I had a no-hitter going. I had thrown three no-hitters in high school. I think John Bentley had a one-hitter the day before; he lost the no-hitter in the 9th. At Florida State, all of the pitchers just pushed each other. You always felt you had to do better than the other guy before you had done. So, I walked three batters in, making sure to be careful and save the no-hitter. I struck out 11 on curveballs. The neat thing was that game was on TV, and whenever they showed the stands on camera, my grandma was there cheering for me. She passed away a short time thereafter." (FSU won 13-0. Current Rays manager Kevin Cash went 3 for 4 with 5 RBI and a 2-run homer)

A Memorable Start to 11's Record-setting Season

"What I love about 11 is the way he enjoys seeing the players with their children. If I visit the dugout, and I don't have Noah with me, he'll tell me to get out and go get him. People don't realize how much he loved his players and their families. He embraces Noah as much as he does me."

Chris and Noah visited 11 in the dugout before the first game of 2018, the record-setting season. FSU went out and no-hit Maine. It was the first season-opening no-hitter, but they used three pitchers. The last single pitcher, a nine-inning no-hitter, was Chris Chavez over 20 years before. Chris says he still pulls for any Seminole Pitcher who has a no-hitter going.

June 16, 1999, College World Series,
FSU vs Cal State Fullerton

"This game is probably my personal favorite FSU memory because of what it meant to me and what it meant to 11 and the team. The night before the game, I went to 11's hotel room and knocked on the door. Carol answered and looked surprised, like, "Chris, what are you doing here." I asked to come in and speak to 11. I told him I had studied Cal St. Fullerton, and they had lots of righthand hitters, and if he would give me the start, we would beat them."

(True to his word Chavez pitched a complete game for a 7-2 win, and as 11 said, "We're like the Bee Gees, song "Just Staying Alive." Fullerton coach George Horton said: "Chris Chavez had a lot to do with our frustration" as Cal. State packed their bags.)

"When I got back to the room, I had about five phone calls from friends   All of them wanted to talk about all the camera time my mom got on ESPN's telecast of the game"

(His mom was too nervous to sit in her seat, and the cameras followed as she paced through the stands).

11: Making Baseball History

11's Greatest Influence on Chavez

"How he conducts his married life. How much he loves Carol and his family is something I take away from his example and how I love my wife and son. They are everything to me."

In four seasons, Chris Chavez made 109 app; 296 ip; won 24 games and struck out 312 (still in Top 10 over 20 years later).

Zach Diaz (1996-99)

- Lakeland, FL.
- 116 app; 208.1 ip; 3.72 era; .249 opp. avg
- Winning pitcher in 11's 1,000th win

What It Was Like Playing for 11

"Playing for Coach Martin was a wonderful experience. Coach Martin is Florida State baseball. The chance to play for a program that has that reputation. To take the program to the World Series regularly, you have to play at the highest level against the best competition. And to be successful. It is one thing to play them, but to be successful against them is a rarity."

11's Impact on Zach's Life

"It was absolutely pivotal in the course my life took. Coming to Florida State to play baseball was a dream come true. It prepared me for the minors and prepared me for life. Coach Martin is not only a great coach, but he is a good man. He teaches his players to be gentlemen."

Being a part of historic Wins

"You don't think a whole lot about it when you are in it. After the game was over, you realized to be a part of 11's 1000th win was special. When you look back at that 1,000th win, you realize my name is going to be on that scorecard, as the winning pitcher, you helped him get there. I wasn't a guy who got 10 or 15 wins a year, so that was really cool to get one in that game. In middle relief, you don't get a whole lot of wins and losses. Just credited with innings. I had been a part of his 900th win as well."

JIM CROSBY

Zach's Best FSU Memories

"The championship atmosphere. The chance to play with my brother (Matt). The opportunity to play in the College World Series three times. It was definitely a family atmosphere, Coach Martin and all the coaches, really. Coach Shouppe—I would bounce everything off of him.

Having a guy like Clint Purvis (team chaplain) around, as well as Coach Martin making sure we had great faith leaders was remarkable.

The memories of my parents and younger brother coming up to hang out and watch me and visit before and after games. And then to bring my son up to watch a series one year in the Super Regional. Coach Martin had us in the dugout and made my son feel like a million dollars."

Zach Diaz was an extremely valuable member of the Seminole pitching staff for four years. While pitching almost exclusively in middle relief, Pitching Coach Jamey Shouppe called him an "innings eater." If a starting pitcher ran into early trouble, Diaz could be counted on to come in and effectively pick up lots of the innings of work that the starter left on the table. He appeared in 116 games, working 208.1 innings and striking out 170 batters. He appeared in three College World Series and, in his final season (1999), picked up valuable wins over Auburn in the Super Regional and Stanford in the College World Series.

11: MAKING BASEBALL HISTORY

Bulletin: February 21, 2018

TALLAHASSEE, Fla. - Junior left-handed pitcher Tyler Holton will miss the remainder of the 2018 season with a torn ACL, Florida State announced Wednesday. Holton will undergo surgery Thursday morning.

"Tyler is a fine young man, and we're all disappointed at this setback in his career," head coach Mike Martin said. "He's doing the best thing right now. We'll be there for him and help guide him through the rehab process, but as a team, we have to keep moving forward on our goals for this season."

Holton was a first-team All-American in 2017, recording a 10-3 record and 144 strikeouts in helping lead FSU to the College World Series. Warchant.com reported that Holton will have Tommy John surgery in Pensacola.

Not the kind of news that Seminole fans were waiting to hear. Holton was not only the ace of the staff, limiting the opponents to a .063 batting average in his only outing. He was a good hitter who would add some needed offensive punch. In addition, he is a well-liked, easy-going leader who the team willingly follows. The message Holton posted on Instagram provides an example of his character:

"After meeting with doctors, my family and I have decided the best thing for me to do is have surgery. Unfortunately, that means I'll be out for the remainder of the season. That being said, we are Florida State, and our goal stays the same. This team is special and will do great things this year! God has a plan and a purpose for everything He does! Thank you for all the thoughts and prayers. It's not the end of the world, just a setback. GO NOLES!" (Tyler Holton).

JIM CROSBY

MARTINISM #7

Once, when an opponent had ended a lengthy losing streak against his Noles and won the game 11 expressed surprise, saying:

"They hadn't beat us since Hitler was a corporal."

11: MAKING BASEBALL HISTORY

Bulletin from Florida State Baseball

April 2, 2018, TALLAHASSEE, Fla. - The Florida State baseball team announced Monday that it will pair with the Florida State University Black Student Union to honor the Negro Leagues for this Wednesday's game against Jacksonville

Florida State will wear hats that recognize the Negro Leagues Museum in Kansas City, Mo., and honor the African American players of the early 20th century. Fred Flowers, the first African American student-athlete at Florida State, will throw out the first pitch prior to the 6:00 pm game.

Flowers is memorialized as part of the Integration Statue outside the FSU student union.

The Black Student Union at Florida State is celebrating its 50th anniversary in 2018. From its mission statement, the BSU "offers black students a form of identity ... and seeks to develop unity among black students so that jointly and strongly they can express concerns and problems faced on campus."

The BSU opened a new 5,600-square-foot building on campus in November 2017.

JIM CROSBY

RELENTLESS PURSUIT OF THE RECORD

76 Days Later ...

A Historic Evening—Win # 1,976

It took a while, but they did it. Martin's guys persevered. They knew they were going into one of the toughest places to win a game on the road. Clemson, South Carolina. Making it even more difficult was the pressure associated with the occasion. Just one win, and Mike Martin would become the winningest coach in the history of college baseball. He knew it. His players knew it. And the Clemson Tigers knew it.

CLEMSON—TOUGH PLACE TO SET A RECORD
Three Game Series, May 5-7, 2018
Doug Kingsmore Stadium
Clemson, South Carolina
FSU (31-14, 14-10) vs Clemson (34-11, 17-7)

The Opponent: Clemson, Tigers: The Seminoles and Tigers will tangle for the 143rd time on Cinco de Mayo Saturday, May 5th. Florida State leads the series 74-67-1. FSU is 39-20-1 in Tallahassee, with Clemson leading at home 33-22. Added excitement is Coach Mike Martin needing just one win to set the all-time record for most wins. The series begins on Saturday and runs through Monday this year due to its scheduling during final exam week. The finale on Monday is scheduled for National Television on ESPN2.

Game One: History is Made

Nobody said this was going to be easy, and it wasn't. First of all, the overflow crowd of 5,379 was not very friendly. Obviously, they did not want Coach Martin to set the record for most wins in Tiger territory. And when it was over four hours and twenty-one minutes later everybody was exhausted and only one team was a winner: Florida State.

11: MAKING BASEBALL HISTORY

It took 13 innings to complete, but Florida State came out victorious, 3-2, on a home run by right fielder Steven Wells. Coach Martin can claim coaching genius on the move he made to elevate Wells in the batting order to lead off after spending much of the season batting ninth.

As he stood before the media holding the game-winning baseball, 11 said: "This one (ball) the first one (win) when we beat Miami in 1980. That was given to me by James Ramsey's (2009-12) daddy, Craig (1977-80)."

Then Martin added: "If it sounds corny, I don't care, it's about family, we are Florida State family. This university has given me every chance to be successful and what's more important to me is when people read the record, it'll say Florida State (next to my name)."

Fans witnessed some exceptional pitching with five scoreless innings before FSU scored in the 6th on the double by Rhett Aplin, followed by an RBI single by Cal Raleigh. Reese Albert homered in the 7th to make it 2-0 FSU, and that would be all the scoring for the Seminoles until the thirteenth.

Clemson scored single runs in the seventh and eighth to tie the game. That was all the scoring for the Tigers that night.

In the 13th, with one out, Wells, who was 0-for-6 on the evening, got a pitch that was up in the zone and sent it high over the left-field fence for what turned out to be the game-winner. He said he felt "Relief, it was such a long game, and we were battling. My previous six at-bats did not go my way."

It was a moment he would never forget, nor would Seminole baseball fans everywhere.

Later a smiling Wells said: "I got some texts from my dad and my aunts. It hasn't really hit me yet. It's awesome to see him (Martin) hit this milestone; he brings so much passion to the game every day."

Pitcher Drew Parrish allowed only one run in 6.1 innings while striking out eight. He has only given up six hits and one run while fanning 21 in his last 14.1 innings. Equally impressive was freshman C J. Van Eyk's clutch relief performance as he kept beating back Tiger threats. Van Eyk allowed just one run and 4 hits while striking out 7 in the final 6.1 innings.

After letting out a big sigh Coach Mike Martin laughed: "Yes, I'm glad it's over."

The long journey to that arduous accomplishment was done. Now it was time to focus on trying to keep playing at a high enough level to secure a place in the postseason.

Now Mike Martin, with 1,976 wins, has more than anyone in college baseball history. It took him 39 years to set the record surpassing the late Augie Garrido, who had taken 48 years to achieve the record Martin passed. And he ain't done yet.

FINAL: FSU 3 Clemson 2 (13 innings). FSU (32-14, 14-10). Clemson (34-12, 17-8)

Martin's Magic Number: 0. Now has 1,976 wins.

11: MAKING BASEBALL HISTORY

MARTINISM #8

Mike Martin explains one of the keys to success at Florida State:

"We don't allow negative thinking at Florida State, no complaining, no griping. I don't want to hear that it is too cold or too hot, or the mound is too high, or the batter's box has holes in it, and you can't get comfortable. The other team has the same situation. If you feel like you can't get it done, you won't get it done. There's no room for excuses."

The Stars Speak

Jonathan Johnson (1993-95)
FSU Hall of Fame 2006

- Ocala, Florida
- 57 app; 362 ip; 391 k, 34-5 W-L
- 3 time All-American

First Impression of Mike Martin
"My first impression of 11 when I walked on the field. He was a guy that was always in control of the situation. I think that was the biggest thing. I always felt confident not only that we were prepared for that ball game—that anything that happened in the game, he had seen it and done it. That was my biggest impression I got from 11."

After That
"First getting to know him and just the pride that he had in that Florida State uniform—garnet-and-gold—just pouring that into you as a ballplayer. Getting you not to play for yourself but to play for that school. I think that is why we had the guys perform the way they did.

Guys like me, and Charlie Cruz, Mickey Lopez, Doug Mientkiewicz, and Paul Wilson. So many names … guys that came in there and sold out for the program. We did not have a single prima donna on the team while I was there that was just worrying about getting drafted."

Seminole Pride

"You just had pride in the accomplishments of those who were there before you—Guys like Richie Lewis. I used to look up and see his stats and the other great pitchers of the past, and I was like: 'Man, I want to catch them and surpass them. It was like you didn't want to let them down. Would see guys like Chris Brock, Kenny Felder, Tim Davis, and Roger Bailey, and it was like man, I want them to think that I'm carrying on.' It carries on today. 11's legacy, his leadership, the way he pays attention to detail, handles you as a player and how he prepares."

How JJ Became a Seminole

"Got an invitation to the select camp. Went there hoping to catch the eye of a coach.

The only college that had actively recruited me was Central Community College right there in Orlando. So, I go up to Tallahassee, and there were some big names there. But 11 saw my breaking ball, and he said, 'Jamey (pitching coach Shouppe) get that boy's number. We are gonna need it.' When I signed, Florida State was the only four-year school that recruited me."

Jonathan Johnson Elected into the FSU Hall of Fame in 2006

Jonathan Johnson combined a great pitching arm with a love for competition that would eventually place him among the finest pitchers in the storied history of the Florida State baseball program.

Johnson signed with Florida State out of Forest High in Ocala, Florida, and made an immediate impact on the Seminole program. As a true freshman in 1993, Johnson was named ACC Rookie of the Year, placed in the top 10 in eight of 11 ACC pitching categories, and culminated the year with a place on the Baseball America and Collegiate Baseball All-Freshman teams.

He followed his rookie campaign with a 12-1 record and 137 strikeouts as a sophomore earning second-team All-ACC and third-team All-America honors from Baseball America, Collegiate Baseball, and the National Collegiate Baseball Writers Association. He was selected to Team USA that summer and finished with a 6-3 record. He overcame a broken ankle in his third and final season at Florida State to finish with a 12-3 record, leading Florida State to the ACC Championship in 1995 and a berth in the College World Series. He was a finalist for the 1995 Golden Spikes Award and first-team Baseball America and second-team Collegiate Baseball All-American.

11: MAKING BASEBALL HISTORY

Johnson would win 34 games and lose only 5 at Florida State with a 2.63 ERA and 391 career strikeouts, which ranked fourth on the all-time ACC career list. He was selected by the Texas Rangers with the seventh overall pick of the 1995 draft. He went on to debut in the big leagues with the Rangers in 1998 and enjoyed a six-year professional career. (Nolesports.com).

The Stars Speak

Jeff Ledbetter (1979-82)
FSU Hall of Fame 1991

- Largo, FL
- Still holds 8 records, including 42 HR (season) 97 (career)
- 1st round draft pick by Red Sox in 1982

Called "Treetops," Ledbetter has 8 Hitting Records Still Standing

"I thought my home run record (for a season) might still stand because it just seemed like that year everything I hit hard went up into the air. I wasn't hitting line drives or ground balls. Then they put that screen up (on the RF fence), and I thought this was not good because it didn't give the guys the same opportunity I had. I don't know if anybody will ever break that record."

Destined to be a Seminole, But ...

"I was always a Florida State fan. The tradition of Florida State. I was recruited by all the other teams, but I didn't want to go out of state. I didn't want to go to Miami. That left Florida. My sisters (Laura and Pam) both ran track at FSU. I kept waiting and waiting (for a letter from FSU). That worried me a little bit. The Seminoles held out on me because my sisters had told them I was going to come here. They didn't send my letter for a long time. I was three days away from signing with the Gators. Thank God that didn't happen."

Playing for Dick Howser

"Coach Howser was one of my favorite people. He never gave you his word unless he could make it happen. After my freshman year, I was bound and determined to go home. I was homesick. I had my car loaded out in the

JIM CROSBY

parking lot. Coach Howser called me into his office. I sat down and laid my car keys on the desk.

He kept telling me reasons why I should stay. I didn't notice he had slid my keys over to his side of the desk. Then he said: "Have you ever known me to say anything if I couldn't make it happen?"

I said, 'No, coach.' He said: "I want you to give me your word you are coming back, or I'm not going to give you your keys back.' I said, 'Coach, I'm gonna stay.'"

From Howser to Martin

"We all loved Coach Martin. He wasn't much older than us, so he was a friend of ours. He was more laid back when we were playing as long as we were doing what we were supposed to, then he wasn't like a drill sergeant out there."

11's Impact

"He was always there for us. It seems like I was always in trouble every year at Florida State. Coach Martin was always there and handled it in a way that we respected what he said.

He has definitely evolved with the times. It is almost a crime that he didn't win the College World Series because he got us out there so many times."

1982—One Heckuva Year

(Ledbetter started with 12 home runs in the first two series in which he batted .655).

"I remember I was a couple of home runs behind Mike Fuentes (Golden Spikes winner 1981) for the College record. In my first game (Feb. 13, 1982, vs GA. State), I had four home runs, and when I came up in the 8th, the pitcher threw me three straight balls, and even his own team was yelling at him to get it over. They wanted to see if I could hit another."(FSU won 23-0)

What It Means to Be a Nole

"You come to places in your life where there is a fork in the road, and you take one of those forks. It kinda scared me. What if I hadn't gotten that letter? I was that close to being a Florida Gator. The greatest thing about Coach Martin is I always knew, for 40 years, if I went up to Tallahassee, he was always there to welcome and appreciate. He had a profound effect on me. He was our lifeline to the program. The Hall of Fame is something that can never be taken away from you. Most proud of that. Records are outstanding but being a Hall of Fame member is what sets you apart."

Jeff Ledbetter Elected into Florida State Hall of Fame, 1991

When Jeff Ledbetter was a freshman pitcher and outfielder at Florida State in 1979, he blasted 13 home runs. Four years later, he had racked up 97. Each of his four years with the Tribe was very successful, but to say that Jeff had a "successful" year in 1982 would be the understatement of all time.

During his senior year, Jeff, nicknamed "Treetops" for his prestigious blasts into the pine trees behind the right-field wall at Seminole Field, set varsity records in almost every category available. In addition, he placed himself in NCAA record books for home runs in a season (42), home runs in a career (97), home runs in a game (4), RBIs in a career (346), most total bases in a season (273) and most total bases in a career (346).

Ledbetter capped off that outstanding 1982 season by being named All-Metro, All-Metro Tournament, Metro Player of the Year, All-American, and Sporting News Player of the Year. Drafted in the first round by the Boston Red Sox, Jeff spent three years with the organization. Today, many of his records still stand in FSU and NCAA record books as a challenge to current and future sluggers (Nolefan.org).

JIM CROSBY

THE LAST ROUNDUP: 2,000 WINS & BEYOND

The Decision

"In 2017, I went to Stan (Wilcox-former Athletic Director), and we talked about making 2018 the retirement year," Martin recalls. "One thing led to another, and as we got into the year, we didn't talk about it that much."

In 2017 Florida State, under Martin, would once again top the 40-win mark. It was Florida State's record-setting 40th consecutive season, winning 40-plus games and the 38th under Martin. The Seminoles 38th consecutive regional appearance and 16th visit to the College World Series in Omaha.

Martin recalls, "With about three or four weeks left in the season, Stan and I were talking in his office, and he basically said it this way: '40 is not a bad number.' I was so excited that a man who was running our athletic department was saying that he would like for me to stay another year (past the previously decided on 2018 -his 39th year). I, of course, said I will talk to Carol."

"So, I said to her Stan wants me to stay another year. We had not made firm plans yet, but we had researched some things about retirement. Then when Stan and I got back together, he said, 'and 2,000 sounds real good too.' That made me feel so good. It gave me a warm and fuzzy feeling that he wanted me to come back. That's basically how it went. We both knew that this (2019) would be the last year. Yes, 40 years sounds good."

And apparently, 2,000 wins sounded pretty special also.

Carol Martin's approach to "another year" was: "To be truthful, I'm looking forward to it being the last, and I'm dreading it being the last. I am ambivalent about it because that has been our whole lives."

Over the years before each home game started, 11 could be seen looking into the stands. There is one person he is looking to see. When he sees Carol in the first row, which is almost every time, he knows it's time to play ball.

Thinking about the future, Carol said: "I know it will be hard for him. The transition will be difficult for him because he has been such a hands-on coach. To go from 100 mph all the time to five mph is going to be really difficult."

So, with 39-years behind him, approaching 2,000 wins and with his Best Girl in the stands and his son coaching third base, the man who had dedicated the best years of his life to Seminole baseball eagerly approached his final season as head coach of an elite baseball program that will always carry forward his stamp of excellence.

The Final Team

One thing that the 2019 Seminole baseball team would always have that none of those before them could lay claim to—they were 11's final team. How would that story be written?

Would it have a fairy-tale ending? Could they become the first and only Martin team to win that elusive College World Series title?

While other Seminole teams were on hand to celebrate historic Martin victories such as his 500th, 1,000th, and 1,500th wins and every player from 1980 forward could lay claim to helping tell the story and add to the legacy of Mike Martin, no other team could say they were the last team standing at season's end.

No doubt, when the final chapter is written, the total accomplishments of Mike Martin will outshine any who coached the game. Just the fact that he stayed in one place as head coach for 40 years is amazing in this day when coaching turnover runs rampant and time in one place is often short-term. Coaches continue to move around seeking their best fit and greatest financial gain.

While the Martins not only stayed put, but they also donated large sums of money back to the school's baseball program and athletic department, as well as giving money to their church and various worthwhile community agencies.

So, on February 15, 2019, the Seminole team that suited up and prepared to make history was already a historic one. The 35-man roster was dominated by youth, with 22 underclassmen dressing out—14 freshmen and eight sophomores. There were only four seniors and nine juniors on the team. It was one of the youngest teams that Coach Martin had gone into a season with.

Surveying the youth, Martin said: "It is a very young club. We don't say in our program that we are a year away. We don't use that analogy. Our job as coaches is to prepare our team to get to Omaha. If we had 25 freshmen on our team, we are still going to say that."

2019 Florida State Seminoles

The Roster

No	Name	Pos	B-T	Hgt	Wgt	Cl	Ltr	Hometown
12	Tyler Ahearn	P	R-R	6-2	185	So	*	Jupiter
23	Reese Albert	OF	L-L	6-2	197	So	*	Jupiter
40	Jack Anderson	P	R-R	6-3	185	Fr		Tampa (Jesuit)
51	Nico Baldor	F	L-R	6-2	195	Jr		Tampa
37	Tim Becker	OF	L-R	6-0	185	Sr		Wellington (Palm)
18	Cole Beverlin	P	R-R	6-4	180	Fr		Port Orange
19	Elijah Cabell	OF	R-R	6-2	195	Fr		Winter Park
2	Nander De Sedas	IF	S-R	6-2	192	Fr		Panama City
5	Shane Drohan	P	L-L	6-3	195	So	*	Jupiter
8	J.C. Flowers	OF/P	R-R	6-2	185	Jr	**	Orange Park
36	Jonathan Foster	C	R-R	6-0	205	Sr	*	LaGrange, GA
3	Dakota Gaillard	IF	R-R	5-11	155	Fr		Jupiter
31	Conor Grady	P	R-R	6-2	187	So	*	Tampa
14	Troy Hamilton	IF	R-R	5-11	155	Fr		Royal Palm Beach
33	Chase Haney	P	R-R	6-6	225	Jr-R	**	Winter Garden
46	Gage Hutchinson	P	R-R	6-1	185	Sr-R	*	Port Orange
17	Clayton Kwiatkowski	P	L-L	6-2	205	Jr	**	Tampa
26	Robby Martin	OF	L-R	6-3	200	Fr		Tampa
20	Kyle McMullen	P	R-R	6-2	175	Jr		Jupiter
22	Drew Mendoza	IF	L-R	6-5	225	Jr	**	Minneola
63	Mattheu Nelson	C	R-R	5-11	195	Fr		Largo
43	Drew Parrish	P	L-L	5-11	180	Jr	**	Rockledge
29	Austin Pollock	P	L-L	6-3	180	So	*	Tallahassee
21	Chris Ruckdeschel	OF	R-R	6-1	190	Fr		Davie
16	Mike Salvatore	IF	R-R	6-0	186	Sr	*	Ewing, NJ
24	Alec Sanchez	IF	L-R	5-11	195	Fr		Jacksonville
25	Chase Sanguinetti	IF	L-L	6-0	190	Fr		Tampa
13	Jonah Scolaro	P	L-L	5-9	180	So	*	Valrico
35	Carter Smith	C/IF	L-R	6-1	175	Jr		Fort Myers
9	Cooper Swanson	IF	R-R	6-1	205	So	*	Fort Myers
15	CJ Van Eyk	P	R-R	6-1	185	So	*	Lutz
30	Antonio Velez	P	L-L	6-1	185	Jr		Brandon
27	McGuire Weaver	IF	R-R	5-11	155	Fr		Tampa
38	Corey Yawn	P	R-R	6-1	180	Fr		Seminole

(Nolefan.org)

11: MAKING BASEBALL HISTORY

The Record-Setting Staff-2019

Mike Martin's final staff knew that they would go down in College Baseball history as assistant coaches on the team that put the finishing touches on the record for most wins by a head coach. However, none of that mattered as they embarked on this historic season. That didn't matter to them because it was business as usual. Let's play Seminole baseball. Here are the ones who helped make it happen:

Mike Martin Jr.: 22nd season on the staff as assistant coach and recruiting coordinator. "Meat," as he was called by everyone, also worked with hitters and catchers. His invaluable contribution saw the last FSU recruiting classes ranked in the Top 10. Meat saw 62 of his hitters taken in the MLB draft. He was an All-American catcher at FSU 1993-95.

Clyde Keller: 4th season on the staff, was promoted to pitching coach in August 2018. The Fair Oaks, California native, was a pitcher/infielder in 1988-89. He was 23-5 as a pitcher and hit .315 as an infielder. He was selected by the St. Louis Cardinals in the MLB draft and spent five years in the minor leagues. He has written three books on the fundamentals of baseball.

Tyler Holt: First Season on the FSU staff. Holt will be an undergraduate assistant coach working on a degree in sports management. Holt, the last Seminole to bat .400, will work with hitters and coach first base. He was drafted by the Cleveland Indians and spent parts of three seasons in MLB.

Chip Baker: Director of Baseball Operations. 35th season at FSU. The Big Shooter begins his 17th season in the current position overseeing all the administrative aspects of the program. He has participated in 15 CWS and 11of those in 18 years on the field as 3rdbase coach and instructing catchers. Recognized in 2006 for a Quarter Century of Leadership in Baseball.

MARTINISM #9

Some thoughts from the winningest coach on how he got here:
"It is amazing how the competition can be us. Approaching a season, I'd like to have been able to look back over the success we had and relax. But I knew if you had a couple of bad years, they would be saying: 'Too bad the game has passed him by, or he's too old for the job, he's had a good career. We could not afford to have bad years. Our job was always to be positive.

One of the most positive individuals I ever coached was Deion Sanders. He's a little different, but he always believed in himself. With the game on the line, he wanted to be at bat. He is also a good person."

GETTING STARTED

The Stuff Legends Are Made Of

With over 40% of the team having never played a college baseball game, the Seminoles were introduced to the 4,809 home fans at Mike Martin field in Dick Howser Stadium on February 15, 2019. Martin's final season-opening series would feature four games (doubleheader on Saturday) against the Maine Black Bears. 11's starting lineup had four true freshmen in it.

However, the current recruiting class included five junior college transfers, which, when added to the 15 freshmen, made the new 20-man class the largest in program history.

Even though they were young, the good news was that the 2019 edition of FSU baseball was a talented group. Baseball America ranked the Seminole recruiting class as Number three behind LSU and Vanderbilt. It was the highest-ranked class in the Atlantic Coast Conference and two slots ahead of their down-state rivals, the Florida Gators.

And What a Start It Was!

If you believe in omens, you will find the first game of Mike Martin's final season full of them: Number 11's team went into the season opener ranked 11th in the nation. They won the game by the score of, yep, you guessed it, 11-0. But that's not all for those who are omen-oriented. The Seminoles tossed a no-hitter! Three Nole pitchers combined to pitch the 10th no-hitter in the program's history and the first-ever on opening day.

11: MAKING BASEBALL HISTORY

Was it coincidence that before the game Chris Chavez, who was the last Seminole pitcher to toss a solo no-hitter, visited Coach Martin in the dugout? Chris brought his son Noah, who is a little league pitcher, along with him.

And if all of those weren't coincident challenging enough, the leading hitter that night was named "Martin." Freshman Robby Martin served immediate notice that he will be a player to be reckoned with in the Seminole lineup. All Martin did in his first game in a Seminole uniform was go 3-for-4 and drive in five of the 11 runs.

Drew Parrish, the All-American ace of the staff, got things rolling with a three up-and-three down first inning. He would toss five innings of no-hit ball with one walk and five strikeouts. He was followed by sophomore RHP Conor Grady's three-innings with four K's, and Jr. RHP Chase Haney completed the no-no with a 1-K ninth.

Afterward, Martin said: "This was so much fun. It's very special. The closest that I think we've come to a no-hitter on opening day was us getting 1-hit. It was a great memory tonight."

Informed of 11's comments after the game, Parrish laughed and said: "I mean, the guy's been around baseball longer than I've been alive, times two." Then he added: "For him to say that, after all, that he's seen, all the great players he's coached, it's just something you are going to remember the rest of your life."

After the game, FR catcher Matthew (Mat) Nelson gave 11 the baseball used for the final out. That triggered another memory. After he took the ball from Nelson, Martin flashed back 40 years when another Seminole catcher gave him the game ball from a significant victory... his first one as the Seminoles head coach.

In 1980 after his first win as head coach, a 9-8 defeat of the Hurricanes in Miami, catcher Craig Ramsey gave him the ball. Now he will make room in the trophy case for another one.

Mike Martin's season-opening record improved to 36-4. He was now only a dozen wins from 2,000.

Lots of Baseball, Lots of Fans

Game One of DH vs Maine, Game Two of 2019

While the weather was iffy (cloudy, 72 degrees) for the first weekend of baseball, that didn't matter to the true baseball fans. Over 5,000, mostly garnet-and-gold clad, cheering fans came to the ballpark for this double-header.

After one inning of the first game, the score was 0-0. That was the last inning that the Seminoles did not score. Over the next seven innings, the home team would draw 14 walks, collect 10 hits (2 HRs by Senior Mike Salvatore and Freshman Elijah Cabell) and have six batters hit-by-pitches. It all added up to a 16-3 win for Florida State.

Second baseman and lead-off batter Salvatore had four RBI, as did the number two hitter in the lineup, Reese Albert, and freshman shortstop, #9 hitter in the lineup Nander De Sedas.

RHP CJ Van Eyk picked up where he left off last season with 5 innings (84 pitches), allowing a couple of runs on six hits and three walks while fanning eight. It was his 7th win as a Seminole with zero losses thus far

Game Two of DH vs Maine, Game Three of 2019

In this seven-inning game of the double-header, the Seminoles jumped off to a 2-0 lead in the second inning. At that point, it seemed the Seminoles were in complete control and could run away with another relatively easy win.

Not-so-fast My Friend

Local product sophomore LHP Austin Pollock, who has hopes of nailing down the #3 pitching slot and become the usual "Sunday Pitcher," did not help his chances. Still leading 2-0 going into the 4th inning, Pollock gave up a grand slam to LF Jake Posey and left after giving up 5 earned runs, five hits, and two walks. He threw 71 pitches and faced 18 batters. Fortunately for Pollock and the Seminoles relievers, Jr. LHP Clayton Kwiatkowski and sophomore RHP Tyler Ahearn, did not allow any runs or hits during the rest of the game.

After adding single runs in the 4th and 6th to close the gap to 5-4, the Seminoles went into the home half of the seventh and by schedule last inning. With the home crowd led by the Animals of Section B cheering them on,

Cabell started the 7th with a walk. Playing RF this time, Robby Martin hit a double off the right-center-field wall to tie the game.

SR CF JC Flowers pinch-ran for Martin and advanced to third on a balk. With a 1-2 count on him, FR catcher Mat Nelson hit a fly ball to CF just deep enough for the speedy Flowers to tag and race home with the winning run.

So, now the Seminoles were 3-0, and their coach, Mike Martin, with 1,990 wins now needed only 10 wins to surpass 2,000.

Game Four: Opening Series 2019 vs Maine

The Seminoles wasted no time in nailing down a sweep in Mike Martin's final season-opening series. Freshman left fielder Elijah Cabell doubled in two runs in the first inning against Maine. That would be sufficient for the win, but just to make sure FSU scored seven runs in the seventh for a 9-1 win and a four-game sweep. Freshman Robby Martin had a three-run double, and JC Flowers singled in two runs to highlight the 7-run-7th. 3B Drew Mendoza reached base three times, driving in two runs with a single up the middle and scoring twice.

LHP Antonio Velez picked up his first win as a Seminole with 4-innings of 3-hit, 1-run relief work.

Afterward, Robby Martin told www.seminoles.com, "It was very exciting for all of us. We had a little bit of jitters, kinda just more excited to get out here as freshmen and play our first series of college baseball. It was kind of like a statement setter (getting the sweep) that we are going to be a great group of ballplayers."

MARTINISM #10

THERE WERE SOME LOSSES TOO

It is not all a bed of roses—lots of success but some failures too.

"Everybody gets knocked down. I wonder how Bobby Bowden would feel if he had as many losses as I have (736). Every loss affects me just like it does anyone else. The key is staying positive, knowing you will get it done."

THE STARS SPEAK

Marshall McDougall (1999-00)
FSU Hall of Fame 2011

- Valrico, FL
- 143 games; 596 ab; .383 avg; 43 hr; 173 rbi
- 6 hrs. in one game-most in NCAA baseball history.

Coach Martin's Impact on McDougall

"I think 11 is a very hard worker. Great at working you in practice. I think I learned more defensively. I think what he built is legendary. The way he runs the program is traditional, and he runs practice the right way. He puts the right kind of pressure on you in practices.

I think it is amazing how long he has done it. I think it is a testament to how much dedication Coach Martin has to the program and the people of Tallahassee."

Marshall's Miracle-May 9, 1999

In one game, on a May afternoon in Maryland, Marshall McDougall put his name in the FSU record books in six different categories. The most amazing of those records, which still stands in 2020, is the unbelievable 6-homers McDougall hit that day ... in one game! Even in the Major Leagues, the most HRs in a game are still four.

After hitting a single in his first at-bat, McDougall had a solo homer in the second, a three-run homer in the fourth, a solo homer in the sixth, a three-run homer in the seventh, a bases-loaded homer in the eighth, and a three-run homer in the ninth. His record six homers accounted for 16 RBI and 25 Total Bases. All of these are still stand-alone records. In addition, his nine at-bats, six runs scored, and seven hits in a game still are tied for first in their category. And, oh yeah, Marshall helped FSU win the game 26-2.

20 Years Later Marshall Remembers

"Early on, it was just a normal game. I believe we were up 4-2. First time around, I hit a single, I believe, and it wasn't any big deal. We just started batting around, and it seemed like everybody who came up got on base. It was just one of those things where anything that could happen in our favor went our way. It seemed like every inning; I was up with people on base. The thing I remember most is the celebration of the players. The thing that makes me feel most proud, aside from the baseball aspect, was the look on their faces.

Nobody's Perfect

"Oh yeah, I did make an error, so I wasn't perfect in that game. I did make a mistake."

Marshall McDougall Elected into the FSU Hall of Fame in 2011

No player in the history of baseball accomplished what Marshall McDougall did from the plate in his first year with the Seminoles. McDougall, a Jacksonville native, is best known for his performance against Maryland in 1999 when he blasted an NCAA record six home runs in one game. He also had a record 16 RBI and 25 total bases in the game played on May 9, 1999, that shattered the NCAA records.

The Seminole second baseman went on to win the ACC triple crown in 1999 along with ACC Player of the Year honors with a .419 batting average, 106 RBI, and 28 home runs. He started all 71 FSU games and led the nation in RBIs and hits (126).

He was voted Most Outstanding Player of the 1999 College World Series and was a consensus All-American, a Golden Spikes, and an NCBWA/Dick Howser Player of the Year finalist. McDougall and Florida State reached the National Championship game of the 1999 College World Series, losing to Miami 6-5 and played four games in Omaha his senior season.

McDougall was drafted in the ninth round of the 2000 draft by the Oakland Athletics and reached the major leagues with the Texas Rangers in 2005 (Nolefan.org).

Jose Zabala (1995-98)

- Miami, FL
- 239 games; 539 ab; .312 avg; 46 hbp
- Stole home with winning run for 11's 1,000th win

Zabala's Views on 11

"People might say he was lucky to win 2,000 or more games. But it really does take a great team manager. A person that is going to prepare you to practice in a situation. These are the things that Coach Martin did because when it came right down to the game, you were ready to go."

Why FSU?

"The minute I set foot into Howser and I met Coach Martin and Chip Baker, that was it. I didn't have to go any farther."

Jose Gets His Chance

"11 called me into the office one day, and he said: 'Zabala, if you get on base, you can play.' I said: 'Coach, I can do that for you.' I did what I had to do. I did it for the team, and that is what he wanted. I could not have had a better coach or mentor. I went into coaching, and I learned so much baseball from him that he brought to the game. No one deserves this record more than he does."

Hit by Pitch 46 Times

"Getting hit by pitches was a way I could contribute for the team. Coach Martin was a great coach and is fully deserving of the record." (46 HBP is still 3rd best over 20 years later and his 24 HBP in a season is #1.)

Big Question Answered—Who's taller, Baker or Zabala?

"Here's the thing as you get older, you tend to get shorter. I don't know why that happens. I think he has got me now. I'll have to be honest with you. I remember he used to tell me when I would get to 3rd base in the game, and he was coaching third. 'Zabala get off the base.' I would say why? He'd say: 'Because the base will give you another inch (in height), and I don't want you to have that on me.'"

Zabala Sums It Up

"There are great coaches who come and go, and then there is 11."

Zabala gave 100% effort for four full seasons in Tallahassee. His sparkling personality made him one of the most popular players. Everybody likes Jose. And yes, he did live up to what he promised 11 when he told him that he would get on base for him.

His on-base-percentage for four years was .466, and in his final season (1998), it was a sparkling .491 as he was on base almost half of his opportunities. In addition to 46 hbp, he drew 115 bb, had 168 hits, and stole 22 bases. He also played 3b, 2b, SS, RF, and DH and batted .312 during the 239 games and 539 At bats as a Seminole.

No one represents Florida State and the Seminole Spirit better than Jose Zabala.

Youngstown State Penguins
February 22, 2019, 4 pm, Friday, Mike Martin Field, Howser Stadium
80 degrees, Sunny, Slight Breeze

After rain washed out the Seminoles' second series of the season, a scheduled game in Jacksonville, FSU welcomed Youngstown State to Dick Howser Stadium. It was the first meeting between the two teams. The Penguins from Ohio brought an 0-3 record in after getting swept by Mississippi State in Starkville. Florida State looked to add to the 4-0 start against Maine.

Game One of Three

The Seminoles bats were quiet for the first five innings as 4,012 fans waited patiently for the hometown favorites to put some runs on the board. YSU scored a couple of first inning runs as 3B Blaze Glenn tagged Nole ace Drew Parrish for a two-run homer.

The Seminoles overcame that with a couple of two-run homers of their own. 3B Drew Mendoza tied the game in the 6th with his 18th career round-tripper. Freshman SS Nander De Sedas sealed the win for the Noles in the 7th with his first homer as a Seminole. JR transfer Antonio Velez picked up his second win with four scoreless 2-hit innings.

An advance look at threatening weather ahead for Sunday prompted the two teams to schedule a doubleheader for Saturday. Today's win was Mike Martin's 1, 992nd.

Saturday, Game Two of Three, First of DH, 1:02 pm

No contest! Only way to describe this one. FSU put it out of reach with seven runs in the first after the Penguins scored one. The Noles added 1 in the 2nd, 4 in the third, 3 in the 4th, and topped it off with nine in the 6th. The game was completed after seven innings due to a run-rule that saw the Seminoles grab a 24-2 win.

Much to the delight of 4,914 fans, the Seminoles put up 18 hits, six of which were four-baggers. Reese Albert and Drew Mendoza hit back-to-back HRs in the 1st inning. Albert to right field and Mendoza to left field. DH Robby Martin had a two-run homer also in the 7-run 1st.

Nander De Sedas had his second homer in two days to right center in the 4th. Carter Smith, pinch-hitting for Drew Mendoza in the blowout, smashed a homer to RF to lead off the 6th. Then, later in the 6th, freshman Elijah Cabell put a cap on the homer-hitting parade with a long grand slam to CF.

Final 24-2, with CJ Van Eyk picking up his 2nd win of the season and 9th as a Seminole with no losses.

Saturday, Game Three of Three, Second of DH, 4:38 pm

Looking for the sweep, it looked a little dicey for a while at Mike Martin Field. Sophomore Lefty Austin Pollock lasted only one inning while giving up three runs. The Seminoles got one in the first and another in the second on a solo homer by Mat Nelson.

After tying the game at 4-4 in the 5th, the Noles scored the go-ahead run in the 6th. JC Flowers singled through the left side scoring two runs in the 8th. Then RHP Chase Haney set the Penguins down in order in the 9th, striking out two for the save. It was a good start to Mike Martin's final season with a 7-0 record to creep up to within six of the 2,000 wins mark.

JIM CROSBY

Martin Named ACC Player of the Week

TALLAHASSEE, Fla. – Florida State freshman Robby Martin earned Atlantic Coast Conference Player of the Week honors Monday after going 8-for-12 with eight RBI against Youngstown State this weekend. He is the first Seminole freshman to earn Player of the Week honors since current Baltimore Oriole DJ Stewart won the honor twice in 2013. Martin hit .667 for the week, including a combined 7-for-8 as the Seminoles completed a three-game sweep of Youngstown State by winning both ends of Saturday's doubleheader. Martin delivered a two-run homer in the first inning of game one, then added an RBI double in the second inning and a three-run double in the third to become the first Seminole with six RBI in a game since teammate Drew Mendoza in 2017. Martin added two more RBI in the nightcap and led the ACC with 17. The Tampa native's 15 hits for the season are also tops in the conference thus far. Nationally, Martin ranks third in RBI (17), fifth in doubles (5) and RBI per game (2.43), sixth in hits (15), ninth in sacrifice flies (2), and 10th in hits per game (2.14). Louisville pitcher Reid Detmers was named the league's pitcher of the week (www.seminoles.com).

11: MAKING BASEBALL HISTORY

Martin Marches On
March 2019

Mercer Pays a Visit
March 1-3, Dick Howser Stadium
Three Game Series
Mercer (8-1) vs FSU 8-0

The Mercer Bears from Macon, GA, have one of the longest standing non-conference relationships with Florida State of any school outside of the Sunshine State. Mercer and FSU first met on the baseball diamond in the Seminoles first season of baseball, 1948, in Macon. The Seminoles outlasted the Bears 14-12.

The two teams are meeting today for the 69th time in a series that heavily favors Florida State. The Noles have won 60 and lost only eight. In Tallahassee, they are 49-4 and have a 22-game win streak in the series.

Friday 6 pm, Game One of Three

Drew Parrish tossed six innings of 5-hit, 3-run baseball while striking out 8 batters to pick up his 2nd win of the season and run his career mark to 13 wins as FSU won 9-5.

Florida State scored three runs in the first inning. Robby Martin had an RBI single to center to start the scoring. The freshman from Tampa would go on to drive in three runs, running his season total to 20—4th in the nation. His 3-for-5 day at the plate was tops. J. C Flowers and Mat Nelson had two hits apiece

Leading 5-3, the Noles broke the game open with a four-run 8th. The key hit was a two-run pinch-hit homer by Sophomore Cooper Swanson. It was the Seminoles' 14th homer of the season, with 10 different players having at least one homer for the season.

It was decided that game two of the series would be moved to 2 pm from the original 1 pm start to accommodate fans attending the FSU basketball game at noon vs N. C. State.

Game Two of Three vs Mercer
Saturday, March 2, 2 pm
72 degrees, cloudy and wet

Not ideal baseball weather. In fact, two rain delays totaling 74-minutes probably whittled the original crowd of 4,047 down considerably. Nevertheless, those who remained enjoyed the all-Seminoles outcome, 12-1.

The Noles started the Bears' downfall with a 5-run third inning. Cooper Swanson, being rewarded for his HR the night before, got the start at first base. He repaid Coach Martin's confidence with a 482-foot, 3-run HR over the left-field scoreboard.

In the fourth, Drew Mendoza hit a two-run homer to increase the Seminole lead to 7-1. It was his 20th career homer.

Despite a 25-minute lightning delay in the second inning and a 49-minute delay in the top of the third, C J Van Eyk worked five solid innings to get the win and go 3-0. He threw 70 pitches, only surrendering one run and five hits while striking out eight.

FSU improved to 9-0 with the 12-1 win over Mercer, who fell to 8-3.

Game Three of Three vs Mercer
Sunday, March 3, 2019
1 pm, 79 degrees, cloudy

Attendance for the Mercer finale was 3,956 as the home team went for the sweep and hoped for a perfect record through 10 games.

The fans were rewarded with four-Seminole homers and a 5-1 win. FSU struck first in the third inning for three of their four runs when Drew Mendoza hit a two-run shot. Elijah Cabell followed with a 466-foot solo shot to left center.

Cooper Swanson homered for the third consecutive game in the sixth inning. Then Drew Mendoza hit his second of the game and third of the weekend in the seventh.

Shane Drohan tossed three and one-third innings, giving up three hits and no-runs. Conor Grady got the win with 2.2 innings of scoreless relief.

The Seminoles remained one of seven teams nationally without a loss. Their 10-win record put Mike Martin just 3 wins away from the 2,000 wins mark.

11: MAKING BASEBALL HISTORY

Next up: North Florida on Wednesday, March 6

What's an Osprey?
Wednesday, March 6, 2019, Dick Howser Stadium
North Florida (8-5) vs FSU (10-0)
6 pm, 55 degrees, winds 6 mph blowing out to RF

The brief history of FSU vs North Florida began on March 28, 2006, with a 14-8 Seminoles win. FSU has won 8 of the 10 games in the series, with only two games being played on NF's home diamond in Jacksonville. The Seminoles have scored in double figures in four of those games. The last meeting, April 7, 2010, was a 9-2 Seminole victory in Tallahassee.

Looking to keep their perfect record going, FSU fell behind the Ospreys 3 to 0 in the first inning with 3,896 fans looking on at Mike Martin Field. Seminole starter Antonio Velez failed to complete the first inning retiring after surrendering three earned runs on four hits.

The Seminole bullpen would hold the fort as Jonah Scolaro, Conor Grady, Clayton Kwiatkowski, and Chase Haney held the Osprey's scoreless over the final eight and one-third innings. Haney would receive credit for the walk-off win, his first of the season.

SS Nander De Sedas singled in a run in the second. LF Elijah Cabell tied the game in the 7th with a two-run home run that brought a relatively quiet crowd to its feet.

It remained for the freshman De Sedas to be the star of the night. With the game still tied, 3-3, in the bottom of the 9th and two runners on (Nelson on an E6, Flowers a BB), the Panama City, Panama native De Sedas lined a game-winning double off the right-center-field fence for the 4-3 victory. The Seminoles perfect season, 11-0, continued while Mike Martin moved to within 2 wins of 2,000.

By the way, an Osprey is a large fish-eating bird of prey that catches fish with its talons.

History-Making Weekend

The Historic Weekend

Lots of excitement in Seminole territory as the weekend approached. The Seminoles got their ACC schedule underway with the Virginia Tech Hokies coming to town. The Friday night contest would be the 58th time these two teams had hooked up. FSU leads the all-time series 43-14. But the Hokies won two of the last three played in 2017.

Of course, the major focus of Seminole fans was that Mike Martin was just two wins away from 2,000. The fans were certain this would happen, and close to 10,000 of them showed up for the series at Mike Martin field in Dick Howser Stadium to cheer the team on.

Game 1

The Seminoles brought a sparkling 11-0 record into the series. Virginia Tech was 8-3. Friday, March 8, 2019, it was LHP Drew Parrish (2-0, 3.00 ERA) vs. LHP Ian Seymour (2-0, 2.77 ERA).

In the opening game, the Hokies served notice that this would not be a cakewalk for the Noles. Uncharacteristically, Seminole Ace Drew Parrish would leave after six innings and 98 pitches trailing 4-3, having been touched for 6-hits, two of which were homers.

Heading into the bottom of the eighth, FSU found themselves trailing by 3 runs, 6-3. Even though both teams hit three home runs in the first four innings (Cooper Swanson's fourth, Elijah Cabell's fifth, and Jonathan Foster's 1st), it was beginning to look like win #1,999 would have to wait another day. But the Noles rallied in the 8th to tie the game at 6-6. The key hit was a two-run double by Drew Mendoza.

Still tied after regulation, the Hokies applied the heat again in the 10th with two runs.

However, this is not a Seminole team that can be counted out until they turn off the lights. After a walk to Mike Salvatore, with two outs, Cabell was hit by a pitch. Then walk-on senior Tim Becker drew a walk to load the bases.

With the pressure on CF, J.C. Flowers blasted a double off the center-field wall scoring all three runners and giving the 12-0 Seminoles their 3rd walk-off win of the season.

11: MAKING BASEBALL HISTORY

Mike Martin Was One Win Away from 2,000

Doubleheader Day

GAME 13 – Virginia Tech at Florida State, Saturday, March 9, 2019. RHP CJ Van Eyk (3-0, 3.00 ERA) vs. RHP Luke Scherzer (1-1, 4.76 ERA)

With 72 degrees, sunny skies, and a light breeze game one of the anticipated historic doubleheader day got underway at 12:02 p.m.

The Hokies showed the 5,500 fans in attendance that this might not be as much fun as they had anticipated. With 4 runs in the first three innings and lefty Chris Girard keeping the Noles hitters off balance by mixing up his assortment of four different pitches, it looked like this game might not be fun for the Seminoles.

In fact, it wasn't until the seventh inning that they got their first hit—a solid single by Drew Mendoza. That was the only hit, and the Noles went down six to nothing. Number two pitcher CJ Van Eyk was not as sharp as usual. In five innings, he walked six, gave up four earned runs on four hits.

The series was even at a game apiece. Fans would have to wait around until 3:45 to see the rubber match game and now had to wonder if Mike Martin would get his 2,000th win today or not. They certainly hoped so because the team would travel to Gainesville on Tuesday to meet the Florida Gators, who had defeated the Seminoles eight games in a row.

Later that Day …

Florida State did not clear the stands between games, so most of the fans stayed and waited out the 45-minute recess while the grounds crew whipped the field into tip-top shape. Fans who had been checking out the first game on television or radio from home or work now realized they could still get in the stadium for Game 2 and possibly see baseball history being made.

GAME 14 – Virginia Tech at Florida State, Saturday, March 9, 2019 LHP Shane Drohan (1-0, 1.04 ERA) vs. LHP Chris Gerard (0-0, 0.64 ERA. Seminole territory got loud as the home team jumped out to a 2-0 lead. Strong man Cooper Swanson (DH) from Fort Myers, FL, brought them to their feet with a long home run over the right-center-field fence, his 5th of the season.

After the game, 11 said: "Swanny is one of the strongest young men. You pat him on the back, and you go 'good gosh.' He could play tight end anywhere. He is a stud, and that bat speed is second to none. He can do some damage." The Noles added another run to take a 2-0 lead.

Nole fans were beginning to feel good until VA Tech spoiled that in the 3rd inning when they knocked lefty Shane Drohan out of the box and tied the game 2-2. But that was all she wrote for the Hokies. The Seminoles were not going to be denied this record-setting opportunity. Freshman SS Nander De Sedas started putting the celebration in place with a double in the 7th. Mendoza doubled him in. Freshman Elijah Cabell drove in another run to make it 4-2.

Coach Martin was determined to nail this win down. He brought CF J.C. Flowers in to close things out in the 8th and 9th. To make sure he did just that, Flowers not only retired six of the seven batters he faced in a performance that included three strikeouts, but he hit a long home run in the 8th to give FSU a 3-run cushion heading into the final inning. Flowers mowed them down, and the celebration began. This 2019 Seminole team had just enabled Mike Martin to become the first coach in any college sport to post 2,000 career wins.

Let the Celebration Begin!

The Celebration

What a scene! Happiness is spilling all over Mike Martin Field at Dick Howser stadium. Fans, Players, Coaches, Media, Administrators, Martin's family. They were all there to celebrate. Florida State President John Thrasher, a huge Martin supporter, and his wife Jean were there in front of the Seminole dugout. AD David Coburn was there. Of course, the guy in the Garnet jersey with the number 11 on it was wearing the biggest smile of all as he hugged everybody. His biggest hug was reserved for Carol Martin, his lovely wife. It was one huge joyful scene. The players surrounded a large banner that read:

"CONGRATS, MIKE MARTIN 2,000 WINS"

The huge video board had the same message but under the wording was a line of pictures of Mike Martin from all stages of his playing and coaching career.

The Animals of Section B were not going quietly into the night. They called for Coach Martin to lead a Noles Cheer. He obliged, and even though it wasn't the best Noles Cheer ever, it was the most effective and well-received one.

Later the media gathered in the Mike Loynd Trophy room to hear and report on what Coach Martin had to say. Here is what 11 said:

Martin's Opening Statement

"You know that is a special group of guys in there. It wasn't the greatest beginning of the day (lost game 1of DH). But that showed what they are all about by getting it done in a very important game. You don't want to lose two out of three in the league. There are a whole bunch of folks that are going to win two and some three. We have to be sharp, and I am very proud.

Before I go any further, I really want to say this from the bottom of my heart to the great fans of Florida State baseball and Florida State athletics … for them to be out here to celebrate with my family, to watch our players play darn good baseball. It is important that we understand that we wouldn't be where we are today without our great fans. They got us going. They knew that the homerun that JC hit was big. You could feel it. You could tell by their reactions that it was a big home run. I just want the fans to know that we appreciate them.

And another thing. We appreciate you guys and ladies (the press) for the great job you do in promoting and writing about Florida State baseball. That is important to all of us. These young men are looking at a lot of responsibility."

Next, two of the game's star players, speaking on behalf of the whole team, met with the press. Here is what they said about how it feels to be players on the team in which the Coach set an all-time record with 2,000 wins …. J.C. Flowers and Drew Mendoza were also on the 2018 team when 11 broke the record for most wins:

THE STARS SPEAK

After the game, players Drew Mendoza and JC Flowers visited the press conference following 11's 2,000th win and shared these thoughts:

Drew Mendoza

"We were a part of the record-setting for wins last year and this year the 2,000th win. Both were extremely special. Any time you have a coach who is getting banners printed out for him on the field, it is extremely special. We'll remember this one."

Drew Mendoza, out of Minneola, Fl., was drafted by the Detroit Tigers in 2016 but elected to come to Florida State and play for Mike Martin. In 3 years, he played in 170 games, batted an even .300, hit 33 Hrs. and drove in 133 runs. He was selected in the 3rd round of the 2019 MLB draft and signed with the World Champion Washington Nationals.

JC Flowers

"That's something we will remember the rest of our lives. To be a part of history like that. A very special moment."

JC Flowers from Orange Park, FL, was drafted in the 2016 MLB draft by the Cincinnati Reds but chose Florida State. He was an exceptional center-fielder who also became the closer on the team in 2019. He had a sterling 1.69 era with 13 saves. At the plate, he batted .245 with 15 Homers that included a grand slam against the Gators in Gainesville. He was selected in the 4th round of the 2019 MLB Draft by the Pittsburgh Pirates.

Three Days Later
March 12, 2019, McKeithan Stadium, Gainesville, FL

Baseball is a humbling game. Just when Florida State's team and fans were feeling good about themselves and perhaps a little cocky, the catchphrase popularized by a former Seminole player, coach, and now television personality, Lee Corso, was apropos: "Not so fast, my friend."

In front of 5,385, mostly Florida Gator fans, the Seminoles' first venture on the road was not much fun. It looked like it was going to be. Before the game, Gator coach Kevin O'Sullivan presented Coach Martin a gift ... a going away present in his final season in college baseball. It was a new golf bag and a Canadian cruise.

Then the Seminoles jumped off to a 6-0 lead against a Gator team that had already lost five games in the season, which was very unusual for a team that had become perennial guests at the College World Series.

Doubles by Mike Salvatore and Drew Mendoza in the first scored a run. In the third, Nander De Sedas homered to make it 2-0. Then in the 5th, a grand slam by CF JC Flowers gave the Seminoles a 6-0 lead, and it looked like they may coast their way to victory.

Not so fast, my friend. Sorry, Corso, to use your phrase again in this situation, but it fits.

The wheels really came off for the Seminoles as the Gators scored five runs in the fifth, eight runs in the sixth, and seven runs in the eight for an embarrassing 20-7 win over FSU. It was the ninth win in a row for Florida over Florida State. It was the most lopsided loss by the Seminoles to the Gators in 39 years.

The two teams still have two games left to play. The next meeting will come on March 26th in Jacksonville. Then the two teams will round out their series of three single games with a game in Tallahassee on April 9th.

A Game for the Ages

Talk about a historic rivalry full of monumental battles. Florida State vs. Florida—Seminoles and Gators baseball is unsurpassed. Through 2019 the two teams had battled it out on the baseball diamond 250 times. And as #11 Michael David Martin Sr. hung up his cleats for the last time, his head coaching record against the bitter rivals stood dead even at 76-76-1. However, adding in his record against the Gators as a player ('65-66), assistant coach (75-79), and head coach (1980-2019), #11 came out on top 96-86-1. In retirement, Martin had preserved the Seminoles' all-time winning record against the Gators, which stands at 128 wins for FSU, 121 for Florida, and 1 tie game.

While there have been many memorable games fiercely contested by these two arch-rivals, one that will always be remembered in Seminole Territory and a game that Gator fans will claim to have amnesia about occurred on Seminole Field 37 years ago.

As Tallahassee Democrat sportswriter George Maselli wrote: "Not even a bad Hollywood scriptwriter could have dreamed up this outlandish scenario."

It is uncertain how many of the 3,229 fans were still in the stands at the finish, although all of them probably would say they were there with the exception of any clad in orange-and-blue.

It looked extremely rocky for the Mudville, oops ... Seminole nine that evening. Heading into the bottom of the 9th inning, which would surely be the last one since 27 runs had already been scored and 16 of those belonged to the Swamp dwellers.

But as Mike Martin has always pointed out, there are 27 outs in a game (unless it goes extras), and his Seminoles will fight you until the final out is made. Well, this night, there was no final out made.

Trailing by 5 runs in the 9th, which started with Mike Yastrzemski, son of Major League Hall of Famer Carl Yastrzemski, slamming a double. Randy Rhino and Mark Barineau drew walks. Then, Hal Cohen, who had homered in the 6th inning, singled in a run to cut the Gator margin to four runs.

Unfortunately for the Gators, up stepped the guy who still holds the NCAA record for most home runs, and that is what Jeff Ledbetter did … hit a grand slam over the fence and headed toward the circus grounds to tie the game at 16-16.

Ledbetter came up again in the 10th, but Florida had seen all they wanted of him and walked him intentionally to load the bases. Then, Jimmy Jones, who had entered the game earlier as a pinch-runner, walked on four straight balls to get the easiest walk-off, game-winner of his career, and Florida State had won 17-16.

Afterward, Mike Martin said: "That's the wildest, longest baseball game I have ever been involved in."

And Jeff Ledbetter added: "I was a little nervous. I hope they don't count on me doing that much more."

More Road Woes
March 15-17, Doak Field, Raleigh, NC

It was a different North Carolina State team that greeted the Seminoles for the weekend series and their 103rd meeting. Florida State had pretty much dominated the series in the past, winning 71 of the 102 contests and losing just 31.

But this Wolfpack team entered the fray ranked #12 and was one of only two unbeaten teams left in the college season. On Friday, they would put a 17-0 record on the line against FSU's 13-2.

The opening game was not pretty for the Seminoles. The hangover from the embarrassing loss to Florida continued. In fact, it hurt even worse when after a scoreless first inning, the Pack put an eight-spot on the board with all of the runs coming off Seminole ace lefty Drew Parrish.

11: MAKING BASEBALL HISTORY

Nothing went right for the Noles as Parrish gave up nine runs on 10-hits in five innings and saw his era balloon to 5.88 while suffering his first loss of the season.

It was another embarrassing loss for Florida State, 16-0. The once high-riding Seminole team committed three errors and had now given up 36 runs in the past two games.

How Would they Rebound from This? Or Would They?

Saturday-Game Two

Before the game N.C. State coach Elliott Avent presented Coach Martin with a golf club and a plaque as a final trip to Raleigh gift.

In retrospect, Saturday could be considered Mike Salvatore Day. The Senior second baseman from Ewing, N.J., was on fire at the plate. He opened the game with a single. In the second inning, he tripled to score Mat Nelson, then scored the Seminoles' fourth run. Things were looking good for the visitors.

But by the 4th inning, the Wolfpack had scored five runs off RHP CJ Van Eyk. No problem! Salvatore to the rescue as he hit a double to tie the game 5-5.

Then with FSU leading 6-5 in the eighth, Salvatore hit a two-run homer to put the lead to 8-5. Salvatore had hit for the cycle, becoming the 9th Seminole to hit for the cycle.

According to Seminole Historian Bob Perrone on NoleFan.org, the previous Cyclers were:

Name	Date	Opponent
1. Mark Lacy	4/4/1982	Georgia State
2. Frank Fazzini	4/21/1983	Mercer
3. Luis Alicea	2/17/1985	Southern Mississippi
4. Paul Sorrento	4/1/1986	Central Florida
5. Jeremy Salazar	4/26/1996	Georgia Tech
6. Chris Smith	3/7/2000	Saint Joseph's
7. Stephen Drew	5/20/2004	Wake Forest
8. Tyler Holt	3/28/2010	Maryland

Unfortunately, the Seminole lead was ephemeral. Pack DH Brad Debo tied the game in the bottom of the 8th with a three-run homer.

The 9th inning was even uglier as RHP reliever Conor Grady walked the lead-off batter, Devonte Brown. Mike Martin was ejected during that at-bat after a heated conversation with plate umpire Craig Barron. It was his first ejection since May 21, 2011.

JC Flowers was called in from CF and walked a batter, then got two force outs and looked like they would get out of it. But CF Tyler McDonough bounced a walk-off single up the middle, and the Seminoles suffered their 3rd loss in a row, 9-8.

Now NC State's unblemished record improved to 19-0 while the Seminoles dropped to 13-4. Sunday's game would be huge for the Seminoles. Could they get back on track?

Game Three

With the Seminoles desperate to end their three-game losing streak and get back on the winning track and the Wolfpack wanting to keep their perfect, 19-0 record alive, the two teams faced off under sunny skies with 57 degrees. The Seminoles struck first with three runs in the second inning. The still hot Mike Salvatore had an RBI single, which was followed by a Reese Albert's two-run double, and it was 3-0, Noles.

In the fifth inning, FSU pushed the lead to 6-1 on a JC Flowers HR to left field and doubles by Nico Baldor and Nander De Sedas. Then, De Sedas had an RBI single in the sixth to extend the lead to 7-1.

Conor Grady allowed three runs in the sixth, and the Pack scored another in the eighth. But JC Flowers shut them down in the 9th, and the Seminoles left Raleigh with a losing-streak-ending 7-5 win. The record improved to 14-4 while NC State had a still-sparkling 19-1 record.

Weekday Baseball

After the weekend war with their ACC opponents in Raleigh, NC, the Seminoles were happy to return to the friendly confines of Mike Martin Field at Dick Howser Stadium for two weekday opponents—the University of Central Florida (UCF) on Tuesday and Florida International University (FIU) on Wednesday.

11: MAKING BASEBALL HISTORY

FSU (14-4) vs UCF (14-6)
Tuesday, March 19, 2019

Florida State and Central Florida had met 43 times, with the Seminoles winning 37. Since 2011 FSU had won 17 of 18 and currently held a nine-game winning streak in the series. The Seminoles hoped to use the two weekday games to get back on a winning track.

The game of baseball is full of surprises, as Florida State fans would rediscover. One of the surprises was the large crowd. Since it was the second day of Spring Break and most of the student body was out of town, the attendance of 4,517 was a pleasant boost for the home team on this cloudy evening with a game-time temperature of 66 degrees.

An unpleasant surprise was the six-spot the Knights posted in the fifth inning to open up an 8-3 lead. Florida State had plated two runs in the fourth on a bases-loaded walk and a balk to take a 3-2 lead. It would be their last lead of the game.

Seminole starter Antonio Velez lasted 4.1 innings allowing seven runs (five earned) on six hits. The one bright spot for the Seminoles was the work of relief pitcher Chase Haney who held the Knights scoreless over the final three innings.

The Noles tried valiantly for a 9th inning rally as they loaded the bases, scoring one run before their number three and four hitters, Mendoza and Cabell, struck out, ending the rally and giving UCF a 9-7 win.

The Seminoles, now 14-5 on the season, would have to wait another day to start winning again. UCF celebrated on the field and left town with a 15-6 record that ended the Seminoles nine-game winning streak over them.

FSU (14-5) vs FIU (10-9)
Wednesday, March 20, 2019, Howser Stadium, Mike Martin Field

Getting Back on Track

Things were getting a little frustrating for the Seminoles and their fans. Since their loss to the Gators eight days ago, the Noles had lost four of the five games they played. Mike Martin had seen his team drop from 13-1 and Top 10 in the rankings to 14-5 and #19. They were seeing win streaks against teams end and a losing streak against a rival increase. It was time to put a stop to this.

The Florida International University Panthers returned to Tallahassee for the first time since 2012. The two teams had met 22 times, with Florida State winning 16 and losing 6. A crowd of 3,899 showed up for this three o'clock matchup.

Everything was coming up roses for the Seminoles in the second inning when they jumped out front four-zip. An RBI double by SS Nander De Sedas and an RBI single from Jonathan Foster accounted provided the fireworks. But the roses wilted in the third as FIU came back with four runs of their own. After allowing only one hit in the first two innings, Tyler Ahern gave up a home run, two walks, and a single and departed, having allowed four earned runs.

FIU took the lead in the fifth on a two-run homer by 3B Austin Stento off Clayton Kwiatkowski.

The Seminoles added single runs in the fifth and seventh, with Robby Martin scoring the game-tying sixth run after hitting a double.

So, going into the 8th inning, the game was tied. With two men on, Drew Mendoza, who had struck out four times in the previous game against UCF, the last one coming with the bases loaded in the 9th inning, made amends with a solid, no-doubt-about-it, high and long HR over the RF fence. The three runs sealed the deal for a 9-6 Seminole win as JC Flowers got his 4th save in the 9th.

It was a nice way to close out the homestand as the Seminoles prepared to go to frigid South Bend, IN, home of the Fighting Irish of Notre Dame, for the weekend.

Fighting the Irish
FSU (15-5, 3-3) at Notre Dame (8-10, 4-2)
March 22-24, Frank Eck Stadium

Friday
Game postponed. Inclement weather. Rescheduled as a double-header on Saturday noon.

Saturday
Game 1: 12:07 pm
Ace Lefty Drew Parrish was back in form on a sunny but chilly for Floridians, 40-degree afternoon. Parrish retired the final 13 batters he faced

from the second to sixth inning while fanning a season-high nine batters. Parrish shutout the Fighting Irish on 2 hits and picked up his third win of the season with one loss.

Drew Mendoza hit his team-leading 8th homer of the season while Elijah Cabell added his sixth. Mike Salvatore continued his hot hitting going three-for-five, his ninth multi-hit game of the season. Robby Martin drove in three runs with two doubles raising his team-high batting average to .373.

The Seminoles picked up their 16th win and got ready to play game two 45 minutes later.

Game 2-3:40 pm

RHP CJ Van Eyk continued to experience control difficulties walking 6, allowing three hits, seven runs (six earned), and taking a loss with 3.2 innings of work. LHP Clayton Kwiatkowski struggled in relief, giving up five hits and two runs in one inning.

Notre Dame scored two runs in the first, third, and fifth innings and plated three runs in the 4th and 6th innings to coast to a 12-3 win and even the series at a game apiece.

With inclement weather expected later on Sunday, the series finale was moved up to an 11 a.m. first pitch.

Game 3-Sunday, 11:02 First Pitch

An overcast 40-degrees greeted the teams for the early start to the final game of the series. Left-hander Shane Drohan got the call to finish the deal for the Seminoles, and he responded with a sterling effort. He pitched a career-high 5.1 innings and had a no-hitter going until the sixth inning. He was lifted after throwing 100 pitches, striking out 6, and giving up just one hit and one run. Conor Grady was stellar in relief, tossing 3.2 shutout, hitless innings keeping the score tied a 1-1 through nine innings.

Elijah Cabell hit a triple and scored on a wild pitch in the sixth for a run that was matched in the bottom of the inning by Notre Dame on an RBI double by cleanup hitter Eric Gilgenbach. That would be the only hit and run of the game for the Irish.

The 10th became a nightmare inning for Notre Dame shortstop Jared Miller who committed back-to-back throwing errors that plated two Seminole runs after a single by Reese Albert.

#10 FSU took a 3-1 lead into the bottom of the 10th and looked to their closer JC Flowers to close it out. Coming in from the outfield to pitch on a chilly day was not the best recipe for a sterling relief pitching performance.

Flowers was shaky to start with two walks putting the tying run on with the winning run at the plate. But Flowers was able to get ground ball outs for the save.

Final FSU 3   Notre Dame 1

Seminoles improved their record to 17-6, 5-4, and scurried out of frigid Indiana, coming home to Tallahassee for a day before heading to Jacksonville to play the Florida Gators again.

Baseball in Jacksonville
#21 Florida (16-10) #24 Florida State (17-6)
March 26, 2019, Baseball Grounds, Jacksonville, FL

It was the 249th meeting between these two state universities, and 8,041 fans, the largest crowd to witness a college game in the Sunshine State in 2019, turned out for the 6 p.m. contest.

Even though Florida State held a nine-game winning advantage (128-119-1), the Tribe had fallen on hard times in recent years in the series. The Gators came in sporting a nine-game winning streak over the Seminoles.

The two teams battled to a scoreless tie through the first four innings. LHP Jonah Scolaro, making his first collegiate start, only gave up three hits and one unearned run before departing in the fifth. A fielding error by SS Nander De Sedas followed by an RBI double by the number eight hitter in the lineup, LF Austin Langworthy, put the Gators ahead 1-0.

In the bottom half of the fifth, #9 hitter C Mat Nelson walked, and lead-off hitter 2B Mark Salvatore put the Seminoles ahead, 2-1, with his third homer of the season, over the right field fence. Unfortunately for Florida State, those would be the only runs they scored.

The Gators took the lead for good with three runs in the seventh. With two outs and a runner on first, some poor fielding kept the inning alive and, as it turned out, lost the game for Florida State. 3B Drew Mendoza's error kept the inning going. Then Salvatore threw away a slow roller to allow the tying run to score. Florida scored two more on a double to CF by SS Brady McConnell. That made it 4-2 Florida and was pretty much all she wrote for the Seminoles, who headed back to Tallahassee, smarting from their 10th straight loss to Florida.

Back Home against Boston College
Three games
March 29-31
All Time: FSU 33 BC 5
2019: FSU 17-7, 5-4. BC 12-12, 3-6

Friday Night

It was anticipated, at least by Seminole fans, that FSU would get back on track, especially in the ACC, with Boston College coming to Howser Stadium to play. After all, FSU not only had a five-game winning streak against the Eagles but also had won 15 of the last 16 games between the two teams. The Seminoles were in for a big surprise.

Before the 4,165 fans got settled in their seats, the Eagles had scored three runs off Seminole starter Drew Parrish. After a walk and a single cleanup hitter Gian Martellini, the catcher hit a three-run homer.

That would not bode well for the Noles key pitcher as Parrish did not get out of the second inning. Coach Martin's second visit to the mound would send Parrish to the showers after surrendering five hits and five runs. Austin Pollock came in.

BC got another run in the third, and suddenly, the Seminoles, before they had been through the order even once, found themselves trailing 6-0. After BC ran it up to 7-zip, scoring in every inning, the Noles fought back and scored three in the 4th. The key hit was a two-run double by Robby Martin.

Trailing 8-3 in the eighth, FSU rallied, with a crowd-pleasing four runs. Once again, Robby Martin drove in two runs, making his RBI total for the night four. And lead-off batter Mark Salvatore doubled in two more. Just like that, the Eagles margin had been cut to 1.

The Seminoles would go into the ninth trailing 8-7. But just as the hopes of the Seminole faithful had flared up, they took a hit as BC scored two in the 9th to make it 10-7.

The home team got two runners on in the bottom of the 9th, bringing the tying run to the plate with one out, but the next two batters flied out to end the game. The Seminoles went to their homes shell-shocked with a 10-7 defeat. They would have to win the next two to keep from losing the series.

JIM CROSBY

Saturday—Game Two 6 p.m.

Looking to even the series and have a chance to win a series at home, remembering the 7-0 deficit from early in Friday's game FSU struck for three runs in the first. With C. J Van Eyk dealing, that lead would hold up until the 7th inning.

Van Eyk departed after the 6th inning, having given up only one unearned run. Jonah Scolaro came in. BC tied the game at three in the 7th touching Scolaro for two runs; one of those was unearned.

With most of the Saturday night crowd of 5,312 fans still in their seats and making noise, the Seminoles came up in the bottom of the 9th, needing only a walk-off run to break the tie and win. BC had 11 hits while the Noles were held to 3, but the score still stood 3-3.

Tim Becker walked to start the inning and advanced to second on a sac bunt by Mat Nelson. That brought up lead-off hitter Mark Salvatore, who was hitless with a walk in four trips to the plate. As the Animals of Section B sang their revised version of Dean Martin's "That's Amore:" "When the moon hits your eye like a big pizza pie—Salvatore." The object of their affection, the Seminole's second baseman punched the first pitch into right field for a walk-off winning single and RBI. 4-3 Florida State!

The Series was even, and FSU edged above the 500 mark in the ACC 6-5 while BC dropped to 4-7.

Sunday Game 3—Noon

Sometimes in baseball, a pitcher just has your number. That's what happened on Sunday, but it wasn't the Seminole pitcher who had it. BC RHP Mason Pelio tossed seven sterling innings of 2-hit, shutout baseball, walking just one, and fanning 8.

Seminole LHP Shane Drohan matched him for 5.2 innings allowing six hits but no runs, 2 walks, and fanning 8. Conor Grady came on to close out the 6th inning, but the 7th was a different story. He gave up four hits, including a two-run shot to CF Sal Frelick, giving BC a 3-0 lead.

The Eagles added four more off LHP Clayton Kwiatkowski and one-off Jack Anderson in the 9th to walk away with an 8-0 win and the series.

The Seminoles lost the regular-season series to the Eagles for just the second time since joining the ACC and the first time since 2009. An obviously upset Coach Martin (seething inside but showing a calm appearance on the outside) said simply: "There will be some changes made."

11: MAKING BASEBALL HISTORY

After the game, Mike Martin was in for a surprise. As the two teams formed a line for the obligatory post-game handshakes, Boston College coach Mike Gambino came back over to Mike Martin, gave him a hug, and said: "11, I might be a little emotional, but I just wanted to tell you how much I appreciated the way you made me feel comfortable in my coaching position when I first came into the league. I have always appreciated that."

Then when he stepped aside, the entire Boston College team had lined up behind him, and one-by-one they shook hands with Coach Martin and expressed their appreciation individually for what he had done for college baseball.

JIM CROSBY

MARTINISM #11

11 Talks About the Importance of Goal Setting

"I'm a big believer in having the players write their goals down each year. They put them in their hat or locker, but they need to make them realistic. I tell them anybody can quit.

Look at the great people like Thomas Edison, who failed on hundreds of inventions. How about Abraham Lincoln, who had a nervous breakdown, went bankrupt, lost 18 elections. Yet the day we celebrate my birthday, we celebrate his. He never quit."

The Stars Speak

Ricky Kimball (1988-91)
- Lithonia GA, HS in Stone Mountain, GA
- 113 App, 280 ip, 307k, 23 wins, 32 saves
- Baseball America-1st team Freshman All-American, 1988

From Stone Mountain, Ga to Tallahassee
"They didn't know much about Florida State and Tallahassee in Atlanta (in the 80s).

But my dad was a huge college football fan, and we love Bobby Bowden and Wally Woodham, and Jimmy Jordan. I was a QB in high school and loved watching teams that threw the ball. Back then, Florida State was one of the few that threw it."

How Coach Martin Sealed the deal
"Played a summer ball game in Tallahassee against Jerry's Caterers (FSU's summer team) and pitched well. Coach Baker talked with me and turned me over to Coach (Rod) Delmonico. Rod said they thought I could be the next Richie Lewis.

Coach Martin flew up, came to one of my practices, and came to my house that night. He met my mom and dad. When he left, I remember Mom said: "You know, I like him." My Dad said he did too. I said, good. I had a twinkle in my eye about Florida State."

11: MAKING BASEBALL HISTORY

11's Impact

"I just thought he was real. He had a commanding presence. I knew he was religious—not in a force-it-down-your-throat way. But I knew it was important to him. Whereas a lot of other coaches have a commanding presence, they're a little saltier. He was personable.

I met his wife, Carol, and I remember thinking. 'You know they are not fake. That's who they are.'"

Martin's Competitiveness

"It is not so obvious when you're watching TV. He looks very calm. But you have no idea what is going on inside. He is projecting leadership. So yes, he is being competitive, but he wasn't going on like a maniac, ranting, and raving because then it becomes just noise, and it's chaos. And people think, well, we don't have a leader. He is losing his mind."

Kimball at Florida State

Ricky came in sporting a 94-mph fastball that blew away high school batters but didn't have a breaking ball. Pitching Coach Mike McLeod, former Seminole pitcher and pitching coach in the minors, helped him develop a curveball that he could throw for strikes on any count. Before he left, working with new pitching coach Jamey Shouppe he added a changeup.

Because the Seminoles had a good starting rotation, they asked Kimball to become a reliever. "I didn't want to at first because I had been a starter all my life. But Coach Delmonico explained that I would get more playing time as a reliever, and they needed someone to finish games."

So, Kimball became one of the best relievers in Seminole history. His 32 saves are still a record 30 years later.

"I remember my last year I got a save at Miami, and that was the one that clinched the FSU saves record," he said. "That makes me feel good."

Martin's Unbreakable Rule

"Coach Martin had a strict NO CURSING rule. There were a few times on the field in practice when guys let a couple of them slip. He wouldn't jump down your throat if you cursed. He would simply say it, in the nicest way: 'If you want to play here, you'd better drop the cursing.'"— Ricky Kimball (1988-91)

John-Ford Griffin (1999-01)

- Sarasota, FL
- 190 GP; .427 AVG; 31 HR; 168 RBI
- Consensus All-American

Any Chance You Wouldn't Become a Seminole

"There was absolutely no chance that I was not going to Florida State. I got drafted pretty high, but my family was a big advocate of my going to college. My readiness to play professional baseball was not there. I came from a winning tradition playing under Hall of Fame Coach Mike Metcalf (Sarasota High), and I wanted to be a part of another winning tradition."

First Impression of 11

"I met Coach Martin on my visit. Went to his office. Ate dinner. In baseball, you compartmentalize the game so much. There's your baseball life. Your family life. Your student life. With coach Martin, it was always family. His beliefs. And he just had this way about him that was so calm that you just felt like you belonged. There is nobody more competitive than him when it comes down to wanting to win. At the same time, outside of the game, you just felt welcome. He didn't talk about baseball as much as he talked about life."

Why So Consistent as a Hitter?

(Griffin batted over .400 every year)

"As I was growing up, hitting was just something I felt natural with. It was just one of those things that was like a language to me. I speak it pretty well. (Griffin now teaches hitting at IMG Academy). One of the things I loved about 11 was he said: 'Don't let anything get in your way. See how far you can go with this.' He condoned my total commitment to hitting."

11's Influence

"Wish I was still up there. When you grow up, you kinda lose touch, but there isn't a time that goes by when I'm coaching or teaching players where his philosophy doesn't come out. He was so funny. I don't think people know that about him. He has got such a personality that just makes you laugh. He makes you feel good. He's got that fire about him. When he gets fired up, he gets you fired up. And he's got that voice. I don't think anybody could mimic that voice. Everybody knows how 11 talks. He has got that awesome voice. And he will call you by state. "Hey, California. Hey, Florida."

1999 College World Series

"Still talk about it to this day (lost championship game to Miami, 6-5). We all wanted to win it so bad for 11. Chris Chavez, Nick Stocks, John McDonald. That was an absolute sound team. It just had chemistry. We knew we were better than Miami even though we lost.

When I got to pro ball, I felt like I had come from somewhere. It was like playing for the Yankees in college baseball. You played for 11."

How 11 Prepared You for the Pros

"Coach Martin did not hold you back. That was 11. The respect. The integrity. The moral principles that you have to have to be a good baseball player. He would tell you to go out there and play the game and if you make a mistake by being aggressive. I will never hold you to that. I will never argue with it. I'll support you."

Being a Seminole

"I'm as proud of being a Florida State Seminole as I am of anything else I do in my life. I can walk around anywhere, and even if you don't like Florida State, you have to respect the name. The one thing that makes us brothers and bridges the generation gap is that we played for 11, and we played for Florida State."

John Ford-Griffin Elected into the FSU Hall of Fame in 2012

Outfielder from Sarasota … lettered for three years and started for two and a half years for the Seminoles … batted over .402 all three years and had a career .427 batting average … his top 25 season records include Batting Average (3rd-.450 in 2001, 12th-.403 in 2000— even though he hit .436 in 1999 he did not have enough at bats to qualify for the top 25 list), Slugging Percentage (6th-.797 in 2001), At Bats (11th-300 in 2000), Hits (4th-121 in 2000 and 11th-113 in 2001), Doubles (33 in 2000 and 30 in 2001), Home Runs (18th-19 in 2001) and Total Bases (8th-200 in 2001 and 18th-187 in 2000) … top 25 career marks include Batting Average (1st-.427), Slugging

JIM CROSBY

Percentage (8th-.686), On Base Percentage (4th-.506), Runs (25th-193), Hits (10th-292) Doubles (1st-78), Home Runs (23rd-31), Total Bases (11th-469) ... had a 23 game hitting streak in 2000 ... helped lead the Seminoles to the College World Series in 1999 (2nd place), 2000 (3rd) and the Super Regional in 2001 ... ACC Player of the Year in 2001 ... earned 2nd team All-American honors in 2000 and NCAA Consensus All-American honors in 2001 ... played two years with the Toronto Blue Jays (Nolefan.org)

The Griffin Family Clubhouse

Former Seminole first-team All-American John-Ford Griffin grew up in a Garnet & Gold home. Both his father Bill and mother Carla attended FSU as well as his two sisters. So, it seems appropriate that one of the greatest Seminole baseball players, along with his entire family, have their names adorning the Seminole Clubhouse.

Out of appreciation to the family for a generous gift when the school was renovating Dick Howser Stadium, FSU named one of the nation's top locker rooms in honor of the family as Seminole players now prepare for games and practices in the Griffin Family Clubhouse.

The clubhouse is one of the most impressive in the nation, with personalized wooden lockers, a big-screen television, a state-of-the-art sound system, and every comfort current and future Seminoles could ever ask for.

"Phenomenal" was the first word that came to mind when former Seminole Doug Mientkiewicz first toured the Griffin Family Clubhouse. "I walked into the clubhouse for the first time, and I said, 'This is better than 95% of the big-league clubhouses.' The clubhouse at Fenway, when we won the World Championship in 2004, was about the size of this room. If it's not the best, I'd like to see the best in college baseball. To me, this is the best place to be, and this is the best place to play" (Seminole Baseball '19 Florida State University Media Guide).

Jeremy Salazar (1995-98)

- Lafayette, Louisiana
- 224 games; 680 ab; .303 avg; 33 hr; 172 rbi.
- 1st team All-ACC and 1st team All-American

Why FSU from Louisiana?

"Brooks Badeaux and I were friends for many years, and he started going to FSU baseball camp. One year, he asked me to go with him; I was a freshman in high school. When we got there, it was like, 'wow, this is a big campus.' It was kind of impressive. After one practice, Coach Chip Baker said, 'Big Shooter, come ride with me.' And he asked me if I wanted to be a

Seminole, and he said, 'I'm going to do everything I can to get you here.' From then on, there was nothing else in my heart but FSU baseball."

Playing for Coach Martin

"It was a pleasure to be able to work hand-in-hand with Coach Martin. What can you say about being able to work hand-in-hand with the greatest coach of all time? He is the best teacher of the game that I have ever seen. I think every player who played for him when they got to pro ball would be doing things that we already knew."

11's Coaching Style

"He stressed the bunting, the baserunning, little things, and little parts of the game that most people overlook. That was a valuable experience we had every day listening to the way he works.

The second thing I learned from him and one of the most impressive things because in baseball, there is a lot of pressure and use of profanity as you go to different levels. But, not from 11. In four years, there were a lot of stressful situations. He always kept his composure, and he was a true professional. He played the game the right way, and he taught us how to play the game the right way. We were truly blessed to have four years with him."

Best Memories from FSU Days

"I was on third base when J. D. (Drew) hit his 30th home run that set the 30-30 record (30 HRs & 30 stolen bases). I remember thinking I am going to remember this moment. 'Cause things can fade away pretty quick. It is been over 20 years now.

"I remember Chris Chavez's no-hitter like it was yesterday. (13-0 with 11 Ks over Charleston Southern Feb. 18, 1998). His curveball was really working good that night. Bruce Ravan (was the umpire) behind the plate and Chris kinda hung the curveball for the last pitch but struck the batter out."

Martin the Teacher

"I think every player who ever played for him when they got to pro ball, they (the teams) would be doing things that we already knew, and they would say where did you guys learn this from. We would tell them, 'We've been doing this for four years in college.' We were advanced in the minor league level compared to these other guys because we did it so often at FSU.'"

Catcher Jeremy Salazar improved in each of his four seasons at Florida State. He played 224 games and ended up with a .303 AVG. In 680 at-bats, he garnered 206 hits, 33 homers, 173 runs batted in, and had a .526 slugging pct. He hit for the cycle and had eight RBI in a game against GA Tech in 1996.

Salazar helped lead the Seminoles to three College World Series appearances and was a 1st Team All-American.

Brooks Badeaux (1995-98)

- Lafayette, Louisiana
- 254 GP; 938 AB; .299 AVG; .425 OBP; 59 SB
- 10 yrs. MLB; 7 teams

From Louisiana to Florida

"First of all, going to Florida State was like the nicest college facilities I had ever seen. Florida itself just fits the model. You are going to (the state of) Florida; you figured it would be beaches and palm trees everywhere. Geographically speaking, that's how I perceived it at first. Then you get there, and I learned so much baseball from those camps. Actually, going there and playing for 11 made the transition from college to pro ball easy as far as the learning curve."

Playing at Howser

"Hands down (Howser) is the best place to play in college baseball. The fans had knowledge of the game. Their passion and pride. Their whole knowledge of the game. It was just an awesome experience. I think the visiting teams would say the same thing. The fans applaud good baseball."

What You Learned from Martin that Will Help You as a Coach

"To sum it all up—attention to detail. That's it in a nutshell. That's what makes the difference between a good player and a great player. A great player gets the details and applies them. A good player doesn't. He isn't results-oriented. A ground ball is hit to you, and you throw the guy out. But you didn't do it correctly. 11 is going to let you know. He wanted it done correctly every time because he knew that would come back to haunt you. He was a very good coach all around."

Why Players Played Hard for 11

"It seemed like he never took a day off. There were some days when it was freezing cold or steaming hot, or it was raining. There were some coaches that would call it a rain-day and take the day off. Well, we were inside working on the mental aspect of the game. We did what we could do. It was always 100%, and he gave us his all every day, which I think is a direct reflection of how and why the players gave him their all every day.

I can honestly say there was much I learned in (10 years in pro ball) because I learned so much in college. I considered myself a student of the game (I knew a lot about baseball) before I got there. I was wrong."

What It Means to Be a Seminole

"It means that you had the courage to get out of your comfort zone and play with the best . And play against the best. Secondly, the tradition. Everybody knows the war chant, the chop, and the history of the school. It just kind of breaks the norm for a lot of people, especially those around here in our home state. It is just something unique and different that I am very proud of."

Brooks Badeaux and Jeremy Salazar live about 10 minutes from each other in their home state of Louisiana. Brooks has been named head coach of his high school Alma Mater Teurlings Catholic High School. Counting his four years at Florida State and 10 years of pro ball, Brooks played 14 years of baseball. He participated in 1,145 games, had 4,094 official at-bats, collected 1,112 hits, and scored 683 runs.

Dolphins Swim into View
Jacksonville (18-10) at Florida State (18-9)
Tuesday, April 2, 2019, 6 pm

The Seminoles were looking to get back on a winning track, having dropped three of the last four games after a 12-0 start to the season. The Jacksonville Dolphins looked like the likely suspects for the Noles to return to early season form. After all, FSU held a large all-time winning advantage over the Dolphins, having won 127 against just 37 losses. Under Coach, Martin FSU was 90-24 against them.

Martin experimented with center-fielder/closer JC Flowers as starting pitcher. Flowers came through with three scoreless innings surrendering just a hit and a walk while fanning three (27 of his 46 pitches were strikes).

The Noles struck first in the fifth inning when Mark Salvatore followed a Mat Nelson bunt hit with a two-run homer. Other than that, it was an exercise in futility for the home team striking out 13 times and leaving nine runners on base. Martin said: "It looked like one of those games in which we were pressing. We were trying to do things instead of letting the game come to us."

JSU would score a run in the fifth off LHP Jonah Scolaro, FSU's third reliever. Then they tied the game in the eighth with two doubles off the fifth Noles pitcher of the night, Antonio Velez.

The game proceeded into extra innings as FSU went to their sixth pitcher of the night RHP Conor Grady. In the top of the 11th, Grady was touched for a double and a run-scoring single to give JSU a 3-2 lead. The Seminoles went quietly in the bottom of the 11th, and JSU had its first win in Tallahassee in three years.

The Seminoles record now dropped to 18-10 while JSU improved to 19-10. An unhappy Mike Martin added this comment in the post-game press conference: "In all the years I've been here, I've experienced losing five or six in a row. It's called life. And there's another saying that we have here with our baseball program. 'Shut up and play.' And that's what we intend to do."

Back Where it all Started
FSU (18-10, 6-6 ACC) vs. Miami (18-11, 5-7 ACC)
Miami, FL-Mark Light Stadium, April 5, 2019, 7 p.m.
Game One-Friday 7 pm, 80 degrees, Mostly cloudy, Attendance: 3,227

Thirty-nine years ago, Mike Martin brought his first Seminole team into this stadium for his first series as Head Coach of Florida State. That team lost the first two games but would win the Sunday finale on a 3-run Mike Yastrzemski homer. Who knew that would be the first win in the start of a legendary career that would see 11 go on to break all the records for victories?

Entering the 2019 season, these two teams had met 286 times, with Florida State holding a 152-130-4 victory margin. Strangely this final series between a Seminole-coached Mike Martin team and the Miami Hurricanes in Coral Gables would mirror that first series 40 years earlier.

On February 22, 1980, the Canes bombed the Noles 10-0. On April 5, 2019, it was Miami 11 FSU 0. The way the game started, it did not look like there would be a lopsided outcome at all. Seminole ace LHP Drew Parrish was sharp, as usual. He faced the minimum through four innings, giving up only a hit to CF Jordan Lala, who was out stealing. There was little to indicate what lay ahead for the Nole's ace.

After all, three Seminole batters struck out in the 5th. The door would come off the hinges for Parrish and FSU. #3 in the order, RF Adrian Del Castillo started it off with a single to RF, and 3B Raymond Gill followed suit-—single to RF. Both runners advanced on a ground-out, bringing up Catcher Michael Amditis. FSU elected to intentionally walk him to load the bases and set up a possible double play. But 1B Alex Toral, the #7 batter in the order, foiled that strategy with a grand slam.

That took all the wind out of the Seminole's sails. They would only get two more hits, a total of four for the game, while Miami had a six-run seventh and added a run in the eighth to seal an 11-0 shutout.

The two teams left the field that night with identical sub-.500 ACC records at 6-7. Overall, FSU dropped to 18-11, while Miami was 19-11.

Game Two-Saturday-April 6, 2019-7 pm
80 degrees Mostly Cloudy, Attendance 4,115

Flashback-February 23, 1980: Game 2 in Mike Martin's career. Saturday evening in South Florida. Final score: Miami 4 Florida State 3.

The Saturday game in 2019 in Coral Gables would resemble the one 40 years ago in two ways. Miami scored four runs. Miami won. But for the second day in a row, the Seminoles were shutout. 18 innings without a run. Once again, they only collected 4 hits; that's eight hits total in two games.

RHP CJ Van Eyk, FSU's #2 starter lasted 4.2 innings; although he fanned seven and only surrendered four hits, he gave up all four of Miami's runs and was replaced by LHP Clayton Kwiatkowski, who went 3.1 innings to finish the game only surrendering 2 hits and 0 runs while fanning five.

Miami's first run came in the third inning on a solo shot by #8 hitter LF Gabe Rivera, his second HR of the season. The three-run 5th inning finished the scoring for the evening. The Seminoles were shutout again, 4-0.

Miami evened their ACC record to 7-7 and overall won #20 against 11 losses. FSU fell to 6-8 and 18-12.

Game Three-Sunday-April 7, 2019-1 pm
83 degrees Mostly Cloudy, Attendance; 2,781

Flashback: February 24, 1980: Game 3 of Martin's first series in Miami as head coach. Seminoles get a thrilling come from behind win, 9-8 on a Yasztremski 3-run homer. Final: 9-8 Seminoles.

2019: History repeats itself. After falling behind twice in the game, the Seminoles pulled out a 6-5 win and avoided getting swept. JC Flowers had a starring role hitting his sixth home run and earning his sixth save. It was the 4th time that Flowers had homered and earned a save in the same game. Conor Grady recorded his 5th win by striking out the only batter he faced in the seventh inning.

Alec Sanchez, making his first start of the season in RF, had a three-hit game, and 3B Drew Mendoza and SS Mark Salvatore contributed two hits apiece.

Prior to the game, the City of Coral Gables recognized head coach Mike Martin with a proclamation in honor of his 40-year career as Florida State head coach. Former FSU Board of Trustees member Les Pantin helped spearhead the movement.

It was a satisfying conclusion for Number 11 on his final visit to Mark Light Stadium in Coral Gables as the Seminoles ran their all-time victory margin over the Hurricanes to 21wins (153-132).

Here Come the Gators
Florida 21-13 vs FSU 19-12
Tuesday, April 9, 2019, 6 p.m.
Mike Martin Field at Dick Howser Stadium

Barring a post-season matchup tonight, Mike Martin faces the Florida Gators for the final time. The Gators are 2-0 against FSU in 2019. It will be the 250th meeting between these two Sunshine state rivals. The Seminoles have won 128 times compared to 120 by the Gators. In 1974 the two teams played to a 0-0 tie in Tallahassee.

In recent times, the Gators have enjoyed an advantage in the series, having won 10 of 11 and 15 of the last 16 games. 11 comes into the game with an even 76-76 record against the Gators.

Coming into the game, Gator Coach Kevin O'Sullivan told www.FloridaGators.com: "I've been thinking about this night for a long time, being the last time we get a chance to compete against coach Martin."

After the game, O'Sullivan, whose team had just been swept by Ole Miss, said: "I'm obviously really excited we played better tonight, number one, but all the games we've competed against Florida State over the years have been extra special, and this has really been special tonight for a lot of different reasons."

RHP Conor Grady got the ball and pitched seven impressive innings for Florida State, giving up just 2-hits and one unearned run while striking out 9. He left after throwing 88 pitches, 60 of which were strikes. The Gators struck first in the 4th inning through no fault of Grady's.

SS Brady McConnell reached base on a rare dropped ball by CF JC Flowers getting to second on the play. He was sacrificed to third and scored on a passed ball by catcher Mat Nelson.

The Seminoles tied the game in the 5th when SS Nander De Sedas walked, went to second on Nelson's single, and they both moved up on stolen bases. De Sedas scored on a fielder's choice at first base by Alex Sanchez.

The game stayed tied until the 9th when Florida scored two on a couple of doubles sandwiched around an intentional walk to make it 3-1. When Florida State went down in order in the ninth, Florida had its 11th straight win over FSU.

It was a bitter pill to swallow for Martin, who said after the game: "I don't know when I've been this frustrated in 40 years as a head coach. And then I'll say to myself just like I say to the players. Shut up and play. That's what I'm going to do, and that's what they're going to do."

Later, when a reporter asked him to express his feelings over the loss to Florida, he said: "I haven't had this much fun since I was mugged in Afghanistan." Then he left to get his team prepared for another bitter rival. The Clemson Tigers were coming to town for a weekend series.

Clemson's Last Visit
#16 Clemson (25-8, 11-4 ACC) VS FSU (19-13, 7-8 ACC)
Friday Night, April 12, 6 pm, Tallahassee
Game 1 of 3

With the exception of their in-state rivalry with the Miami Hurricanes, the Clemson Tigers might be considered the Seminoles bitterest rivals in the Atlantic Coast Conference. Coming into this three-game set, the two teams had played 150 times. Florida State held a 76-69 lead in the series.

At home, FSU leads the series 39-20-1, while on the road, the Tigers hold a 35-29 lead. And when playing at a neutral site, the record was dead even 14-14. The numbers alone attest to how fiercely competitive the games between these two teams have been.

Drew Parrish looking like the Parrish of old, with all of his pitches working and totally in command, led the Seminoles to a 6-2 series-opening win. In front of 4,246 delighted fans, Parrish went a season-high eight innings recording 12 strikeouts, also a season-high.

11 said, "I thought Parrish pitched as well as I've seen him pitch since he's been here. He went out there determined to get it done. He really picked us up tonight."

Parrish said: "Throughout the season, I've definitely had my ups and downs, but to come out and pitch a game like that is a mental confidence boost."

Drew Mendoza provided all the support Parrish needed at the plate with a three-run homer over the left-field wall in the fourth inning. He said: "My mindset was just to stay short and put a good barrel on the ball."

Teams had been putting on a shift with Mendoza up, and he showed that he could beat the shift with his homer to the opposite field and a bunt single to the third-base side.

A happy Mike Martin admitted his team felt like they had their backs to the wall. Then he added with a smile: "This is nice. I'll go home and pet the dog."

Game Two-Saturday 2 pm

Not to be outdone by his pitching partner Drew Parrish, C, J. Van Eyk tossed a gem on Saturday afternoon. The big difference between the two games was the run support for Van Eyk, which made it easy.

Winning 16-2, FSU broke the game open in the 4th inning with five runs, followed by three in the fifth, four in the sixth, one in the seventh, and three more in the eighth inning.

Van Eyk showed that he could do the eight-inning thing too. He completed 100-pitch 8 innings, his career-high allowing just four hits, walking one, and striking out four. It was his fourth win. After the game, he said: "It felt really good. I felt like I was letting the ball go pretty well today and commanding the zone."

Coach Martin said: "What was encouraging, and impressive was he was throwing 97,98 MPH in his last inning in the eighth. I can't sit here and tell you I've had a number of those guys. I haven't."

Leading the 14-hit parade for Florida State was lead-off hitter Mark Salvatore with a four-for-five afternoon, including his fifth HR. JC Flowers went three-for-four, including 2 HRs and five RBI. He and Cooper Swanson had back-to-back homers in the five-run fourth inning.

"I feel like we were firing on all cylinders. I just believe hitting is contagious. When you see someone else hit, it just makes you more focused and makes you want to get a hit, "said Flowers. The Seminoles hit .444 with runners on base and .615 with runners in scoring position.

Game Three-Sunday 1 p.m.

There was joy in Seminole Territory on Sunday as the home team completed its first three-game sweep of Clemson since 2008 and its first sweep of the Tigers at home since 2001with a 6-4 win. Likewise, it was the first home sweep of an ACC opponent since 2016.

With the Tigers having taken a 3-0 lead off FSU's starter, LHP Shane Drohan, the Seminoles bounced back with a four-run second inning. The key hit was by Drew Mendoza-—a two-run shot to give FSU a 4-3 lead.

Mendoza commented after the sweep, "It's tough to really get a lot of emotion going when you are not scoring runs. Just to break it open on Friday, it just opened everybody up. Everybody took that deep breath, and we kept it rolling the rest of the weekend." The Tigers sent Drohan to an early shower in the third with a run that tied the game at 4-4. Enter Conor Grady. Exit any more scoring for the Tigers. Grady pitched 5.1 innings of shutout ball while throwing 70 pitches and striking out 11 Tigers. Added to Drohan six Ks and two by Flowers in the 9th, who picked up his ninth save, the total Clemson whiffs was 19. The Tigers only got one hit and one walk over the last six and one-third innings.

"All three pitches just happened to have been working this week. It was one of those outings where everything was working, and I just hope it continues," said Grady.

Told that Grady struck out 11 of the 18 batters he faced, Coach Martin said with a laugh, "That's pretty impressive."

As a result of the sweep in which FSU improved to 10-8 in the ACC, the Seminoles jump up 30 points in their RPI ratings to 67th nationally.

Drew Mendoza summed up the weekend: "Emotions fly, and that's college baseball for you. It was great to be on the good side of that emotion today."

On the Road to Virginia
FSU (22-13, 10-8 ACC) vs. Virginia (22-16, 8-10)
Three games, Davenport Field, Charlottesville, Virginia, April 18-20

FSU readies for its 31st game in Virginia, where they hold an 18-12 lead. Overall, they have met the Cavaliers in baseball 84 times, winning 55 while losing 29. In Tallahassee, the Seminoles' victory margin is 28-9, while they hold a slim 9-8 margin on neutral sites. Game one. Thursday evening, 6 pm under clear skies with winds at 9 mph, SW.

Fortunately for FSU, Drew Parrish was on the flight and turned in another gem. He coasted through six innings of the 14-2 blowout of the Cavaliers. Parrish only gave up 5-hits and one unearned run. He fanned 6 in throwing 96 pitches, 63 for strikes.

Moved to the cleanup spot for the first time, JC Flowers rewarded 11 for the move with a two-run first-inning homer as the Noles struck for three runs before the Cavaliers could get back in the dugout. The Noles would add two runs in the second for a 5-1 lead, put the game away with a five-run seventh, and add a run in the eighth for good measure.

Martin, Cabell, and De Sedas had two hits-a-piece in the Noles hit parade of 13 base hits to go with their 14 runs.

The Seminoles apparently find Charlottesville a hitter-friendly location as they have scored 39 runs in the past three games dating back to 2015.

The win was Mike Martin's 500th regular-season ACC win. In 28 years in the league, he is 500-232-0. The closest competitor is GA Tech's Danny Hall at 405.

Games Two and Three-Saturday April 20, 2019

Due to inclement weather, the Friday game was postponed, and a doubleheader set for Saturday.

The noon game saw a scoreless three innings to start in a pitcher's duel between CJ Van Eyk and Noah Murdock. Despite having a runner picked off third base, Virginia managed to score a run on three hits and take the lead, 1-0, in the fourth.

Florida State would bounce back with two in the fifth and three in the sixth. That completed their scoring for the game. But it was enough for the 5-3 win (Martin's 2,011th) and to capture the series.

Reese Albert, back in the Seminole lineup after recovering from a shoulder injury, gave evidence that the shoulder was fully healed as he had a three-for-four day with a run scored, an RBI, and a walk.

Despite an unseemly five errors, the Seminoles were able to hold on for their sixth straight ACC win, tied for the longest league streak this season and its longest conference winning streak since an eight-game run in 2014.

Van Eyk picked up his fifth win, and JC Flowers got his ninth save.

Game Three of the Series, Game Two of the Double-header

The series finale got underway at 4:20 pm in front of 3,928 fans. Before it was over, the luster was off of the series win because there would be no sweep for the Seminoles. Virginia took the finale 13-3, getting 13 hits off six Seminole pitchers.

Starter Shane Drohan lasted four innings and surrendered 3 earned runs. Jonah Scolaro gave up three earned runs also but in only .2 ip. Chase Haney surrendered 2 runs, and Gage Hutchinson followed by allowing four earned runs. All 13 of the Hoos runs were earned.

The Seminole bats were quiet in this one getting only six hits. They left town with their second ACC series win in a row but were disappointed in the finish of this one.

FSU would return home with a 24-14 and 12-9 ACC record. However, their next nine games would be in Tallahassee, and 12 of 13 scheduled at Dick Howser Stadium.

The Mad Hatters Return
April 23-24, Dick Howser Stadium
Stetson (18-20) vs Florida State (24-14)

Tuesday, 6 pm

A longstanding Sunshine State foe Stetson comes to Tallahassee for the 87 and 88th games. The Seminoles hold a 63-13 edge and are 38-11 in Howser Stadium.

The first game proved that this would not be easy as the Hatters outhit the Noles 13-10; however, playing long ball, the home team pulled off a 9-8 win. Mat Nelson, Reese Albert, and Nico Baldor each had homers. It was the fifth time in 2019 that FSU had three home runs in a game. Eight of the Seminoles' nine runs came with two outs while they stranded a season-low two runners on base. Mark Salvatore led the hit parade with three hits.

The Seminoles ended up using six pitchers, with Jonah Scolaro getting the win tossing three innings in relief. J.C. Flowers came on to finish out the eighth inning in which FSU used three pitchers. He also worked the ninth to pick up the save. It was Florida State's 13 straight wins over Stetson in Dick Howser Stadium.

Game two vs Stetson-Wednesday 4 pm.

In front of a nice weekday crowd of 3,863 fans, the Seminoles finished their two-game sweep of Stetson, their 14thconsecutive win in Tallahassee over the Hatters. The fans went home happy as the Seminoles pulled off a 10-4 win.

The Seminoles jumped out to a 2-0 lead in the first inning, and by the fourth inning, that had increased to 6-1. After Salvatore tripled in the first inning, Mendoza followed with a two-run homer to get the Noles off and running.

The fourth inning scoring was highlighted by a two-run homer from Elijah Cabell, his 7th, and a solo shot by Mendoza, his second of the game, a blast that carried 441 feet over the center-field wall. Reese Albert also had FSU's second triple of the game in that inning and hit another one in the seventh to tie a record of two in a game.

The Seminoles outhit the Hatters 10-8, with seven of the 10 hits going for extra bases. And a rarity occurred when all four of the freshmen in the Noles lineup were hit by a pitch.

The win ran the Seminole record to 26-14, giving them seven wins in the last eight games. Mike Martin's record-shattering all-time win total now reached 2013.

Wake: Another ACC Weekend
Wake Forest (25-17, 11-10 ACC) vs FSU (26-14, 12-9)
April 26, 2019, Howser Stadium
3 Game Series

Game 1-Friday, 6 pm.

The 119th meeting between Florida State and Wake Forest took place before 3,840 fans who chose to start their weekend at the ballpark. The Seminoles owned a 60-victory margin, 89-29), but Wake had won two in a row in Winston Salem. FSU had been dominant in Tallahassee, running up a 47-11 total.

Drew Parrish continued to prove that he was back in form with his third consecutive dominant performance. Parrish shutout the Demon Deacons over seven innings, leaving with a 9-0 lead as he allowed only three hits and struck out 10 batters in a 98-pitch performance. With all his pitches working, he found the strike zone 68 times. He has not allowed an earned run in 21 innings.

The Seminoles added four runs in the eight to come away with a satisfying 13-2 opening game win. The FSU hit parade saw Robby Martin hit his second homer, scoring two and driving in two while batting cleanup. Cooper Swanson hit a long HR over the LF scoreboard in his only plate appearance.

JC Flowers enjoyed a perfect three-for-three evening at the plate, including his first triple of the season. Reese Albert tied his career-high by reaching base for the ninth straight game while going two-for-six. Game two is scheduled for two p.m. on Saturday.

Game Two-Saturday-2 p.m., Attendance: 4,508

The Seminoles continued their aggressive hitting by scoring two runs in the first and a five-spot in the third. After Wake Forest put three runs on the board in the fifth, Florida State came back in the bottom of the inning with two more, and the game was pretty much history, with a 9-3 lead.

The Deacons got two in the seventh, but it was Seminoles all the way with a 9-5 win.

Starter CJ Van Eyk was effectively wild as he walked five but erased them with 11 strikeouts. He ended up throwing 111 pitches with 68 going for strikes in five innings and picking up his sixth win of the season and 13th as a Seminole. Jonah Scolaro finished out the final four innings by striking out six Deacons and running the opponent's strikeout total for the game to 17.

Drew Mendoza led the hitters with three-for-five and his 13th HR. He had a season-high four RBI. Reese Albert continued to swing a hot bat going two for three. Since returning from injury seven games ago (at Virginia), Albert is hitting .407 (11 for 27) with eight runs scored, six RBI, two triples, a home run, and four walks.

The Seminoles have now won three straight ACC series for the first time this season and won the series against Wake for the first time since 2015.

11: MAKING BASEBALL HISTORY

Mike Martin Chalked Up His 2015th Win.

Game three-April 28, Sunday at 1 p.m.

The 4,086 fans in attendance witnessed a wild-and-crazy game. For those who like hitting, it was a fan's delight for those who like a pitcher's duel, not so much. When the final out was made in this four-hour-thirty-seven-minute game, 81 batters had made 28 hits and scored 28 runs.

Unfortunately for the Noles, who had the 16 hits, they were the team with 12 runs as Wake Forest got out of town with a 16-12 win and avoided the sweep.

Reese Albert hit his fourth HR of the season in the fourth, and Robby Martin tagged his third HR in the fifth while going four-for-five.

But the Deacons manhandled eight different Noles pitchers scoring four runs in the third, sixth, and seventh innings. Starter Conor Grady (6-4) was tagged with the loss lasting only three innings and giving up four earned runs on four hits and two walks while throwing 54 pitches.

Now with a 29-15 record, 14-10 in the ACC, the Seminoles have a week off for final exams.

PHOTO GALLERY

Martin family at the College World Series

Homecoming Grand Marshalls

American Gothic—Mike & Carol

Mike Martin (11) & Mike Martin Jr. (4)

11 & Tyler (age 7), now FSU First baseman

Mike Martin speaks to Good Samaritan UMC

11 Coaching

At home in the dugout

Most wins ever!

Thank You very much!

Congrats from President Thrasher

Swinging as a player

Always about the Swing

"This way Nogo!"

"Come On Ump!"

11's 1st team: Fuentes, Ledbetter, & Ramsey

Legends of the game, 11 & Ron Fraser

11 broke Augie Garrido's record

JD Drew, Hall of Famer

Buster Posey (L) & Tyler Holt

Buster with Howser Trophy with Jana Howser & 11

Radio Guys, Lee Bowen & Jim Crosby

11 presents retirement jersey to Jim Crosby

Mongo, of Animals, leads Noles Cheer

Animals request 11 lead Noles Cheer

Wallking from CWS into retirement

Photo Credits

- FSU Sports Information
- Martin Family Photos
- Crosby Photos
- Mike Olivella
- Ross Obley
- Unconquered Magazine
- Hall of Fame Photo

11: MAKING BASEBALL HISTORY

MARTINISM #12
11 Talks about People:

"Everybody is lazy (to a certain extent). People fall into one of three categories. They are either intimidated, frustrated, or motivated. Those who are motivated come in and compliment everybody. They also have a smile on their face, make everybody feel good about themselves."

The Stars Speak

Randy Choate (1995-96)

- San Antonio, Texas
- 56 app, 305 ip, 281k, 29 w,
- Multiple All-American teams, 15 yrs, 8 MLB teams

From Texas to Tallahassee:

"I came to the advanced camp. Went to Pepperdine summer camp on the west coast and Florida State on the east. Pitching coach Jamey Shouppe was calling balls and strikes from behind the pitcher. On a 3-2 count, I threw a curveball and struck the kid out. He said if you can throw a 3-2 breaking ball, you can play at Florida State."

First Impression of 11:

"He was just so nice. Friendly. Personable. Genuine. He was just sitting there listening intently to anything I would answer. He seemed genuinely concerned about taking young men and helping them develop. You could just see how much he cared about Florida State, about the program, and all that. Made you feel at home and that he really loved the place and how great it really was to him."

Main Things You Learned at Florida State:

"The team and family aspect. Here it was like family. Everyone is pulling for the same goal. You are trying to get to Omaha. We would all go to chapel in the tradition room. I needed those three years to grow up. I learned a lot that better prepared me. It was a part of the growing-up process, but you had somebody who was such a great example of how to do it right and how to do it with class. 11 made it easy to respect him because you saw how he went about his life and how he did things and how he approached life in general."

Believing in You Even When Things Were Going Bad

"I remember a game against Maryland (March 15, 1996), and he followed me into the clubhouse, sat me down, and said: 'Listen, this is the first inning, and you are my front end guy. You are not going to get out of here in two innings. I'm leaving your butt in the game. You need to get your head on straight.' I ended up going six or seven innings, and we won even though I gave up six runs.

"That also happened at Duke (May 17, 1996) in an ACC tournament game. I wasn't thinking I was going to pitch, I thought somebody else would pitch, but we got a loss. He pulled me aside and said, "Listen, you are pitching this game. I am not pulling you out or saving you for tomorrow. So, you need to get locked in and get going.' I gave up 12 singles and a double, but they only scored one run in nine innings, and we won the game."

Always a Seminole

"Here's how important being part of the Seminole family is. I had a year to go to graduate when I left to play pro ball. I just finished up on December 13, 2019. I graduated from Florida State over 25 years later (and after 15 years in the Majors) because I didn't want to go anywhere else. I got my degree in Criminology." It was that important to Randy Choate to be able to say he is a Seminole in every way.

Randy Choate earned All American honors from multiple organizations while at Florida State. Coupled with his 29 wins, he struck out 281 batters in 305 innings. Taking those lessons learned at Florida State Choate went on to pitch for 15 years in the Major Leagues. The eight teams he pitched for in the Big Leagues included the Yankees, Diamondbacks, Brewers, Rays, Marlins, Dodgers (two stints), Cardinals, and Blue Jays.

11: MAKING BASEBALL HISTORY

PAUL SORRENTO (1984-86)
FSU Hall of Fame 1997

- Peabody, MA
- OF, 234 gp, .352 avg, 795 ab, 48 hr, 222 rbi.
- Baseball America, 1st team; 11 yrs in MLB, 4 teams

Paul Sorrento graduated from St. John's Prep High School in Danvers, Ma. He established himself as a college-ready player early, batting .349 with 17 homers as a freshman and earning Baseball America's 1st Team All-American.

11 on Sorrento
"In the words of Coach Mike Martin, he (Sorrento) 'hit our fall conditioning program hard. He lost weight, got stronger, and picked up some quickness. By his junior year, he was the straw that stirred our drink'" (Allen Cohen in "Society for American Baseball Research).

Sorrento's Consistency
Sorrento had many stellar performances while compiling a .352 average with 48 home runs. He had 73 multiple-hit games, 16 with 3 hits or more and two in which he went 5-for-5 (South Carolina May 11, 1985; UCF, April 1, 1986).

In 1986 the Seminoles returned to the CWS for the first time since 1980. Sorrento came in batting .392 and unloaded a triple in the 3-run 7th to give the Seminoles a lead they would not relinquish in the 5-3, Game 1 victory over Indiana State. Afterward, Paul said: "It was well worth the wait. We have a couple of games to win, but this team is really confident." The Seminoles would take it to the championship game before bowing out and finished #2 in the rankings.

Sorrento Elected into the FSU Hall of Fame in 1997
Paul Sorrento, the Seminoles' starting right fielder from 1984-86, was one of the most feared hitters in Florida State history.

Sorrento, a left-handed hitter from Peabody, MA, began his Seminole career with a bang as he hit 17 homeruns and drove in 68 runs in his freshman campaign to earn a spot on Baseball America's Freshman All-American team. In 1985, he set a school record by reaching base 13 consecutive times in the Metro Conference Tournament and garnered all-tournament team honors for his efforts. Sorrento earned All-Metro Conference and All-Metro Tournament team honors in each of his three seasons with the Seminoles.

Sorrento was the club's power man as a junior, leading the Seminoles with 22 homeruns and 86 RBI in 1986, as Florida State came up a game short of a national championship in the College World Series. His achievements of that magical season earned him Baseball America All-American (2nd team) honors. He finished his three-year career at Florida State with a .352 batting average, 48 homeruns, and 222 RBI.

The California Angels organization selected Sorrento in the fourth round of the 1986 amateur draft, and he made his major league debut with the Minnesota Twins in 1989. As a member of the Twins, Sorrento helped the team to a 1991 World Championship. Sorrento played for the Cleveland Indians during 1992-95 and was a member of the 1995 American League Championship team. He played first base for the Seattle Mariners in 1996 and 1997 and finished his career with the Tampa Bay Devil Rays during the 1998-99 seasons (Nolefan.org).

In 2015 Paul Sorrento was hired as the Los Angles Angels hitting coach.

11: MAKING BASEBALL HISTORY

The Bell Rings Again

May 3, 201, Howser Stadium
Pitt (16-28, 4-17 ACC) vs FSU (28-15, 14-10)
3 Game Series

Game 1-Friday 6 pm

Billed as the return of Mike Bell to Mike Martin Field at Dick Howser Stadium, where he was a pitcher (1994-95) and the most recent pitching coach (2012-18). The expectations were that the teacher would give the pupil another lesson, as Martin faced off with Bell and his team that only had four wins in the ACC in Bell's first season.

Make that five ACC wins for Pitt as Bell's charges gave FSU what the Voice of the Seminoles, Gene Deckerhoff, would call a "woodshed whipping." Final score of Game 1: Pitt 10 FSU 0.

Seminole Ace LHP Drew Parrish was not his usual self as he saw his streak of 22 innings without allowing an earned run end in the second inning. Instead, he picked up his fourth loss in surrendering three runs and six hits, walking three, striking out seven with 104 pitches.

The Panthers went on to score seven more runs off three Seminole pitchers and run away with a shocking 10-0 win.

Afterward, Bell said: "Lot of emotions. It is. Any time you spend time, invest time at a place, there's a lot of great memories here," he told the Tallahassee Democrat, "We continue to create great memories and that's what we did today. This isn't about me; this is about my team."

The weather forecast for the weekend showed heavy rain predicted for Sunday, so the two teams agreed to play a doubleheader, Saturday.

Saturday—Game 1 of DH, game 2 of Series

Florida State was anxious to get back on the diamond on Saturday to put all thoughts of Friday night's abysmal defeat behind them. But the weather had other ideas. Twice the game was delayed by rain. After getting started and playing for 21 minutes, the game was halted for two hours and 49 minutes. Then, played for 44 minutes before a final weather delay pushed the game to a Sunday doubleheader.

Sunday, Noon, Resuming Game Two of the Series
Game 1 of a DH

When play resumed on Saturday, the Seminoles decided to take out their frustrations on the baseball and, as the saying goes: "knock the cover off the ball." They jumped on Panther pitching for three runs in the first inning, adding single runs in the second and third before putting the game completely out of reach, scoring 10 runs in the final two innings (4 in the 7th & 6 in the 8th). Final score was 15-6.

The Noles banged out 20 hits, with five of those going yard. JC Flowers led the homer parade with two bringing his season total to 11 and enjoying a three-for-five day with three RBI. Robby Martin set the stage with a three-run first-inning homer, his fourth. Mat Nelson hit his third homer of the season in the seventh, and Reese Albert blasted his fifth in the eighth inning.

CJ Van Eyk pitched three innings and picked up 10 strikeouts with 70 pitches. Conor Grady notched his seventh victory of the season in pitching the middle three innings.

Although it took two days to finish this game, the official amount of playing time was listed as 3:45. The rubber match would follow in 45 minutes.

Sunday 3:30 pm, Game 2 of the Doubleheader
Game Three of the Series

Announced attendance for the day was 3,845. Not sure how many were around at the conclusion of the Seminoles doubleheader sweep of Pitt, which sealed the series 2-1. Those who stayed the course witnessed almost seven hours of playing time (over two days) with a forty-five-minute intermission as well as two rain delays when the game started on Saturday evening.

Once again, the Seminoles parlayed two big innings, a five-run fifth and a four-run sixth, into a 12-6 win. When all was said and done, FSU had put 27 runs on 29 hits on the books in the doubleheader.

Shane Drohan started and pitched 3.2 innings leaving with FSU trailing, 3-1. Jonah Scolaro picked up the win, his third against no losses, with a couple of innings of relief. He was the beneficiary of the Noles 5-run fifth which basically put the game away.

Drew Mendoza was the hitting star with a three-for-three game, including four RBI. It was a big weekend for the junior third baseman from Minneola, FL. He hit .800 (8-for-10) with six runs scored, five RBI, and three walks. This propelled his batting average up from .289 to .321.

11: MAKING BASEBALL HISTORY

Florida State ran its record up to 30-16 with a 16-11 ACC mark. Mike Martin's career wins mark moved to 2,017. Next up, another doubleheader at Howser. JU on Tuesday.

JIM CROSBY

Mendoza Named ACC Player of the Week

TALLAHASSEE, Fla. – Junior third baseman Drew Mendoza hit .800 with five runs scored and six RBI last weekend against Pitt, earning Atlantic Coast Conference Player of the Week honors for the first time in his career. He is the fourth different Seminole to be honored by the league this season.

Mendoza had two of FSU's six hits in Friday's opener before finishing the weekend 6-for-6 with six runs scored and five RBI in the final two games. He walked three times and added a sacrifice fly, reaching base at a .786 clip in the series while slugging 1.000. His batting average jumped from .289 to .321 in the three games.

The Minneola, FL, native set a career-high with four runs scored in game two of the series and tied a season-high with three hits in both of the final two games. Mendoza has started at third base in all 108 games over the past two seasons.

Mendoza is the fourth Nole to earn weekly league honors this season, joining Robby Martin (Feb. 25), Conor Grady (Apr. 15), and Drew Parrish (Apr. 29). FSU is the only team in the ACC to have four different players earn Player or Pitcher of the Week honors in 2019.

PLAYING TWO WITH THE DOLPHINS
May 7, 2019. Dick Howser Stadium
FSU 30-16 vs Jacksonville 25-22
Doubleheader

Game 1- 2 pm 89 Degrees and Sunny

Florida State and Jacksonville University ordinarily play one game apiece at home. However, the February 19th game scheduled to be played in Jacksonville was rained out. Consequently, rather than lose a game off of their respective schedules, the two teams agreed to play a doubleheader instead of a single game in Tallahassee.

These two teams had met 164 times, with FSU dominating the series, 127-37. They first started playing each other in 1964. The Seminoles won the first 10 games and held a commanding 80-10 record in games played in Tallahassee as head coach Mike Martin won 9 of the first 10 against JU. His teams racked up winning streaks against JU of 19 games (1994-2002), 18 games (2002-06), and nine games (2010-14). The Seminoles entered today's game with six wins in a row over JU.

Although it was close, in the first game of the doubleheader, the Seminoles got off on the right foot. In a pitcher's duel, FSU earned its second shutout of the season and first since the opening day, combined no-hitter vs Maine.

Antonio Velez got his third start of the season and pitched six innings for the win. Both games, by earlier agreement, were scheduled as seven-inning games. Velez picked up his third win, shutting out the Dolphins and allowed just four hits. J. Flowers earned his 11th save.

Nico Baldor went two-for-two, scoring a run and driving in one. FSU scored single runs in the second, third, and fourth innings to nail down the win in one hour fifty minutes in front of 3,759 fans.

Game Two

Those fans who stuck around for the second game that started at 4:44 pm under sunny skies and 91 degrees did not leave as happy as they expected. Florida State grabbed a 1-0 lead on a Mike Salvatore sac fly scoring Elijah Cabell. Unfortunately, that was all of the Seminole scoring until they plated a too-little-too-late run in the final inning and lost 3-2.

The Dolphins had scored a run in the sixth to tie the game, then put two on the board in the top of the seventh by piecing together two singles, two walks, and a sac bunt. The Seminoles tried to rally in the bottom of the seventh, but the game ended with the bases full of Noles, and JU escaped with a 3-2 win. FSU dropped to 31-7. Jacksonville headed home with a 26-23 record.

ROAD GAME WITH THE HATTERS
May 8, 2019, Melching Field Deland, FL
FSU (31-17) vs Stetson (20-26)

5 pm Sunny, 83 Degrees, Easterly Winds 13 mph

The Seminoles matchup with Stetson was their sixth game in six days. They came into Deland looking to make it another season sweep of the Hatters. They were unpleasantly surprised.

Although they got good pitching, the Seminoles seemed to have left their bats in Tallahassee. The team that just five days prior had scored 27 runs on 29 hits in a doubleheader against ACC opponent Pitt not only could not manage to score a run against Stetson, but they didn't get a single hit.

Thirteen Seminole batters struck out as the Hatters used three of their best pitchers in a determined effort to beat FSU. That was an unusual but satisfying move for Stetson, who, with an important conference game coming up on the weekend, did not follow the usual procedure of using down-the-line pitchers for a weekday game.

Hatter batters didn't fare much better, collecting just five hits yet scratching out a 1-0 victory in front of 1,472 delighted home fans.

Freshman Jack Anderson made the first start of his career, and while he gave up the only run and four of their five hits, struck out four and showed off his potential for the future. Tyler Ahearn and Chase Haney held the Hatters scoreless on just one hit in the final five and two-thirds innings.

The bus ride back to Tallahassee was not a happy one as a dejected team pondered a missed opportunity to pick up their 32nd win and earn a sweep against an unranked team.

Back Home to Close the Season
May 10, 2019, 3-game Series
Mike Martin Field at Howser Stadium
Richmond (25-19) vs FSU (31-18)
Friday 6 pm 78 Degrees, Mostly Cloudy

Although the Richmond Spiders had only played Florida State 20 times (19 of those in Tallahassee) this series would be a historic one. It marked the final home games of Mike Martin's illustrious career. At this point, it had become evident the Seminoles record would not warrant a national seed that would entitle them to host a regional. In fact, it was still up in the air as to whether FSU would be playing in the postseason at all.

Consequently, this series took on more significance than it normally would. Even though Florida State had defeated Richmond in all 20 of the games, they had played each other. The two teams had not met since March 11, 1992.

FSU wasted little time in taking control of game one with two-run first and second innings. By the end of the sixth inning, they were up 8-2, and that would be the final score.

Drew Parrish tossed six innings and gave up only 2 hits and 2 runs and using 93 pitches to strike out 8 and picked up his seventh win against four losses.

The Seminoles had ten hits, with Robby Martin banging out two of the four doubles. Mat Nelson hit his fourth homer of the season. Mike Salvatore picked up his 60th hit driving in Elijah Cabell, who had doubled.

The Seminoles picked up their 32nd win and Martin's 2,019 before 3,788 fans.

Prior to the game, the graduating Seminole players were recognized. They included Chase Haney, Gage Hutchinson, Jonathan Foster, Tim Becker, Mike Salvatore, Drew Mendoza, and Coach Tyler Holt.

Saturday, Game Two, Noon, 83 Degrees, Mostly Cloudy

Today's game was moved to noon because of the evening gala scheduled for the Donald L. Tucker Civic Center. It was a celebration of Mike Martin's career called: "A Night with 11 and Friends: a Celebration and Roast."

Once again, the Seminoles jumped on the Spiders early, scoring two runs in the first and second innings, then scoring four in the third and one in the fourth, sixth, and eighth innings for an 11-1 win.

CJ Van Eyk ran his record to 7-3, picking up the win with five innings of work. He was touched for only three hits and zero runs while fanning 8 batters. He threw 80 pitches and got three innings of relief from Shane Drohan and one from Gage Hutchinson.

Mark Salvatore had four hits finishing a homer shy of the cycle. Salvatore's hits included his fourth triple of the season. Carter Smith started at first base and chipped in three of the Seminoles' 15 hits. The Noles ran their record to 33-18, and Martin got win #2,020.

The game was over in 3:43. Plenty of time to make it to the Martin Celebration and Roast. Over 600 people were expected, including 100 former players and the current team.

JIM CROSBY

A NIGHT WITH 11 AND HIS FRIENDS
May 11, 2019

To say the Mike Martin Roast hosted by Florida State Boosters, Florida State Seminoles, and Florida State Seminoles Baseball was a gala event would be understating it. However, this event held at the Donald L. Tucker Civic Center was definitely a "come early stay late event."

As expected, 600 RSVP-ers enjoyed a full evening of fun. It was advertised as an "event including dinner, access to a cash bar, and a special program featuring a variety of Seminole legends from past and present who will be offering unique insights into the career of "11."

The celebration and roast will pay tribute to our legendary skipper, who is coaching his 40th and final season with the Seminoles. Coach Mike Martin has had one of the most successful runs in college baseball history, becoming the winningest coach in college baseball last season, achieving his 2,000th win this season, and averaging over 50 wins since 1980."

A Celebration and Roast

Among the former Seminole baseball players who gathered at the Tucker Center to honor Coach Mike Martin were:

- Luis Alicea   1984-86
- J D Drew   1995-97
- Ken Fischer   1978-81
- Marc Giordano   1987-88
- Lane Green   1967-68
- Richard Holloway   1978-79
- Tyler Holt   2008-10
- Bruce Huff, Sr.   1976-79
- Lincoln Jarrett   1962
- Jonathan Johnson   1993-95
- Greg Jones   1976-78
- Doug Kasimier   1968-71
- Jeff Ledbetter   1979-82
- Mike Martin Jr.   1993-95
- Blair McCaleb   2000-02
- John McKnight Jr.   1977-78
- David Mobley   1977-79
- Jeremy Morris   1994-97
- Jack Niles   1993-94
- Eduardo Perez   1989-91
- Craig Ramsey   1977-81
- Jeremy Salazar   1995-98
- Craig Saxner   1985-86
- David Smalley   1980-83
- Gary Sprague   1986
- Allen Swindle   1980-82
- Woody Woodward   1962-63

11: MAKING BASEBALL HISTORY

Buster Posey's Video Message to Mike Martin
May 11, 2019, at "An Evening with 11 and Friends"

"Some of my earliest memories of Florida State were the December camp. I remember 11 and Meat and Coach Shouppe being out on the field. Having that nervous excitement to perform in front of them, I hoped to be noticed. Fortunately, things went well, and I started a relationship with them. I still just think about the excitement I had when I was offered a scholarship to play baseball here.

"Following Florida State as a child, I remember the Drews coming in. Stephen Drew was about 4 years before me. I followed his career and knew what kind of a great player he was ... a shortstop. I wanted to live up to some past players.

"I think 11 had such great attention to detail and the repetitions that he put his infielders through daily. I can still remember now being out on a practice in August, and it was about 120 and throwing the ball across the infield. And this is kind of gross, but the sweat was just coming off the jersey. 11's excitement and passion just for those practices still stick with me today.

"November of my sophomore year Mark Hallberg who I met up in the Cape Cod league…and Mark is still one of my best friends today. I think they liked Mark a little bit more at SS than they liked me. Mike Martin Jr came up to me and said, "What do you think about catching?" I don't know why I was as open to it as I was, but I really took to the position and had a great teacher and mentor in Mike Martin Jr. I still use a lot of his teachings today and can really fall back on a lot of the fundamentals he taught me."

Florida State Baseball Fans

"I have guys come up to me continuously, older or same age younger, and they talk about how great an atmosphere it is there. The Animals in Section B with their chants. They make it fun. I also think guys will go on and play at a higher level. It gives you a feel like what those high-intensity games are gonna be like. I was very lucky to play in front of a Collegiate fan base that enjoys baseball as much as they do.

"I think we (11 & him) both show a passion for baseball. It is fun for me to talk to him about the game. Still get his perspective on what he thinks about things. Even some of the ways that the game has changed just in my career. What a great baseball mind. But I always go back to how passionate he is and how much he cares about the sport itself. But even more so, the students that come in, you could tell he was in it for the right reasons. I was very fortunate to have played under him.

"11, congratulations on 40 years. What an amazing run. I am so humbled and feel very fortunate to have been a part of it for three years. Even more fortunate to call you a friend now. I hope you enjoy this last year as much as you can. I'm really looking forward to spending some time with you when you are done. Hopefully, we can get on the golf course. But as we all know, you are going to have to give me a few strokes."

The Stars Speak

The Last .400 Hitter
Tyler Holt (2008-10)

- Gainesville, FL.
- 2008-10, 199 GP; .359 AVG, 21 HR; 117 RBI; 79 SB.
- All-American, 3 yrs in MLB
- Assistant Coach 2018-2020

Eight years after last playing for head coach Mike Martin, Tyler Holt returned to Florida State in July 2018 as the Seminoles' undergraduate assistant coach as he worked toward his degree in sport management. Holt returns to Tallahassee after playing parts of three seasons in the Major Leagues for the Cleveland Indians and Cincinnati Reds.

Holt, from Gainesville, Fla., was a three-year letter winner for the Seminoles (2008-10), hitting .359 with 59 doubles, seven triples, 21 home runs, and 117 RBI in his career. Holt was a freshman All-American in 2008 by the NCBWA and a second-team All-American in both 2009 and 2010.

Holt is the last Seminole to hit .400 in a season, hitting .401 over 237 at-bats in 63 games in 2009. As a sophomore in 2009, Holt won the ABCA/Rawlings Gold Glove Award for his outstanding defense in center field.

Holt was the 10th round draft pick of the Indians in the 2010 draft and made his major league debut on July 6, 2014, for the Indians. A midseason trade in 2015 sent him to the Reds, where he played through the 2016 season.

Holt hit .228 with seven doubles and three home runs while appearing in 156 games in his MLB career. Holt on Buster Posey (at the Martin Roast):

"I was not the original speaker scheduled for this slot. He had to cancel. I'm thinking, what has Buster Posey got to do that is more important tonight? Not sure why Buster Posey got the first call. He's not that much better than me. He doesn't have a Gold Glove in College in the outfield. He doesn't have a natural cycle. He didn't spend parts of two or three seasons in the Big Leagues" (Each comment drew laughter).

Holt on 11 (at The Martin Roast)

"11 made one mistake when I was a player. I was batting leadoff in my freshman year and sophomore and junior years. My freshman season, we were going into postseason ACC play; the biggest line was that freshmen always choke, which I did. I was 0 for 12 going into the last game. I think he gave Buster Posey the day off. We had lost the first two, but we were going into the Regionals, so he gave Buster a chance to rest.

"We came up with the bases loaded or maybe runners on second and third. I get a tap on the shoulder. Buster is warming up. I think he was hitting .460 with 20 A's (HRs). I don't know. I don't really care. So, I'm sitting there on the end of the bench, and he has a 3-1 count. I'm saying I bet he doesn't get a hit. He hits a laser to left; two runs score, we tie the game. We end up losing the game. Good call, Coach! (claps).

"So, we go into the Regional, and like I said, I batted leadoff every game in my freshman, sophomore, and junior year, except one time. (pauses) It takes a lot to admit you are wrong—that you made a mistake. In the first game of the Regional, we lose to Bucknell, 8-0. I batted ninth. The only time all year, 2008, we got shutout."

Press Conference, Sitting Next to 11

He closes with this. 'Tyler Holt has been our leadoff man since he got here. He will be our leadoff man the rest of the way.'"

From a Player to a Coach

"Now, going from a player to a coach, I was going to say a lot about how much 11 means to me. But I get emotional. He knows I love him. So, I came back and was taking 5 courses, and Mike Bell gets the job at Pittsburgh. I go to 11 and say I would like to get into coaching. He said, 'I wish you had come to me earlier. Ramsey had already spoken to me You can't be a volunteer coach if you are in school.'

"So, I am in my room pouting, and I get a call. It's 11; he said we are going to try to work this out for you to be a student assistant coach. I think I am the first and only to hold that position. At this point, I didn't really care if I got the job. He didn't owe me anything. I played for him. Just him calling and saying we are going to try to make this work for you speaks volumes about the kind of guy he is. It has never been about him. It has always been about us."

Going from player to a coach. Some things come back to me. 'Line drive in the dirt. Stay short. Come on, lefthander. Hit the cutoff, man. We haven't done anything yet. There's a lot of baseball left. Don't give up on us yet. We are right where we want to be. You know how the Seminoles play in the postseason. And my favorite, I heard twice. "We're Going Back"' (Holt's comments can be seen on 'A Night with 11 and Friends on YouTube").

Link Jarrett (1991-94)
- Tallahassee, Florida High
- 276 GP; 989 AB; .278 AVG; 275 H; .364 OBP; 165 R.
- 2nd Team All-American 1993-94
- Assistant Coach: 2002-03

Link Jarrett played his high school baseball in the shadow of Dick Howser Stadium over at Florida High, where he played in two State Championships and was the team MVP in his senior season. He was the first freshman under Mike Martin to earn a starting role at shortstop, where he played for 201 games.

Jarrett led the team in hitting with a .325 average in his sophomore season. He was one of the best defensive shortstops in the nation and one of the most consistent ones to play at Florida State. He was a switch hitter who was versatile enough to bat in any spot in the order. Jarrett played in three College World Series during his four seasons as a Seminole.

Link on 11

"He's tremendous. He's an elite-level coach, and I'm trying to get to that point. I'll call him throughout the year if something's going on. He's called me about things. He's always going to be a resource. His in-game sense and people skills are just phenomenal. That's why he's the best" (www.burlingtonfreepress.com-Mike Berardino Indy Star July 15, 2019).

Link as a Student of the Game

"I wasn't a great player, but I was a great student. I studied, and I felt like Coach Martin had a knack for putting us in the best position to win. I pulled bits and pieces everywhere I went, and you feel like when you get your shot as a head coach, you have to find out what works for you with your personality. You pull the traits from some of those great leaders and put them in what you do" (ndsmcobserver.com).

Link Jarrett was drafted by the Colorado Rockies and played six seasons in the minor leagues. He played in 488 games, had 1,754 plate appearances, and advanced to AA for three seasons. After that, his coaching resume filled up. In 1999-2001. he was an assistant coach at Flagler. Then he came back to coach with Mike Martin at FSU in 2003. Then Mercer for 2004-05, East Carolina 2006-09, and Auburn 2010-12, where he was named SEC Assistant Coach of the Year in 2010. In 2013 Jarrett was hired as head coach of UNC Greensboro, where he coached for seven seasons. His teams broke 29 school records there, and he was named Southern Conference Coach of the year twice. On Jul 12, 2019. Link Jarrett was named the head baseball coach at the University of Notre Dame.

JIM CROSBY

MARTINISM #13

11 Talks About Decisions in Life that People Must Make

"You must make a decision. There are six things you can choose to do to be successful:

1) You can be constructive
2) Positive
3) Committed to Excellence
4) Help others succeed
5) Be trustworthy
6) Believe in yourself."

Sunday, May 12, 2019-Game Three vs Richmond

Over 4,000 fans came out on a warm, cloudy Sunday to pay tribute to Mike Martin in his final home game in the garnet-and-gold. It was a sluggish start for the Seminoles and had begun to look like Richmond would spoil the celebration of Martin's farewell game. Then came the "O Canada" inning, the fifth inning. As the Animals of Section B sang the Canadian National Anthem as a rallying point for Florida State—the team responded with six runs.

Mark Salvatore and Drew Mendoza hit back-to-back home runs, and JC Flowers doubled in a couple of runs as the Seminoles basically put the game away, taking a 6-2 lead. The final score would be 7-2.

Conor Grady picked up his 8th win, tops on the team with five innings of work. With the three-game sweep of Richmond, the Seminoles upped their record to 34-18, and it began to look like 11 might get his 40th 40-win season after all. He now had recorded 2,021 wins. After the game, Martin tipped his cap to the cheering fans, and with his wife, Carol walked around the field that bears his name for the final time. Next up, Louisville on the road for three games, then the ACC tournament in Durham, NC, hopefully, followed by a Regional Appearance.

11: MAKING BASEBALL HISTORY

CLOSING ON THE ROAD
Thursday, May 16, 2019, Louisville, KY
Patterson Stadium, 6 pm, 81 degrees, partly cloudy
Florida State (34-18, 16-11) vs Louisville (41-12, 19-8)

Game one of a Three-game Series

Florida State and Louisville have met 34 times, with FSU winning 27 times. Only eight of those games were played in Louisville, where the Seminoles hold a 6-2 edge. In Tallahassee, it is 16-5 Noles, and they are 5-0 at neutral sites.

However, this series was different. Louisville was ranked 8th, and the Seminoles were now unranked. The series got off to an auspicious beginning mainly because Florida State's hitting, as well as their pitching, were conspicuous by their absence in game one.

Louisville hit four home runs, with three coming in the first inning off Seminole ace Drew Parrish. Then the Cardinals followed up the four-run first with seven runs in the second and one in the third. That was pretty much all she wrote, as FSU only scored a single run in the eighth. Final Score Louisville 14 Florida State 1. There were two more games to play there. Yipes!

Mark Salvatore and Robby Martin had 2-hits apiece, and that was half of the Noles' total hits for the game.

It was the worst outing of the season for Parrish, who only lasted through 6-batters in the second inning, giving up 10 runs (9 earned) and 9 hits. The loss was his 5th against 7 wins.

To make matters worse, the game was delayed for 86 minutes in the bottom of the seventh inning by rain, with FSU trailing 13-0. After an ugly game like this, Mike Martin would point out that the good thing about baseball is that you get to play again the next day, unlike football where win or lose, you have to wait a week to play again.

Game Two of the FSU-Louisville Series
Friday, 6 p. m.

What a difference a day makes. In this game, the Seminoles played like the Cardinals did the night before and vice versa for their opponents—final score: Florida State 14 Louisville 3. The Seminoles matched their most runs in a road game since the Virginia game on April 18. In a nutshell, the

Seminoles improved to (35-19, 17-,12 ACC), dropping the Cardinals to (42-13, 20-9). The battery-mates for FSU played heroic roles in this one.

Catcher Mat Nelson had two homers, and pitcher CJ Van Eyk went six innings to ring up his 8th win. Since April, Nelson is hitting .362 with 5 HRs. The Seminoles' 16 hits were the most in a road game since a 2017 game at NC State. The win evened the series and gave Mike Martin his 2,022nd career win.

Game Three: FSU at Louisville
1 pm, 86 Degrees and Suunny

You could pardon Seminole Skipper Mike Martin if he said, "Excuse me, but this is where I came in" and beat a hasty retreat out of town after the game. Once again, the Seminoles were never in this one.

Louisville started the game with a four-run first and a two-run second, and this game was history mainly because FSU had two hits and no runs all day. Final: LOU 11, FSU 0.

Conor Grady only lasted an inning for FSU and surrendered four runs on three hits. Louisville starter Bobby Miller only gave up 2 hits and 0 runs in six innings to run his record to 5-1. Three Cardinal relievers followed with three perfect innings to seal the deal.

Florida State leaves town with a 35-20, 17-13 ACC record as Louisville improves to 43-13, 21-9. Next up for both teams is the ACC tournament in Durham, NC, where Louisville has now secured the number one seed.

The Stars Speak

James Ramsey (2009-12)

- Alpharetta, GA
- OF, 245 gp, 781 ab, .339 avg, 34 hr, 202 rbi
- Consensus All-American

Ramsey: A Seminole Legacy

"I feel like I was a Seminole when I was born. Then to play here was golden. My dad played here (Craig (1978-81), and my mom played Tennis (Mary Beck, 1977-80) at Florida State.

When I got to paint my room as a kid, I painted it Garnet-and-Gold. I have some good memories of sitting in the FSU dugout with my dad. I went through the recruiting process and had lots of interest from topflight schools, but I have kind of always made my decisions from my heart, so definitely, to this day, FSU and Tallahassee is a special place for me."

11's Influence

"I think as a player, he was always trying to push me to reach my full potential. I think it might sound cliché, but he always followed up on that. There is the understanding if you're gonna be a Seminole, you have to hold yourself to a set of standards. There's a certain way you have to carry yourself. There are certain expectations for how you approach practice and the way 11 just came to the field every day really excited to just get better. I think that was something that helped me in my career."

The Role Martin's Faith Played

"Yeah, I think his faith was a big part of it. We talk about improvements on the field, but spiritually and internally just really helped me embody a lot of things that Florida State was and is. Being a good steward of when you go to Florida State where the people before you were the ones that built the walls and put the money into the facility. They hung the banners and got the trophies before you. To me, that comes from a spiritual place. Any time we go somewhere, we want to make sure that we leave that better and impact others."

Playing at Howser

"There is nothing like it. It is just a different feel. Everybody there right on top of you. Passionate fans. They are classic. Even if a team came there and shut us out, the fans would applaud like, "Hey man, well done." But when the weather gets hot, and pressure is on the line, the crowd just seems to elevate itself. I know 11 even said, when we faced Stanford in the 2012 Super Regional, that it was one of the loudest crowds ever. "(FSU beat Stanford 17-1 & 18-7 to advance to the CWS).

Noles in Omaha

"We went there twice, once we were there seven days (2010) and the other for 10 days (2012). There you have more days off than you would in a weekend series. We could have spent that time watching film or scouting the other teams. But we were always doing community service, visiting hospitals, and one time we had a lunch for underprivileged families."

Being a Seminole

"It plays into the Unconquered spirit. You can tie that back to 11. He was such a big part of the mentoring and coaching process. There are so many of us, no matter what the lifestyle, that he truly did impact to this day."

James Ramsey had a stellar four year-career in which he was a consensus All-American and the ABCA National Player of the Year in 2012. In four years at Florida State, Ramsey batted .339 in 245 games. In 781 at-bats, he had .265 hits, 34 homers, a .570 slg%, and .458 obp. He was a first-round draft pick of the St. Louis Cardinals and played for eight different teams over 10 seasons. He is currently an assistant at GA. Tech coaching hitters and outfielders.

Craig Ramsey (1978-81)

- Atlanta, GA-North Springs HS
- Catcher; 172 games; 483 AB; .267 avg; .418 slg%; .380 obp
- Played on 11's first team as head coach

From Atlanta to Seminole Territory

"I was playing in a high school all-star game, and Mike Martin showed up." (he was Woody's assistant coach and chief recruiter). I thought I was going to start as a catcher, but the coach started his own catcher and put me in leftfield. I'm 'like wait a minute I don't play outfield I'm a catcher,' "So I'm out there and the batter, with runners on 1st and 2nd, hit a rope to left-center that the centerfielder wasn't going to get. Somehow, I got over there, caught it, and whirled around threw the ball as hard as I could, doubling the guy off of second. Then I got a couple of hits.

"So, Woody (Woodward) and Mike sat me down and say: 'We want you to come down and play behind Terry Kennedy' (All-American catcher).' Then I told my mom and dad, I'm going to Florida State."

11: MAKING BASEBALL HISTORY

Played for Three Coaches in Four Years

"Woody was all business. He was first class. He came in there and really changed the profile. The first fall, he brought in advertising. We had this chain-link fence (in the outfield), and he put together fundraising, getting sponsorships (for signs on the fences). He was a businessman as well as a coach, which is what the program needed during the transition period.

"Then came Dick Howser. What a great person! Other than my dad, he was probably my greatest influence. He was gregarious, related well with his players on a personal level, and made you feel comfortable.

"Bringing Mike Martin in was so exciting. He just cared about you as a person and obviously as a player. He brought his family into it, and we were an extension of him. Had that tradition there that played off of what Bobby Bowden did in football. What a great set of role models to have."

11's First Win

"That first win down in Miami, when he won his first game, I could see that look of pride and comfort that came across his face. I got the game ball, gave it to him, and said: "11 here's the first. I know how much you wanted and earned it. Then the next year, I gave him the game ball for his 50th win and later was able to give him the ball for his 100th."

The Competitor

"Mike would not only try to beat you in anything he was playing you in, he would win. It didn't matter if we were playing pool at his house or on the golf course he won."

11's Style

"I watched him change over time. He was still as competitive as ever, but he adapted. I think that over time, as the game changed, 11 changed too. You can't be good at your trade if you don't adapt. That's the one thing I found remarkable about Mike. He could still be who he was yet continue to learn and feed that back into the game and to his team. I think that is a key attribute."

JIM CROSBY

Always Looking Out For You

"We were scheduled to play the Gators in Gainesville, and it got rained out. They decided to stay overnight and play the next day. I had a final exam that day at 8 am, and I told 11. He said: 'Hold on a minute,' and he went over and came back with Dick Howser's car keys. He handed them to me and said, 'Drive home tonight and come back after your final exam.'"

Ramsey's Last At-bat at Home- vs Tulane, May 7, 1981

"My last at-bat, I pulled a Babe Ruth (sort of). I told Ledbetter in the dugout. 'I'm going to hit one out.' He said, 'no way you are going to hit one out of here.' Son of a gun, if I didn't"

MARTINISM #14
11 Told a Sales Group

"The one thing we all have in common is time. We all have 24-hours a day and 60-minutes in each hour. We all have the same amount of time. The only difference is how each person spends it. Our players have little time to put their feet up and enjoy television until after 9:30 pm. They have classes, practice, conditioning, study hall, an hour for lunch and 45-minutes for supper."

The Stars Speak

BLAIR VARNES (1999-2002)

- Pascagoula, Mississippi
- 4 yrs, 2 as #1 Starter
- 76 app; 446 ip; 41 w's; 326 k's

FSU—a No Brainer

"My grandfather was a Biology professor at Florida State. My dad went to Florida State, and my mom and dad were from Eastpoint (FL) and Carrabelle (FL), respectively. We had season tickets to Seminole football growing up, and Terrell Buckley (football) was from Pascagoula. It was a 4-hour drive to Tallahassee and five to six hours to Mississippi and Miss. State. When I heard from Coach Martin, then I started getting offers from LSU and Alabama, and others. But Florida State was my dream school."

Rough Start for Varnes

"In the fall ((1998), when I got there, I was all excited, and during the first couple of practices, my elbow started hurting. When I went home for Christmas break, I knew something was wrong because it was hurting more. In January, a month before the season, I had Tommy John surgery and took a redshirt. So, the team opened the season in the Disney World Classic in Orlando on television. They went down there, and I was sitting in a dorm room alone with a sling on my arm. It was the most depressing day of my life."

How 11 Ran the Program and Strategized Games

"I think it was the mental preparation (that excelled). Sometimes we would go on the road, and he would tell us before we got off the bus, not to acknowledge the fans, like in Miami. Gave us little tips on how to handle things. Before games, he always had good insight. He might tell me something about just one pitch like this batter can't hit an outside curveball."

Good Advice from the Coach

"I almost flunked out (as a freshman). But 11 was there for me. We had meetings, and he would talk to me and tell me to let my actions speak louder than words. He said, make your yes be yes, and your no be no. Make your words mean something with action behind them."

Memorable Games

"The 2002 Super Regional game (June 9, 2002) against Notre Dame because it was the last game, I would pitch in Howser Stadium."(FSU won 12-5, Varnes went to 10-3, and it was the team's 60th win, only the 2ndtime FSU had that many wins. Stephen Drew had a 5 for 6 night).

"Then there was the 2002 Super Regional game vs Miami in Tallahassee that helped send the Noles to the CWS. I had lost the National Championship Game to them in my freshman year. Coach Martin gave me the ball on Friday night, and I had one of my better games. We beat them 9-2."

Varnes Braces Himself to Pitch in the 2001 National Championship

"Messed up my knee in the Super Regional. They told me I had a torn ACL you can't pitch in the College World Series. I didn't even bring my glove or cleats. I'm kinda mad because I'm walking around with a knee brace, and I wanted to pitch.

"Our game against Stanford (14-11, 13 innings) was the 5th game. Coach Shouppe said to me: 'We just pitched (starters) John McDonald, Nick Stocks, and Chris Chavez. We don't have any pitching left.'

" I said, 'Coach, I've been telling you all week I can pitch!'

"With a brace on his leg Varnes gave the team six innings before Miami edged them out 6-5).

"He recalls: 'I pitched better with a brace in the spotlight than I did against them earlier with no brace when I didn't make it out of the first inning (April 18). They had a good team."

11: MAKING BASEBALL HISTORY

Martin said afterward of Blair: 'Wasn't that gutsy or what? Is that what it's all about?' That's typical of our baseball team all year."

Varnes record: 41 wins (4th); IP 446 (2nd); 75 starts (2nd) 326 Ks (6th) 1st team All-American.

Jody Reed (1983-84)
FSU Hall of Fame 1992

- Brandon, FL
- SS, 147 gp, 570 ab, .323 avg, 98 rbi, 56 sb
- 11 seasons in MLB w/Red Sox, Dodgers, Brewers, Padres & Tigers

Jody Reed came along in Mike Martin's 3rd year as head coach. After transferring from Manatee Community College, where he was a two-time all-division and all-state player, he stepped in as starting shortstop and held that key position for 147 games.

Reed didn't miss a beat going 2-for-3, including a double and home run in his first game as a Seminole (2-12-83 vs Southern Mississippi). He began to really crank it up, and after going 4-for-6 two days later against Mercer, his batting average soared up to .538.

The Seminole coaches were patting themselves on their collective backs at getting this talented player, who had been drafted twice (Giants '82 and Rangers' 83), to turn down the pros and come to play for Florida State.

In the 1983 Metro Tournament, Reed hit .421 with two homers and seven RBI. Then in 1984, he was the Metro Tournament MVP.

Reed made it to the Majors in 1987, where he played for 5 different teams in an 11-year career. He played for the Red Sox, Dodgers, Brewers, Padres, and Tigers. Reed's MLB career ended with 1284 games, 4554 at-bats, 1231 hits, and he scored 566 runs.

Jody Reed Was Elected into the FSU Hall of Fame in 1992

Jody Reed stands as one of the great all-around baseball players ever to attend Florida State University. After working his way through the minor league system, Reed was a mainstay in the Boston Red Sox infield for five years. A transfer from Manatee Community College, Reed was drafted twice before he stepped on the field at Florida State. He was a two-year starter at shortstop for the Seminoles, leading FSU to a pair of Metro Conference Tournament titles.

"If there is one factor you can credit to the success of our club, it's the addition of Jody Reed," FSU Head Coach Mike Martin said of Reed during the 1983 season.

Reed was an All-South Regional selection in 1983 and Metro Conference MYP in 1984. In 1983, Reed led the club in runs scored (97), doubles (23), walks (68), and stolen bases (31). With Reed at short, FSU turned a school-record 88 double plays.

Drafted in the seventh round by the Boston Red Sox, Reed immediately began his climb to the major leagues. He continued to love the game, quickly becoming Florida State's most recognized major leaguer (playing 11 years with five different teams Red Sox, Dodgers, Brewers, Padres, and Tigers). Reed went on to manage in the minor leagues and was named Manager of the Year by the Arizona league in 2011 as manager of the Arizona League Dodgers (Nolefan.org).

ACC Tournament

May 21, 2019, Durham, NC
Wake Forest (30-25) vs Florida State (35-21)

Two-time defending champion Florida State drew Wake Forest for the tournament-opening game at 4 pm on Tuesday. Less than a month ago, the two teams met in a 3-game series in Tallahassee, with the Seminoles taking two of three, losing the finale in a wild 16-12 defeat.

The Demon Deacons jumped out on top with a 3-run second inning off of Drew Parrish, then added another run in the 3rd to make it 4-0. In the fourth inning, the Seminoles tied the game 4-4 with a two-run triple by JC Flowers, and Nander De Sedas had a two-run homer.

A frustrating seventh inning for the Noles put the game away for Wake. They scored the go-ahead runs on two bases-loaded walks and a passed ball. When the dust settled, the Demon Deacons had a 7-4-win evening the season total against FSU, 2-2.

Coach Martin said: "I sat there when all that was going on and there was no 'woe is me.' It was, 'I don't think this has ever happened to me. We could not throw the ball over the plate. And I honestly don't think in my 40 years when it has been to this extent. Again, it's called baseball. Anything can happen." Drew Parrish's performance was a mixed bag. In 5.2 innings, he fanned 13 batters, one shy of his career-high. He surrendered 8 hits and four runs, although only one of the runs was earned. Jonah Scolaro took the loss. Next up, Florida State will tangle with N.C. State on Friday.

Friday, May 24, 2019
ACC Tournament, Durham, N.C.

The Seminoles and Wolfpack will clash for the 4th time this season. Earlier in Winston Salem, N. C. State won 2 of 3. The Noles got over the initial game in which NC State hit them with 8 runs in the 2nd inning and ran away with a 16-0 win. FSU came back to win game three.

By virtue of their Tuesday night loss to Wake Forest, the Seminoles lost out on a chance to move into the semi-finals and defend their ACC Championship. However, being on the bubble for the postseason, this game was very significant for 11's charges. CJ Van Eyk was on from the start. He allowed only one hit over six innings while his teammates were pounding out 16 hits and scoring 11 runs in a run-rule (7 innings) victory for Florida State.

It was Van Eyk's 9th win as he struck out 11 and allowed only one-hit in a 99-pitch performance. JC Flowers pitched a perfect 7th to close it out.

Martin said: "I think CJ just set the tone right off the get-go. He had three pitches going. I thought he kept his poise; he ran into a little bit of a problem, a couple of walks, but showed what kind of pitcher he is. He gathered himself and got a big strikeout."

Van Eyk said: "I always try to pitch with emotion and keep my team in the ball game, but today it meant an extra something for us to win this game and ultimately contend for a regional coming up."

Flowers and Drew Mendoza each had three hits and three RBI. The Seminoles scored 2 runs in the 1st, 3rd, and 4th innings. Put up 4-runs in the 5th and added a single run in the 7th to close out the 11-0 win.

The win gave Florida State their 36th victory. Still in question was if it was enough for them to stay alive for a 42nd straight regional (includes every year with 11 as head coach), and would they have a shot at putting up 11's perfect record of winning 40 or more games each year?

The Stars Speak

Ryan Barthelemy (1999-2002)

- Miami, FL. Killian HS
- 948 GP, .339 Avg, 50 HR, 261 RBI
- 2002, 3 All American 1st team

How I Ended Up at Florida State

"I was very interested in leaving Miami and growing up and learning how to do laundry. I wanted to be a part of the Florida State Family. As soon as I came on campus, it was just a different world. The people were different. The southern hospitality kicked in and that environment. I fell in love with that."

About Coach Martin—First impression

"He was intimidating because he was the pinnacle of college baseball. When he spoke, we listened. You think you know what you are doing. Then Mike Martin talks, and you realize you had no idea.

Impact on Me as a Player

"He taught me about leadership. He saw something in me, I don't know what, but he taught me to lead by example, and I take that very seriously. He just has a way of extracting the best part of what each person brings to the team and tying it back in to make the whole team better."

Changed as a Person

"(Under Coach Martin) I was changed for life. It was like I am (now) a person who does things the right way, if you are looking at me or not. I carry that same effort today. It gave me the strength and the courage to grow that element of who I am."

Ryan's Time

Ryan Barthelemy was a first/third baseman who was a four-year starter from Miami. He had spent many a night watching the Miami Hurricanes play, and they were in touch with him every week and expected to sign him.

He first came to a Mike Martin camp at Florida State that Chip Baker was running as a junior in high school. When he hit two balls out of the park during batting practice, he got the Seminoles attention, and a scholarship offer followed.

Always a team leader and a clutch hitter. In the classic 17-inning game against Miami, the Hurricanes had taken a 13-11 lead in the 17th. Barthelemy hit a two-run homer to tie the game and set the stage for a game-winning single by Brett Groves. The Seminoles walked off with a 14-13 win.

Barthelemy, a four-year starter, batted above .312 all four seasons finishing with an overall .339 average. He had a 33-game hitting streak and helped lead the Seminoles to two College World Series appearances (1999-2000) and two additional Super Regionals (2001-02). He is tied for most CWS Homers at 5 with Marshall McDougall and J. D. Drew.

Frank Fazzini (1983-85)
FSU Hall of Fame 2015

- Belleville, New jersey
- 234 gp; .369 avg; 884 ab; 326 h; 78 hr; 270 rbi
- All-American all 3 years.

Fazzini's FSU Story

"I was doing well for myself in high school, and colleges were calling. It was between Oklahoma State, who was writing me letters, and Florida State, who was calling me. The difference was the personal touch. Coaches Mike Martin and David Fannin made phone calls. Coach Fannin was coming up to see me play, but we had a snowstorm, and a blizzard canceled three weeks of our season. So, they went on the recommendation of a scout from the Yankees. The first time I met Coach Fannin was when he came up to sign me to a letter of intent."

First Impressions of 11 and FSU

"It was a bit of a culture shock because I wasn't used to the southern accents and the southern hospitality. Coach Martin came up to me and said: 'Glad to have you as a Seminole. We are here to help you in any way we can. We are expecting big things from you.' He was like a father extension. Later on, in life, as I was coaching, giving hitting instructions. I told parents, 'Yeah, he wanted to win, that's his job. He is trusting his livelihood to 18- to 22-year-olds. But you want a coach who you know, when you put your head on your pillow at night, that your kid is going to be OK.'"

Valuable Instruction

"The biggest thing I carried throughout my college career was when 11 told me whenever you have two strikes on, you look outside for the pitch and adjust to the inside. If you are going to hit the ball the other way, you have to let it travel further toward the catcher (before you swing). Most of my balls were hit the other way. I had the strength to hit the ball as far to rightfield as to leftfield."

11: MAKING BASEBALL HISTORY

How Fazzini Ended Up with the 2nd Most Home Runs

"My sophomore year, I remember Coach Martin called me into the office. He said that they want me to hit for average, but we are not concerned as much as we want you to hit with more power. He wanted me to look for balls I could drive and hit them into the gap or out of the park. He wanted the mindset to get in scoring position. He said to me: 'Frank, when you are up at the plate, you are in scoring position.'"

Fazzini Showing Off His Ability

As a freshman, Fazzini hit for the cycle in a game against Mercer on April 21, 1983. That year, he had three home runs in one game vs. Southern Miss (May 2. 1984). But it was in the first game as a Seminole, this one against Southern Miss that his mindset was formed into a slugger. "My first game, I looked at the lineup 11 had posted, and my name was not on it. I'm thinking, how in the hell can I not be in the starting lineup. I was mad. I went out in batting practice and hit nine straight balls over the fence." (Fazzini was not left out of the lineup for the rest of his career except for a one-game suspension for missing curfew.)

Frank Fazzini Elected to the FSU Hall of Fame in 2015

The outfielder from Belleville, NJ, was a three-year letterman and starter and earned All-American honors all three years at FSU. 1st Team Freshman AA from Baseball America in 1983, 3rd Team from Baseball America in 1984 and 1st Team from Baseball America and American Baseball Coaches Association, and 2nd Team from The Sporting News in 1985...All-Metro in 1983 and 85. One of the best hitters ever to wear a Seminole uniform had a .369 batting average, 261 runs, 326 hits, 79 home runs, and 270 RBIs (Nolefan.org).

JIM CROSBY

MARTINISM #15

11 Shares His Philosophy

"Let me share my philosophy for life. I believe God has a plan for each of us, and our job is to do our best. When you lay your head down at night, don't ask yourself: 'Gosh, I wonder what I could have done better today.' Just know that you have done the best you can do when you lay your head on that pillow."

NCAA Tournament
Athens Regional
May 31-June 2, 2019

Opening Game - Noon Friday
FSU (36-21) vs FAU (40-19)

The celebration was shown on television multiple times. Florida State players and coaches erupted into a standing ovation as their name was called to go to the Athens, GA Regional as the #3 seed. It was the 42nd year the Seminoles had made the postseason, but the first time a Mike Martin-coached team was seeded as low as #3 in a four-team regional. Obviously, the expectations, at least beyond Seminole territory, were not great for their success.

They fooled them all. Their determination showed up early as they hit #5 seed Florida Atlantic with a five-spot in the second inning. Thereafter, each time FAU scored in the bottom half of an inning FSU would answer with at least one run in the top of the next inning and most times with two runs.

JC Flowers started the home run parade in the second inning. Then after surprise starter at first base Carter Smith, batting 8th singled, equally surprising LF starter (for the first time all season) Tim Becker hit a two-run homer. That would be an omen for the series as Becker would become a folk legend before the regional was over.

Team Captain Drew Mendoza said: "Every time he (Becker) does anything when he plays, the whole dugout freaks out and gets excited."

Three batters later, in the second inning, Drew Mendoza did something himself. He had a two-run homer making it 5-zip Seminoles. That's three homers and five runs in the second inning. But there was more to come, much more.

In the sixth inning, Mendoza hit his second two-run homer of the game and his team-leading 16th of the season. This majestic homer was a no-doubter from the moment it left his bat and cleared the rightfield fence going out into the trees beyond. It was his third multi-homer game of the season. Now it was 8-3.

Not to be outdone, rock-star Tim Becker hit his second homer in the seventh to put FSU up 10-5. This one looked like a high fly ball out off the bat, but it kept on drifting until it landed on the other side of the centerfield fence. Reese Albert added some insurance in the ninth with his sixth homer of the season. It was another two-run shot that helped put FSU up 13-7 when the inning and then the game ended. Drew Parrish picked up his 8th win despite giving up five earned runs. A quality relief appearance by Antonio Velez earned a save. Now the Noles (37-21) would await the winner of Georgia-Mercer for a Saturday night matchup.

Athens Regional-2nd Day
Georgia (45-15) vs Florida State 37-21)

Game 3-Foley Field

The stands were packed, mostly with red-and-black-clad Georgia Bulldog fans with the exception of a decent contingent of garnet-and-gold Seminoles. Most of the 3,046 fans were followers of the #4 National Seed. They were ready for flame-throwing RHP Emerson Hancock, widely considered to be the 2020 #1 pick in the draft, to blow away the Seminole team that barely made it into the regional.

Both teams had scored 13 runs in their opening tournament games. UGA over Mercer and the Seminoles smashing Florida Atlantic. But, with Seminole fireballer CJ Van Eyck throwing, a pitcher's duel was a possibility. When Bulldog leadoff batter Tucker Maxwell started the game (UGA was the visitors) with a home run, it looked like a bad omen for the Noles. Georgia added a run in the third, and things were looking good for the Dogs. Not so fast, my friends! After that, it was all Seminoles. The fans kept cheering, but it became a hopeless exercise for the red-and-black.

Seminoles' newfound hitting star Tim Becker led off the third with his third homer of the series. Then the Noles added another run to tie the game, 2-2. Georgia was pretty much done, but FSU wasn't. They took control of the game in the fourth when JC Flowers opened with a double, setting the stage for more heroics by the Club Player Becker, who singled in two more runs giving FSU a 5-2 lead.

Meanwhile, CJ Van Eyk, not Hancock (who lasted only four innings), was looking like a future #1 draft pick. He ended up pitching 8 innings, fanning 9 and walking none while giving up just three runs to pick up his 10th win. His strikeout total for the season climbed to 115. This, combined with Drew Parrish's total of 112, made them one of only two pairs of teammates nationally with more than 110 each.

That win was made certain in the fifth inning when FSU put five more runs on the board. Working with a skeleton crew, the Animals managed an almost recognizable version of O Canada, the song that serves as a rallying point for FSU.

The Noles responded with some more heroics from an unlikely source, Carter Smith, who had only started four games and was batting eighth just ahead of the new star Tim Becker. Smith didn't leave Becker much to work with this time as he cleared the bases with a three-run homer. Florida States' 10-2 lead was now, for all intents and purposes, unsurmountable.

Just to make sure, Mark Salvatore added his seventh homer of the season, clearing the pine trees in left field, and Florida State was now all alone in the winner's bracket with a 12-3 win.

Georgia joined FAU in the losers bracket, and their winner would have to beat FSU twice to advance to the Super Regional. FSU improved to 38-21. Georgia dropped to 45-16. Mike Martin rang up his 2,025th win.

Athens Regional-Day Three-Saturday June 2, 2019
FSU vs Georgia
6 pm-Sunny 88 degrees

Nice evening for baseball, but surprisingly just under 3,000 fans showed up for the Bulldogs do-or-die matchup against the Seminoles. The home team recovered from the shock of the Friday night 12-3 blowout administered by FSU. Earlier in the day, the Bulldogs fought their way back by eliminating Florida Atlantic. They would have to beat the Seminoles twice to win the regional in their home park and host a Super Regional.

Still swinging hot bats, the Seminoles tamed the crowd early as Mark Salvatore singled to left and Reese Albert belted a 1-2 pitch high over the leftfield fence, establishing a lead, with just two batters, that Georgia would never recover from.

11: MAKING BASEBALL HISTORY

Albert said: "I knew if we could get something early, it would help keep us locked in."

Salvatore added: "We call ourselves the 1-2 punch; he's just a strong bat in the lineup. You could just see the difference when he was in the order and when he wasn't." Albert had numerous injuries that kept him out of the lineup for 19 games.

While the Seminoles were pounding out 10 hits and scoring 10 runs, RHP Conor Grady matched the effort with a sterling performance on the mound. Grady went seven innings and surrendered only six hits and one run, picking up his 9th victory in the 10-1 Seminole win.

Georgia coach Scott Stricklin said, "Grady was really good for them, and he had all his pitches working against us. Florida State received three tremendous performances this weekend from their pitching staff."

Drew Mendoza added two hits, and along with Salvatore and Albert, the first three batters in the Noles order accounted for six of the Seminoles hits, scored seven runs, had six RBI, and walked four times.

When it was over, the Seminoles had scored 22 runs and clubbed 25 hits off of Bulldog pitching as they secured a spot in the Super Regional against another SEC opponent, the LSU Tigers.

The last words of Georgia Coach Scott Stricklin summed it up; "That's not a No. 3 seed. They were outstanding. The team that played this weekend was one of the best teams in the country."

Mike Martin's team now finds itself one win away from adding a 40th consecutive year of 40 wins or more. But even more important, they are two wins away from his 17th appearance in the College World Series, most of any coach. He added win number 2,026 to his record-setting career totals.

The Stars Speak

Paul Wilson (1992-94)
FSU Hall of Fame

- Orlando, Boone HS
- 55 App; 304 ip; 27 w; 301 k; 2.36 era.
- 1st team All-American; #1 in MLB Draft

At 6-5, 233, Paul Wilson was an imposing presence on the mound. There was no doubt who was in command with Wilson out there as he posted 15 complete games, still 3rd all-time. His six career shutouts still top the record book. These came against Florida, Virginia, and 2 vs Miami in 1993 (4 in a season still a record). Then in 1994, he added shutouts against Coastal Carolina and College of Charleston. Wilson was especially sharp in shutting out the Hurricanes twice in two weeks—7-0 on April 9, 1993, then a 1-0 gem in Coral Gables on April 23rd.

Martin on Wilson's Impressive Shutouts of Miami

"I don't know of any pitcher I've had that could shut out a Miami team twice in two weeks.

Wilson Shines in the Rain as Well

Even the rain couldn't beat Wilson. On March 17, 1993, after a one-hour 41-minute rain delay, he dominated the Virginia Cavaliers, shutting them out while striking out 10. Afterward, Virginia coach Dennis Womack told Democrat Sportswriter David Lee Simmons, "His fastballs always sink, and he throws his breaking stuff around the plate. He doesn't walk many people. Plus, you just can't afford to get behind. We look up in the third inning, and we're seven behind. (Final: FSU 11 UVA 0)

The Gators Couldn't Solve Wilson Either

"It was one of the finest ballgames we've had against Florida. Wilson has to throw that changeup to set up his fastball, and he did that tonight. It was like an artist's drawing," said Mike Martin after Wilson's four-hit, 2-0, win over the Gators. Afterward, the Gator coach said, as reported by Democrat writer Steve Ellis, "It was a tough loss. It was an outstanding ballgame. Both guys pitched their hearts out. Wilson was in control all the way."

Wilson Drafted #1 by New York Mets

When the Mets drafted Wilson #1, it made FSU the first school in history to have the #1 pick in baseball and Heisman trophy winner (Charlie Ward) in the same academic year. 21 years later, Florida State would also have Heisman winner and number one pick in the NFL Draft in Jameis Winston, who also played baseball for Mike Martin. Paul Wilson pitched for seven years in MLB. Despite an injury that kept him out of action in 1999, Wilson pitched in 170 games, with 153 starts. He totaled 941.2 innings while striking out 619 batters and winning 40 games. He pitched 1 year for the Mets and 3 years each for Tampa Bay and Cincinnati.

Wilson Elected to the FSU Hall of Fame in 2000

Paul Wilson was one of the most dominating pitchers in Seminole baseball history. His blazing fastball and command of the game from the mound made him one of college baseball's most intimidating pitchers. Over his three-year career, he led Florida State to some of its greatest wins and capped his career with his selection as the first pick of the 1994 Major League Baseball Draft.

Wilson was selected to the Baseball America and National Collegiate Baseball Writers Association All-American teams, in addition to being tagged All-ACC following an outstanding junior season in 1994. The Orlando native capped his FSU career by being named one of nine finalists for the Golden Spikes Award, presented annually to the top amateur baseball player in the country. Wilson led the 1994 Seminole pitching staff to the College World Series with a 13-5 record and 2.08 ERA in 143.0 innings pitched. He struck out 161 batters while walking just 32. During his three-year career (1992-94), Wilson compiled a 27-11 record with a 2.77 ERA. Along the way he struck out 299 in 304.2 innings of work. Wilson established himself as the ace of the 1993 Team USA pitching staff, starting in nine games. (Nolefan.org).

Richie Lewis (1985-87)
FSU Hall of Fame 1995

- Pitcher from Muncie, Indiana
- 86 App; 38 W; 382 IP; 520K 16 CG
- Freshman All-American '85; First Team All-American' 86-87

Martin's Impact on Richie's Life:

"There is so much that goes into that. The guy has been everything for me at some point and an influence and force in my life. He was like a Father. He was a coach, a manager, and my friend. I loved his family—Carol and all the kids. This is a deeply emotional thing for me."

Why Florida State

"We are going back 40 years or so now. I may have been in 6th or 7th grade, but I remember seeing them on ESPN in one of the first College World Series games they telecast.

"In their bright and ugly yellows, Florida State was there that I would be blessed to wear on Sundays. If they (yellows) had made me look taller, I wouldn't have minded. Anyway, I went down (from Indiana) to a baseball camp in Vero Beach. My dad had bought this as a Christmas gift for me. Rod Delmonico was down there to see Chris Pollack. So, Rod accidentally ran into me. After that, he and my dad started speaking. I remember telling my dad that my number one place to go was Florida State.

"We visited Florida (Gators), and after sitting for two hours in the lobby, Coach Dusty Rhodes (assistant who had taken over at that time) sent word out by the secretary that if I became a number one draft pick, he would get back to me. This was after we had driven halfway across the country to visit. I told my dad, "This is one place I definitely ain't going to."

The Martin Way

Lewis had 20 strikeouts in a game before (1986 vs JU a 9-2 win) and had a chance to match or top that on March 16, 2017, when he went into the 9th inning leading UNC-Charlotte 9-1. With two outs, he had 19 Ks.

"I called my catcher Barry (Blackwell) out to the mound. I said that we were close to topping my record of 20, but they only had one out left. I said, 'I'm going to throw a 2-strike curveball in the dirt, and he is going to swing at it. So, don't block it, and he will get on first base (that would be K number 20), then I'll strike the next one out (for #21).' He said OK.

"So as soon as Barry got back to the plate, Martin came out and called him back. He said: 'I don't know what you jokers are planning on pulling, but I don't want you letting a third strike go by on purpose. That's not the way we do it at Florida State. If you do, there will be consequences for both of you.' We said: 'We would never do that.'"

Lewis struck out the batter. Blackwell caught the third strike, and Richie ended up with 20 Ks again.

Concluding Thoughts on 11

"You know we had our ups and downs because I was a wild child in school and all that. But you know what? In the end, he stuck with me, and that's what family does."

In his Florida State career, Hall of Famer Richie Lewis struck out 520 batters. A record that still stands 44 years later. He pitched for five different teams (Orioles, Marlins, Tigers, Athletics, and Reds) in Major League baseball and closed out his pitching career in 1998. When he retired, Lewis had been a pitcher for 17 years.

Super Regional

June 8, 2019, Baton Rouge, LA
Alex Box Stadium
FSU (39-21) vs LSU 40-24)

Game 1-Super Regional
Winner goes to College World Series

Florida State and Louisiana State have met 18 times, with each team winning nine times. At LSU, the two teams have split four games. In Tallahassee, the Seminoles lead 3-1, and at neutral sites, LSU has a 6-4 advantage. Obviously, these two teams are evenly matched. This year FSU is unranked and was one of the last four teams to make it to the regionals, while

JIM CROSBY

LSU is ranked 13th nationally and hosted a regional. The main advantage would seem to lie in the fact that Alex Box Stadium is a tough place for opponents to win a game.

Coming into the stadium parking lot, Coach Mike Martin was surprised with the number of Tiger fans who showed up to welcome him and his team and to thank him for all he has meant to college baseball.

There were 11,636 loud and raucous fans on hand inside the stadium, ready to beat, not welcome Florida State.

The Seminoles made it even tougher on themselves by falling behind 4-0 as the Tigers scored single runs in each of the first four innings. Drew Parrish surrendered all four runs of those runs before retiring in the 5th inning.

But that was all the scoring for LSU as the Seminoles bullpen crew of Chase Haney, Antonio Velez and JC Flowers shutout the Tigers the rest of the way.

Meanwhile, the Seminoles were being no-hit through five innings, and the crowd, except for a faithful group of Noles fans, led by a core representing the Animals of Section B, was loving it. But in the sixth, the tide turned for the visitors. Drew Mendoza walked, Robby Martin singled him to third, and a Mat Nelson, infield-single plated a run. It was now 4-1, LSU.

In the seventh inning, Tim Becker singled to right, and Mike Salvatore walked to bring up Reese Albert. The battle ensued between Albert and hard-throwing Trent Vietmeier. After fouling off seven pitches, Albert blasted a 92-mph fastball high and far over the rightfield fence, and suddenly, a stunned bunch of Tigers had seen their lead disappear. The game was tied at 4-4.

After the game, Albert reflected on the situation: "I knew I was getting a fastball. He just gave me a pitch I could do damage with, and that was it."

LSU coach Paul Mainieri said: "That at-bat was huge. He fouled some pitches off. He battled hard and got around on one."

In the 8th, the Seminoles loaded the bases, and Tim Becker delivered again with a sacrifice fly to give FSU its first lead of the game at 5-4.

One inning later, Albert went to work again. This time, hitting the first pitch he saw from Zack Hess just over the rightfield wall to give the Seminoles a 6-4 lead that would stand up.

So, Mike Martin now had his 40th win for the 40th season as head coach. Overall, FSU has 40 wins in 42 seasons. The next closest school, Louisville, has 40 wins in eight seasons. 11 also picked up win #2,027, and the Seminoles were now one win away from Martin's 17th World Series appearance.

Game 2 Super Regional
Alex Box Stadium, Baton Rouge, LA

Since the Super Regionals were added to the postseason in 1999, Florida State and Louisiana State have played in this event more than any other school. FSU is playing in its 17th and LSU its 14th. That alone put the spotlight on this series which was an added hurdle to surpass to make it to the College World Series.

Eight teams would move on from the Super Regional. Eight others would pack up their equipment for the summer. LSU was fighting for survival, needing a win tonight while it was one-win-and-you're in for Florida State. 11,713 fans were on hand for this clash. A fired-up Seminole team jumped out to a 3-0 lead in the second inning. Mat Nelson and Mike Salvatore drove in runs with singles in the inning.

LSU got a run in the 4th when Antoine Duplantis, the all-time hits leader at LSU, hit a contested home run that appeared to have curled just foul before passing the foul pole. However, replay held up the call of a home run. Proving to be a tough out, Duplantis would finish with a 4-for-6 night.

The Seminoles got the run back in the bottom half of the 4th on an RBI single by Tim Becker, who continued his fairy-tale postseason adventure.

In the 6th inning, the Tigers scratched out another run. Then in the 8th inning, they added two more to tie the game at 4-4. As the pressure continued to mount, neither team could score due to stellar relief work by LSU's Devin Fontenot, who ended up throwing 98 pitches in 6.1 innings. And FSU's Antonio Velez, who threw 64 pitches in 4.2 innings.

In the bottom of the 12th inning, with one out, the ever-dependable Mike Salvatore hit a one-out single and advanced to second on a wild pitch. Then the hero-of-the-day stepped to the plate. Drew Mendoza, the 94th draft pick of the Washington Nationals, laced a 2-2 fastball into right field as Salvatore raced around third and slid into home plate carrying the Seminoles ticket to the College World Series.

The walk-off winner Drew Mendoza said: "Unbelievable. I don't think anyone in this room, let alone this country, would have put us in this place right now (in Omaha). We are all blessed; it's been an incredible ride. We have always believed in each other, and we just got on a roll and are going to keep it going."

As the game ended and the players finished, dogpiling #11 went over in front of the faithful group of Seminole fans who were still standing on the front rows of the stands and cheering. He looked up and set in his loud, raspy voice: "Thank you for being here and helping me to say my four favorite words—'See You in Omaha.'"

Before heading into the media room for the postgame press conference, Mike Martin asked the LSU Sports Information Director if he could speak with their Pitcher Fontenot. In a separate room, 11 expressed his admiration for the effort that the disheartened Tiger hurler, who was in control through 6.1 innings with 11 strikeouts and 96 pitches before surrendering the two hits and run in the 12th. He told Fontenot that he was a true warrior out there and that he pitched a beautiful game. One that he should be proud of.

So, this Seminole team, who a lot of folks had written off, only won 7 of 20 games in one stretch; a month ago, they were no-hit by Stetson, and they lost 5 of 6 games to their rivals Florida and Miami are now headed to the College World Series for the 23rd time in school history. And #11 is carrying 2,028 wins along in his bag of magic tricks.

The Stars Speak
Doug Mientkiewicz (1993-95)

- Westminster Academy HS, Miami, FL
- 209 games, .348 Avg, 35 HR, 188 RBI
- College World Series All-Decade Team-1990s

From Miami to Tallahassee

"My Dad and I were in the head coach's office at FIU and was ready to sign with them when our old block white cell phone rang. It was FSU's Assistant Coach, Jamey Shouppe, saying they had an offer. My Dad and I walked out of that office, and as we were walking back to the car, I verbally committed to Florida State."

First Impression of 11

"It was almost like I was looking at a baseball god. I remember it. Just the way he handled himself. When he spoke, everybody listened. He commanded respect, and I just loved that aspect of him.

11: MAKING BASEBALL HISTORY

Playing baseball at Howser Stadium

"To me, playing at Howser Stadium is the best experience on the planet. I have played at a lot of places. Been in a lot of big games. I remember my first at-bat there. I hit a double down the third baseline. After that, I settled in. You know that atmosphere is second to none. The Animals make the place unique in its own right."

Martin's Impact on Doug

"From looking at him, you don't realize he is as much of a jokester as he really is. He starts to kind of unfold with his players. I remember one time I had a beard during fall ball. He was in the middle of a speech to the team, and he stopped, looked at me, and said, "Douglas. Are you playing one of the wise men in the church play?"

The Joke

"My junior year, we were playing at NC State on April first, and Terry Harvey or one of their lefties was scheduled to pitch. I will never forget this. I took a lot of pride in hitting third for 11. Chip Baker had us together before infield and 11 put up the lineup that had me batting 6th or 7th. I felt so disrespected. I just snapped. I was so angry. So mad I untucked my shirt. It went on for five minutes. Chip kinda walked me off the ledge. 11 walked up to our huddle for his usual pre-game speech. And the end of his talk 11 said: "Oh yeah, someone put your arm around Douglas and tell him 'April Fool.'" (Everyone was in on the joke except Doug He batted 3rd again.)

Lasting Impression of 11

"Coach Martin was the most prideful man with that uniform on, and it spoke volumes. When you put that jersey on, it meant something. Everywhere we went, people respected us because of him. He always talked about what Florida State baseball meant, and this is how we do things. Coach Martin took us to another level. He is Florida State Baseball.

Elected to the FSU Hall of Fame in 2002

Doug Mientkiewicz had an outstanding career in athletics at his high school Westminster Christian. An All-State football and baseball player who was also named All-City in basketball, he helped lead his prep team to a National Championship his senior year. Though he was a 12th round draft pick out of high school, Doug elected to sign with Florida State and leave his hometown of Miami to become a Seminole.

Mientkiewicz had three very successful seasons at Florida State and led the team in batting each year. In Doug's final season at FSU, he was named the MVP of the Atlantic I Regional, after his three homers, helped lead the Noles to their 14th trip to the College World Series. He led the Seminoles with a .371 batting average, 19 home runs, and 80 RBIs for the year. In 1994, he was a member of Team USA, where he led the team of all-stars with 10 home runs and 41 RBI's and was awarded the Fighting Spirit Award by the All-Japan University Baseball League.

He ranked 10th in the Florida State record book for batting average and slugging percentage and was named to the CWS All-Decade Team of the 1990s.

In 1995, the left-handed first baseman signed with the Minnesota Twins. He made his major league debut in 1998. But one of Doug's brightest moments came when he was selected to play for the USA in the Sydney Olympics and eventually brought home a gold medal.

His major league accomplishments include a gold glove in 2001 and a World Championship ring in 2004 as a member of the Boston Red Sox (Nolefan.org).

Kevin Cash (1997-99)

- Tampa, FL
- 178 games; .299 Avg; 552 ab; 165 h; 27 hr.; .518 slg%
- All American 1999-MLB 9 yrs; Current Mgr. Rays

Kevin Cash was always a solid, dependable player. He had the ability and the mental toughness to be the kind of player you wanted up at bat with the game on the line. He showed that in the 1999 CWS against Stanford. The winner would face Miami for the National Championship. Loser goes home. The Cardinal scored 7 runs in the seventh inning to take a 9-7 lead. With the game on the line in the bottom of the 9th, Cash hit a two-run homer to send it into extra innings. FSU would win in 13 innings, 14-11 (see "Walking Off a Winner" for game story).

11: MAKING BASEBALL HISTORY

In his 178 games in the garnet-and-gold, the versatile Kevin Cash played 3B, DH, 1B, and SS. He was named to the National Collegiate Baseball Writers All-American team in 1999 and was signed by the Toronto Blue Jays.

He played eight seasons in MLB for the Blue Jays, Rays, Red Sox, Yankees, and Astros. In 2015 at 36 years old, Cash was named manager of the Tampa Bay Rays in his hometown. In 2020 Cash was named American League Manager of the Year for leading the Rays to the World Series.

What Cash Learned from 11

"Learning how to practice was the big thing. We practiced better than anybody in the country. He really taught us how to practice, how to work, and how to win."

Cash Brought a New Managing Style to the Rays

"All the teams are looking for an edge right now. And the traditional way of thought is a great way, but if you can bring that thought with maybe those innovative, out-of-the-box thoughts, I think you're getting the best of both worlds." (www.mlb.com)

11 on Cash's Managerial Approach:

"Nobody could have done what he did except Kevin Cash," FSU baseball coach Mike Martin said. "How do you take the game of baseball when it's so set in its ways and do what Kevin has done? Let's start a reliever. He's one of a kind."

David Ross on Cash

"I think Kevin has a unique way of making everyone feel like you've been friends for a long time."

Ross, the current Cubs manager, and Cash were teammates with the Boston Red Sox in 2008.

Martin on Cash Being Always Tough

"Cash had a scare at FSU when he was struck on the left sunglass-covered eye by a batting practice ball off John-Ford Griffin's bat. Coach Mike Martin laughed when he recalled how Cash yelled from the trainer's table, 'Don't you change that lineup!' But 11 called it the most frightening thing he had seen." (Cash played anyway)

Cash Wins American League's Top Award
November 10, 2020

Tampa Bay Rays Manager. Kevin Cash was named American League Manager of Year after receiving 22 of the 30 first-place votes. Under Cash, the Rays had a 40-20 record and a .667 winning percentage which was the best in Rays history and led them to the World Series.

Upon learning that he had received the honor, Cash, in his typical low-key fashion, said: "When you are being voted and appreciated by people that don't always agree with your opinion, and there can be some back-and-forth, I think it says a lot. It's a huge honor."

Cash, who often makes fun of himself and his career .183 batting average during his 8 seasons as a Major League player, refused to take credit for the award. He pointed out the players and the organization as having the most to do with his being the recipient of the award.

His ability to relate to his players and having a loose clubhouse are credited with playing a major role in Cash's success story. He was a master at plugging holes and making adjustments. In a pandemic-plagued season, the Rays had 13 players on the injured list at one point, with five pitchers out for the season. He used 24 pitchers during the season and had 12 different pitchers record a save. Cash had 59 unique lineups in the 40-20 season.

Rays pitcher Tyler Glasnow said: "The scrutiny you're under as a manager and the pressure you're under is enormous. But the way he handles it with his emotional consistency, who he is as a person, and the energy he brings to the field every day, it's very, very relaxed."

ESPN News Services and MLB.com writer Juan Toribio contributed to this report.

11: MAKING BASEBALL HISTORY

MARTINISM #16

At the CWS
(Reported by Wayne McGahee 111, Tallahassee Democrat.)
Mike Martin explaining baseball to the media at the College World Series:

"The only thing that is predictable in the game of baseball is the unpredictability! You never know what might happen."

Seen in Omaha
College World Series
Omaha, Nebraska
June 15, 2019
Florida State (41-21) vs Arkansas 46-18)

The 2019 Florida State Seminole baseball team would enable Mike Martin's favorite phrase, "See You in Omaha," to ring true one more time in his illustrious career. For the 17th time (23rd for FSU), 11 would be the head coach of the Florida State Seminoles CWS-bound team. What FSU fans had not seen since 1999, back in the Rosenblatt Stadium days, was a Seminole team win their opening game in Omaha.

This time would be different. In the fancy new TD Ameritrade Stadium, the Seminoles encountered their third consecutive foe from the powerful Southeastern Conference. Having dispatched #4 seed Georgia in their home regional then heading over to displace #13 seed LSU at home by winning again, they now faced #5 national seed Arkansas.

The hard-hitting Razorbacks had made it to the CWS by pounding the ACC's North Carolina Tar heels in the Chapel Hill Super Regional (scoring 13 runs in the first inning of the Championship game.)

You couldn't blame the fans for expecting a shootout. It was anything but that. In fact, neither team scored a run through the first eight innings of the game. In the ninth inning, FSU scored the only run of the game, without the benefit of a hit.

Drew Parrish (8-5) and Isaiah Campbell (12-1) went toe to toe on the mound unloading their best stuff on the frustrated hitters. Arkansas first baseman Trevor Ezell said:

"He (Parrish) was really tough; he had everything working on us. His off-speed was really good, and you just have to tip your cap." Parrish, who seems to save his best performances for the big games, said with a smile: "I'd say it's one of the best performances of my life for sure. Every kid dreams of pitching at the College World Series, so this definitely ranks up there."

Parrish pitched eight full innings, 113 pitches, allowing five hits, two walks, and no runs. His nine strikeouts ran his season total to 125. His most impressive moment came in the eighth inning of this tense, nerve-racking scoreless battle.

The Hogs leftfielder Christian Franklin led off the bottom of the eighth with a double, then advanced to third base on a ground out. Then with 26,155 fans in attendance and a worldwide audience watching on television Parrish struck out the number two and three hitters in the Razorback lineup, Casey Martin and Matt Goodheart, leaving the potential go-ahead run stranded on 3rd base.

The top of the ninth was strange. J.C. Flowers, who, along with Parrish, was a star in the game, was hit by a pitch. On a ground ball to second by Carter Smith, Flowers slid into the base, and the ball popped out of Kenley (2nd baseman's glove.).

Noles catcher Mat Nelson, who had two hits in the game, laid down a perfect bunt moving runners to second and third. Freshman Nander De Sedas, in one of his biggest at-bats ever, hit a sacrifice fly to right field, and Flowers carrying the go-ahead and game-winning run, crossed home plate to make it 1-0 Florida State.

That was the final as JC Flowers immediately raced to the bullpen to warm up, then came in to save the game. He enticed a ground out and a line out, then got Kenley swinging, and Florida State had its first Opening Game win in Omaha in twenty years.

After the game, Martin addressed the team effort: "The togetherness, the heart that our team has shown, you learn a lot about people when things don't go their way, and there were some things that so-called didn't go our way. But they fought. They're still fighting. They know they haven't decided anything. There's a lot of baseball left. That's encouraging as a coach to know that you have a team like that." It was win #2,029 for Mike Martin setting up a winner's bracket matchup on Monday with Michigan, who had knocked off Texas Tech earlier.

11: MAKING BASEBALL HISTORY

GAME TWO-COLLEGE WORLD SERIES
June 17, 2019
Michigan (47-20) vs Florida State (42-21)

Florida State and Michigan had met eight times, with the Seminoles holding a 7-1-win margin. This time it featured two surprise teams who were among the "last-four-in" to make it into the regionals. FSU had surprised nationally ranked Georgia and LSU, while Michigan knocked off #1 UCLA and defending champion Oregon State.

It's not often that the second pitch of a game decides the outcome. It did tonight. Wolverine centerfielder Jesse Franklin off of Seminole starter CJ Van Eyk. After leadoff batter DH Jordan Nwogu bounced out to third base on the game's first pitch, Franklin hit Van Eyk's second pitch of the game-high into the rightfield stands. It was enough to win the game as the Seminoles didn't score. Michigan added a run in the fifth that basically sealed the 2-0 victory.

Seminole pitchers Van Eyk (10-4), Haney, and Scolaro combined to strike out 17 batters, second most ever in a College World Series game. Scolaro struck out all six batters he faced. The 2019 Seminole pitching staff now has 647 strikeouts, the fifth-most in FSU history.

Florida State could never generate any offense against Michigan Lefty Tommy Henry (11-5). He pitched nine innings of shutout baseball, allowing only three hits, walking none, and striking out 10 with an even 100 pitches.

"He was mixing his pitches and keeping the ball at the knees all night," said Seminole 3b Drew Mendoza. "He kept us off-balance and did a really good job; he deserves credit."

It was enough to keep 23,541 fans on the edge of their seats until the finish. For the Seminoles, the loss snapped a 7-game winning streak and a 6-game NCAA Tournament win streak. They now face an elimination game on Wednesday evening versus Texas Tech.

They are down, but not out, according to Mendoza: "Our mentality isn't going to change; we've had our backs against the wall all season. We will be ready to go on Wednesday and get to play another day."

Game Three-College World Series
June 19, 2019
Texas Tech (45-19) vs Florida State (42-22)

It has been a roller-coaster ride so far for the Seminoles as Mike Martin's legendary career reaches its final stages. Still trying to stave off elimination and keep this love train rolling, the Seminoles battled the Red Raiders of Texas Tech.

In the past, these two teams had only met twice. Both games were in Tallahassee (April 4-5, 2016), with the Seminoles winning 10-1, then dropping the second one 8-4.

The Red Raiders sent Brice Bonnin (6-1) to the mound to face FSU's number three pitcher Conor Grady (9-5). Another pitcher's duel would ensue before the Seminoles suffered a 4-1 defeat while only getting three hits.

The Seminoles tied the game in the bottom of the 4th inning without the benefit of a base hit. Robby Martin walked; Mat Nelson was hit by a pitch. They both advanced on a sac bunt by Carter Smith. Then, with one out, an errant pick-off attempt of Martin allowed him to score. As far as scoring, that was all she wrote for the Seminoles.

The Red Raiders re-took the lead in the 6th inning on a Brian Klein homer to right-center field. They added two more in the 8th for the 4-1 win that ended Mike Martin's coaching career. Two days later, Texas Tech would also exit the CWS with a 15-3 shellacking at the hands of Michigan.

So, Martin's career was over but not before he accumulated 2,029 wins and had an unexpected post-season run with surprising regional wins over highly regarded Georgia and LSU teams. His 2,019 record of 42-23 meant that his teams won over 40 games in every one of his 40 seasons at the helm and also made the post-season tournaments every year.

11: MAKING BASEBALL HISTORY

11's Final Post Game

After congratulating the Texas Tech coaches on their win, Mike Martin returned to the dugout to retrieve his gear. Hearing a chant---"Elev-en, Elev-en" break out in the stands he returned to the field, doffing his cap to the fans, especially those who had come down to the first few rows and mouthing: "Thank You Very Much, I love you" in acknowledgment in each direction.

In the press conference, he made sure, as always, to acknowledge his pride in his team, saying: "I hope the guys don't feel down because of a tough week," he said. "I saw a bunch of guys grow up in front of my eyes. There are a lot of teams who wish their season could end in Omaha."

As the press conference ended, Martin went to each member of the media present and thanked them personally for being there and for all they do for college baseball.

Then as he and his wife Carol, Daughter Mary Beth, and granddaughter Lexi headed for their transportation, another group of fans, most of them from other teams, were outside to greet and thank Martin for all he had done for the game of baseball.

He took time to sign autographs and briefly chat with each person there. He paid special attention, as he always did, to the kids, asking one youngster wearing a baseball cap if he played baseball. Receiving a yes, he then asked what position he played. When the boy said "shortstop." 11 replied: "That's good. You can make a lot of money playing shortstop."

Thus 11 left, and as he headed out from TD Ameritrade ballpark, he probably glanced in the direction of Rosenblatt Stadium, and only he knows what memories were dancing through his head.

JIM CROSBY

MARTINISM #17

11's Challenge to Us All

"When you are challenged in the coming days, ask yourself if you want to give up or really get after it. To do that, you have to work at it. So, trust in God, put your best foot forward and never doubt yourself."

The Stars Speak

Eduardo Perez (1989-91)

- Santurce, Puerto Rico
- 206 gp; 641 ab; .328 avg; 15 hr; 118 rbi
- All-American, 13 years in MLB

The 1989 Seminole Media guide said: "Although still a raw freshman Eduardo Perez most likely will start in centerfield, he adds several dimensions to the everyday line-up with his speed on the base paths and his power at the plate."

All this was said before Eduardo ever played a college game. He did not disappoint. Perez, the son of major leaguer Tony Perez of Cincinnati's "Big Red Machine" fame, would go on to be one of the most popular and committed Seminoles even long after his college career ended.

Perez remained close friends with Coach Martin and always promoted Florida State baseball even through 13 Major League seasons with six different teams and then distinguishing himself with ESPN broadcasting MLB games. He has even been known to give a Seminole chop occasionally on television on MLB game broadcasts after hearing that the Seminole baseball team has won a game.

Perez played all three outfield positions in 66 games as a freshman. Then he found a home at first base for his remaining 140 games at Florida State, batting .346. He was a first-round pick by the Angels.

Eduardo Reflects on What FSU Means to Him

"This is family. This is where I grew up, where a kid became a man. A lot of people who had a lot to do with that are still here. It's home.

I know where they stand in my heart, and I know where I stand in theirs. (www.tallahassee.com Jim Henry, May 29, 2015)

Wearing the same number, 24, same as his Major League dad Tony, Eduardo went on a rampage in the 1990 NCAA South Regional with 10 hits in 22 at-bats, scoring five runs, driving in a pair, walking twice, and stealing three bases.

Eduardo helped lead the Noles to the College World Series in 1989 and 1991. He earned All-American honors in 1991.

The Name is Eduardo, Thank You Very Much

At one point in his college career, Eduardo and his best friend catcher Pedro Grifol approached the radio broadcast team of Lee Bowen and Jim Crosby and told them they had decided they would like to be referred to on the broadcasts as Eddie and Pete instead of their given names of Eduardo and Pedro. So, the broadcasters obliged them, THAT NIGHT.

Before the next game, the players quickly sought out the broadcasters and informed them that their mothers had been listening to the game and they were not very happy about the name change. They were never called Eddie and Pete on the radio again.

JIM CROSBY

Copy of The Letter to Mike Martin from National Hall of Fame
President Jeff Idelson

A letter was read to the FSU team on the field by Eduardo Perez before a game in Gainesville on March 13, 2019. (Image of letter was provided by Cyndi Chambers Sports).

Mr. Mike Martin
Head Baseball Coach
Florida State University

Dear Mike,

Congratulations on making history March 9 when the Seminoles beat Virginia Tech, giving you career win number 2,000 as head baseball coach at Florida State.

With 2,000 wins—more than any coach, in any sport, in history—you are in rarefied air. When you start to consider that only 10 major league managers have won as many games, and all of them are in the Hall of Fame, it shows you the caliber coach you are and the company you are keeping. The 10 in Cooperstown: Connie Mack, John McGraw, Tony LaRussa, Bobby Cox, Joe Torre, Sparky Anderson, Bucky Harris, Joe McCarthy, Walter Alston, and Leo Durocher. That is quite a group with whom you are connected.

You should feel incredibly proud of all that you have accomplished during your illustrious career, and the indelible impact you have had on hundreds and hundreds of young players. As someone who greatly appreciates the role that coaches and teachers play in young lives. Thank you for your four decades of service.

I also thank you for donating the cap you wore and a game ball to the Hall of Fame from your record-setting win in 2018 when you passed legendary coach Augie Garrido, becoming the winningest coach in college baseball history. Both items will go a long way toward reminding baseball fans who travel to Cooperstown about all that you, your coaches, and teams accomplished during your illustrious career, as well as how grandly you have dignified the Florida State baseball program and college athletics, overall.

On behalf of all of my colleagues in Cooperstown, once again, congratulations on a job well done.

Sincerely,

Jeff Idelson
President

11: MAKING BASEBALL HISTORY

EDUARDO PEREZ ESSAY ON COACH MIKE MARTIN
From the College World Series 2019 on ESPN TV

"Mike Martin—11—as you walk off the field for the final time, the Collegiate Athletic Baseball Community salutes you for being the baseball coach that you are for the last 40 plus seasons. But more importantly, the mentor you are, the man you will always be.

"You've set records that will never be broken. But it's the part you have done off the field that will carry on long after you have gone. You have done it with great character, guidance and wisdom. You are a great teacher of the game.

" You are a role model for all. You did it the right way, coach. Just look at how all of college baseball has embraced you this week and celebrated.

"Tallahassee will always be your town. But the dugout is your true home.

"So, thank you, Coach Martin, for all you have done and the way you have done it. College athletics are better because of you. Tonight, we salute you, 11, for your fantastic career." (Text of video essay by Eduardo that aired on ESPN during the 2019 College World Series.)

PEDRO GRIFOL (1989-91)

- Columbus High Miami
- Catcher, 206 gp, ,289avg, 747 ab, 27 hr, 163 rbi
- 1st team All-American 1991

Catcher Pedro Grifol was the High School Player of the Year in Miami and was heavily recruited by the hometown Hurricanes. He committed to the Seminoles in his sophomore year. "The Seminoles came down here every year to play Miami, and I always sat by their dugout and watched Coach Martin and the way they played. I went to some camps and fell in love with Tallahassee."

Pedro Talks about Playing under Mike Martin

"My relationship with 11 was excellent. He trusted me. I trusted him. He allowed me to call my own game. He was there for me if I got stuck. And believe me, we all get stuck at times. He was there ready and available to call a pitch."

How Mistakes Were Handled

"If I called a pitch that 11 thought was not the right pitch, he would say let's talk about it. It was never a second guess. It was always a conversation. When a coach treats you like that and trusts you, the only thing that is going to come out of that is success."

Having Chip Baker to Coach Catchers Was a Bonus

"No doubt about it. Chip was there for me 100% of the time. There was nothing I did behind the plate without talking with Chip about it. He shaped and molded my fundamentals and style of catching. He didn't try to change me but allowed me to do what I could do best."

Pedro improved every year and on May 12, 1991, at Cincinnati, had the best game of his life:

"I will never forget it. I was locked in that day. I hit a breaking ball out to dead CF on my first at-bat. Then I hit a fastball to LF that went out. Next, I hit a slider over the RF fence. And I hit a double off the LF wall."

Grifol's Game results May 12 vs Cincinnati: AB 5 H 4 RBI 4 TB 14 Avg .800; 4 Game Series results: 17 AB 10 H 4 HR 9 RBI 26 TB Avg. 588

Friendship with Eduardo Perez and How 11 Contributed to Their Success

"First met Eduardo in high school. He was there for a semester then went back to his home in Puerto Rico. Six months later, we both ended up in Tallahassee. The trust that Coach Martin had in Eddie and me, with his typical feel for a player, moved us up in the batting order. (Perez to #3 and Grifol to #4). When a coach shows that confidence in a player, he rises to the occasion." (Perez hit .370 in '91, and Grifol was .344 with 16 HR)

Role Martin's Faith Played

"It was really nice to be around a head coach and leader that had so much faith like coach Martin did. I was lucky and blessed to work for leaders that were faith-driven like coach Martin was. Faith, passion, family made for a nice environment for you to relax and just play."

Pedro Grifol is currently the bench coach for the Kansas City Royals.

11: MAKING BASEBALL HISTORY

THE DAY AFTER

First Day of Retirement

My Text to Coach Martin the morning after his career-ending final College World Series Game:

Jim: "Thanks for the memories 11 and for being my friend."

Coach Martin's Reply: "I appreciate your kind words, Jim. Last night was disappointing but thank God life goes on."

A STERLING FINISH

Martin Named 2019 Baseball America Coach of the Year

TALLAHASSEE, Fla. – Former Florida State baseball head coach Mike Martin officially capped his legendary 40-year career by being named the Baseball America 2019 Coach of the Year. It is the second time the publication has named Martin its Coach of the Year and first since 2012.

"For his strong coaching job this season and in recognition of an unparalleled career, Martin is the 2019 Baseball America Coach of the Year," Teddy Cahill wrote as part of Baseball America's announcement.

"Last month, Florida State announced it would induct Martin into the school's athletics Hall of Fame as part of its 2019 class. Martin was also named the Perfect Game/Rawlings Coach of the Year and the ABCA Atlantic Region Coach of the Year after leading the Seminoles to the College World Series for the 23rd time in school history.

"Martin capped his career with 2,029 wins, the most for any coach in any sport in NCAA history. He won at least 40 games and reached the NCAA Tournament in each of his 40 years leading the Noles."

NOLES FINISH IN TOP 10

After winning the Athens Regional against No. 4 national seed Georgia and the Baton Rouge Super Regional against No. 13 national seed LSU, as well as its College World Series opener against No. 5 national seed Arkansas, Florida State finished in the Top 10 for the 25th time under Martin.

Collegiate Baseball and the National Collegiate Baseball Writers Association ranked FSU sixth to end the season; Baseball America and

USA Today ranked the Noles seventh, and D1Baseball and Perfect Game ranked Florida State eighth to end the year.

The Stars Speak

Tim Davis (1991-92)

- Bristol, FL, Liberty Co, HS/Gulf Coast CC
- LHP, 48 app. 18-6, 10 saves, 184 ip, 233 ks, 2.69 era
- Helped lead Noles to CWS in 1991 & 1992
- 6th round MLB pick by Seattle, 4 yrs, 122 ip, 91 ks

Standing 5'11" and weighing just 163 pounds, this wiry lefthander fooled lots of batters with his assortment of pitches. He came to FSU already possessing three pitches—fastball, curve, and slider that he could effectively throw on any count. Then he added a changeup.

"Coach (Jamey) Shouppe tried to teach me a changeup, but I couldn't master his change," said Davis. "I learned to throw a circle-change while throwing the ball back and forth with my pitching teammate Roger Bailey."

Davis' First Impressions of Martin

"Being from a small town (Bristol-44 miles to Tallahassee) as a kid, Coach Martin was like a baseball god to me. Just the way he handled himself and his knowledge of the game."

Coach Martin's Impact on Davis as a Player

"One of the big things was that he always demanded that you do your best. He put you out there because he had confidence in you, and that helped you have confidence that you would be successful. Coach Martin made it easy to pitch for him. He didn't put any extra pressure on you."

Coach Martin's Influence on Davis as a Person

"Just his being a good man. His integrity. His honesty. Being a Godly man. When I coach young players, those are the things I try to bring into it."

11: MAKING BASEBALL HISTORY

Tim Davis—A versatile, Dependable Pitcher

Tim Davis was a reliever and sometimes starter in 1991. He won a key game for Florida State in the 1991 regional. He came into the game in the 2nd inning against Alabama with the bases loaded and got a key strikeout. Then he went on to pitch seven innings, striking out 12, getting the 5-2 win, and being chosen for the All-Atlantic Regional Team.

Why Davis Stayed at FSU Even with MLB Knocking on His Door

Selected by Minnesota in the 1991 draft, Davis, who "always was a huge FSU fan," got a call from Coach Martin and offered him a "full-ride" to come back for the '92 season. He had a big year closing it out with an impressive complete-game College World Series, 9-strikeout win over California. His last game as a Seminole.

Tim Davis Success Continued in MLB

Davis went on to pitch (1994-97) for the Seattle Mariners in MLB. He appeared in 89 games, most of them in relief. He was a valuable member of the Mariner bullpen, striking out 91 batters in 122.2 innings. His ERA was 4.62

Stephen Drew (2002-04)

- Hahira, GA. Lowndes Co. HS
- 168 games; .354; 694 at-bats; 44 hr; 169 rbi
- All-American All 3-seasons

Stephen Drew wasted little time showing that he was not his brother's keeper (of reputation). J. D.'s brother started off with a bang. In his freshman season, he batted .402 with 16 HRs and a slugging pct. of .750. He was named 1st Team Freshman All-American.

Drew got off to a fast start in his first game, as the team opened up on the road in, of all places–Hawaii. He was 2 for 2, three runs scored, two walks, and a triple in the 10-2 win. In the 6th game, he fractured his left foot and was out over 50 days, returning on March 26th. He would go on to have 24 multiple hit games, 9 of them with 3 hits.

On June 9, 2002, in the Tallahassee Super Regional, Drew went

5 for 6, scoring four runs in the 12 to 5 win over Notre Dame. It was FSU's 60th win of the season, second-most of any Seminole team.

Drew got off to a slow start in 2003 and was batting only .297 when the Gators came to town on March 7th. When the 3-game series was over, Stephen had raised his average to .346 by batting .700 (7-for-10) in the final two games.

Stephen was known to his teammates as "Dirt"—a takeoff on the initials of his name S.O.D (Stephen Orris Drew).

11 Learned to Appreciate "Dirt" Early-on:

"He's a guy who can beat you more ways than one," Coach Mike Martin said. "He's a difference-maker."

But Coach discovered a big difference between the Drew brothers:

"While their styles may be comparable, their personalities are different. Martin describes Stephen as a more fiery player. JD would come back to the bench after popping up and calmly put his bat in the rack and be ready to go the next time. There is a lot louder bat putting away and helmet putting away with the other one (Stephen)."

J. D. Drew described his brother in simple terms: "Winning seems to follow him everywhere he goes." (Brent Kallestad, AP writer in Los Angeles Times, May 19, 2002)

Nolefan.org Pointed Out the Stellar Career that Stephan Drew Had

Stephen Drew, Shortstop from Hahira, GA, a three-year starter and letterman., ACC Rookie of the Year in 2002, earned All-ACC honors all three years at FSU and 2nd and 3rd team All-American honors from multiple organizations all three years. He was an outstanding defensive shortstop with good power and speed. Drew finished his FSU career with a .354 batting average, 215 runs, 246 hits, 47 doubles, 19 triples, 44 home runs, 169 RBIs, and 58 stolen bases.

Stephen Drew went on to play 12 years in the Majors for five different teams (Diamondbacks, A's, Red Sox, Yankees, and Nationals) in both the National and American Leagues. Drew played in 1,268 games, 4,917 plate appearances, BA of .252, with 1,109 hits, 435 walks, 123 HRs, and 524 RBI.

11: MAKING BASEBALL HISTORY

THE NATIONAL CHAMPIONSHIP

While no Seminole Baseball team has ever won a National Championship, Mike Martin's teams have come pretty darned close. So close, in fact, it seems that fate was against them when it came to that final game. Still, when you consider that 11's 2,029 wins far outstrip anything accomplished by any college coach ever, it disproves the saying that "close only counts in horseshoes and hand grenades." It counts in baseball as well.

In the overall picture, consider that 297 Division 1 teams compete with aspirations of winning a National Championship. At the end of the regular season, only 64 make it to Regional Tournaments. The field is narrowed to 16 for Super Regional play, with just 8 of those surviving and advancing to the College World Series. Then two teams play for the National Championship.

Mike Martin's teams won 40+ games in all 40 seasons and reached the Regionals every year. Then Martin's Noles advanced to the College World Series 17 times. The following are some thoughts about the Post-Season accomplishments and not winning the final game. Mike Martin said:

"There was a time when I was consumed with winning the College World Series. I was like Captain Ahab (in 'Moby Dick') trying to find that whale every day. Anything that had to do with winning a national championship consumed me. But I realized that the journey far outweighs the destination."

Eduardo Perez (1989-91, 13 years in MLB)

"When I left Florida State, I might not have had a national championship, but I knew I was ready to encounter anything at the professional level. I was fundamentally sound and mentally prepared.

Mike Bianchi (Orlando Sentinel) on Not Winning the CWS

"It's not fair, and it's not right that this spiritual man of faith has been frowned upon by the baseball gods themselves. He's been snake-bit and star-crossed, cursed with what he might call in his Carolina barbecue brogue. 'Dog-gone dad-gum buzzard's luck.' If you root against Mike Martin to win a World Series, you are probably the same person who slams the door in the face of the pig-tailed, freckle-faced kid selling Girl Scout cookies; yells get-a-job to the homeless man begging for quarters, and flips off the little old lady driving her Dodge Dart 20 mph in a 45-mph zone" (May 12, 2018).

Florida State President John Thrasher (2014-2021)

"Mike Martin's abilities are reflected in the fact that he is the winningest college coach in the history of the game, but he has also shown a generation what a program run with pride, class, and proper priorities look like. Coach Martin is a great ambassador for both Florida State University and the game of baseball."

Blair Varnes (1999-2002)

"11 was a legend for the time he did it. 40 seasons! I've had friends or co-workers say something about Coach Martin never winning a National Championship. What was it about him? I say: 'It was nothing about him. The players on the team lost the game.' It's on the players. Mike Martin did not lose the National Championship."

Doug Mientkiewicz (1993-95, 12 yrs. MLB, Olympics Gold Medal

"We won a national championship in high school. Won a World Series in baseball (Redsox). I wanted to be the first to win Coach Martin a (college) World Series ring. The one thing that sticks in my mind is not winning him a ring. It wakes me up in the middle of the night that I am still angry that this is the one ring that eluded me."

Andy Lopez, Florida Coach (1995-2001)

"Every time he got there, I was praying things would work out, and he could catch a break. This is Andy Lopez's opinion-but what Mike Martin has accomplished year in and year out is far beyond any national title. Every coach knows it's not always the best team; it's the hottest team. For that man to win 40 games every single year, it is astounding." (Capital City Bank section in Tallahassee Democrat, May 8, 2018.)

Ricky Kimball (1988-1991)

"In '89 should have won. We had to be beaten twice. We were in the winners' bracket, and when you are up 2-0, you have to find a way. It bothers me that people used to give 11 a hard time for not winning a World Series. He didn't play the game for us. It takes so much just to get there. Some coaches get there then never get back. Give 11 credit for getting there 17 times."

Paul Mainieri LSU Coach (2007-20)

"Some people seem to think that (not winning the CWS) tarnishes his reputation in some way. I'm not one of those people. You have to win an awful lot of big games to win 2,000 games and get to Omaha 17 times. bkubena@theadvocate.com June 6, 2019

Mike Martin Puts The CWS Thing in Perspective

"If I ever said [I had bad luck] to myself, there might be a lot of voices saying, 'You have a nice house. You have the most unbelievable wife a man could ask for. You have three healthy children. You have just about anything a man needs, and you're griping about never winning a national championship?' www.espn.com (Andrea Adelson)

JIM CROSBY

WALKING OFF A WINNER

Some of the Seminoles' most satisfying wins have been those of the walk-off-variety. These are the games that were won in the last at-bat on Mike Martin Field at Dick Howser Stadium. Here are some, not all, of the more memorable ones:

May 19, 1986: In a season in which the Seminoles had a record 61 wins and went all the way to the championship game of the College World Series, the final home game vs LSU was one of the most exciting. Televised nationally on ESPN, the Seminoles took a 4-2 lead into the 9th at Howser. LSU tied it, 4-4, with a two-run homer setting the stage for walk-off dramatics. With a runner on, All-American RF, Paul Sorrento got into a low fastball and muscled it over the RF fence, headed toward the circus tent and winning the game 6-4. Afterward, Sorrento summed up his feelings as: "Top of the world."

April 9, 1995: A game the Martin family will never forget, the Sunday rubber match, was against the rival Hurricanes. FSU ranked #4 Miami #5. It was a battle. 2-2 entering the bottom of the 11th. Mike Martin Jr. was in the throes of a terrible slump—three hits in his last 25 at-bats, steps to the plate.

Canes catcher Rudy Gonzalez says to 'Meat.' "I don't think I can go another inning." Martin replied, "Try catching three games at 165 pounds." Side arming RHP Jay Tessmer, thinking about Meat's .185 batting average figures "With two outs, nobody on I'm going after him." Big mistake as Martin, with one perfectly timed swing, blasted it over the RF fence for a sweet walk-off homer, a 3-2 series-clinching win. It was the first home run allowed by Tessmer in 65 career appearances. 11 said: "I know he's (Mike Jr.) been struggling, but he can hit with anybody once he gets the confidence back." (Steve Ellis and John Nogowski of the Tallahassee Democrat wrote stories on the game)

11: Making Baseball History

Regional Walk-offs

June 9, 2010: When the game is on the line, and you need a big hit, scan the lineup and see when Mike McGee is due up. In the first game of the Tallahassee Super Regional against Vanderbilt, it was just the right time for the Seminole OF/P to be up. McGee, who had two walk-off game-winning hits earlier in the season, delivered again with a blast over the right-field wall for the 9-8 win. He said that he didn't think he would get that good of a pitch to hit, but when he did, he was ready. Freshman Jayce Boyd had put the Noles in position for the McGee heroics with a homer of his own in the 8th inning. The Seminoles would win two of three from Vandy and advance to the College World Series. (Democrat writers Corey Clark and Ira Schoffel wrote stories on the game)

June 10, 2017: In Game One of the Tallahassee Super Regional vs Sam Houston State, it just figured if anyone was going to be a superhero, it would be LF Jackson Lueck. After all, he was already 3-for-4 in the game and was coming off of a sizzling Regional in which he went 10-for-24 with a double, homer, and eight RBI. He already had four walk-off game-winners in his career and two in the 2017 season. Sure enough, with the game tied, 6-6, in the bottom of the 9th, who should stride to the plate but the King of Walk-offs himself. Lueck did not disappoint as he singled in the winning run. It was the first post-season walk-off win by the Seminoles since Mike McGee's homer in 2010. It took all the starch out of the Bearkats and led to an easy 19-0 win by FSU the next day and a trip to Omaha.

College World Series Walk-off Wins

June 18, 1999: It was one of the wildest games in CWS history when FSU met Stanford, with the winner headed to a National Championship game vs. Miami. The Seminoles built a 7-2 lead through six innings, and it looked like they would coast into that final game. Not so fast. In the 7th inning, the Cardinal put up 7-runs to make it 9-7. Neither team scored in the 8th. It was time for FSU's last gasp. Trailing by two in the 9th, Kevin Cash hit a two-run homer to tie and send it to extra innings. Cash later remarked: "This game was all about who wanted to out-clutch who." Both teams scored 2 in the 10th, 11-11. After the 11th & 12th innings were scoreless for both teams, and Stanford was blanked in the 13th, the stage was set for CF Karl Jernigan to be the hero. He was equal to the task, blasting a 3-run homer for a 14-11 wild walk-off win ending the 4.5-hour exhausting, tension-laden game. The Seminoles hit 6-homers. Also clearing the fences were Marshall McDougall (twice), Sam Scott, and Ryan Barthelemy. It set up the Seminoles' 3rdappearance in the Championship game. (The late Steve Ellis wrote a story on this game)

June 14, 2000: One year later, the Noles were back in Omaha, and their battle to stay alive after an opening loss to USC saw them facing the Trojans again, in an elimination game after beating Texas. This game was a good old-fashioned pitcher's duel with 11-game winner Jon McDonald pitching a complete-game four-hitter and limiting the Trojans to 2-unearned runs. Going into the bottom of the 9th tied, 2-2, it was up to Tallahassee native LF Mike Futrell to play the hero role, and "Frenchy" was equal to the task with a game-ending walk-off RBI single. The other two Seminole runs came on two Marshall McDougall's solo homers in the 4th and 7th. This gave him 5 career CWS HRs tying him with J. D. Drew and Ryan Barthelemy in that category.

Martin's Final 2 seasons: Walk-Off Bonanza

In 11's final two seasons, the walk-off machine was well oiled and operating smoothly. His troops treated the fans to seven nerve-racking walk-off wins. Two came in 2018 with five of them saved for his final season:

February 24, 2018: 11's record-setting year got off to a good start, with a #5 ranking and a 6-0 start. Win #6 required some late-inning heroics against Troy. The Seminoles jumped out to a first-inning 3-0 lead, but the Trojans refused to knuckle under, tying the game at 5-5 going into the 9th inning. With the bases loaded following a Mark Salvatore walk, a Jackson Lueck single, and a Cal Raleigh walk, 3B Drew Mendoza got a pitch that he admitted he probably shouldn't have swung at, but he said: "It" was down, but I was fortunate to get a good piece on it." He drove it into RF for his first career walk-off hit and a 6-5 Seminole win. 5,147 fans witnessed 11's 110th win, 26 away from the record.

11: MAKING BASEBALL HISTORY

March 30, 2018: The 29th game of the season was against ACC opponent Louisville (18-7). The Seminoles were 22-5 coming in and had a 4-2 lead through three innings thanks to a SS Mark Salvatore grand slam, his first homer as a Nole. The Cardinals put three runs up in the eighth, so the Seminoles entered the ninth with their backs to the wall trailing 7-6. This time the heroics belonged to Alabama native Jonathan Foster, who played for Auburn for a year and was in only his 10th game and 12th at-bat as a Nole when Coach Martin called on him to pinch-hit. He responded with a walk-off two-run homer for the 8-7 victory. Foster said: "That was a great feeling. I'm thankful for Coach letting me pinch-hit and have that opportunity." They played before 4,469 fans; it was 11's 1,966 win leaving him 10 short of being the all-time winner.

February 16, 2019: In Game 2 of a rare early-season doubleheader against Maine, the Seminoles put up their first walk-off win of 2019. It wasn't pretty, but the final result satisfied the 5,005 fans at Mike Martin field in Dick Howser stadium. It was a seven-inning contest, and the Noles entered their final at-bat trailing 5-4. Elijah Cabell led off the 7th with a five-pitch walk and scored on a double off the RF fence by Robby Martin. JC Flowers ran for Martin and moved to third on a balk, then scored the walk-off winning run on a sac fly by C Mat Nelson for the 6-5 win that kept FSU perfect through the first 3 games.

March 6, 2019: North Florida scored three runs in the first inning, and FSU trailed until the seventh when they got a two-run homer from LF Elijah Cabell to tie the game, 3-3. The Seminole offense was struggling. They struck out 17 times and left 14 men on base. But all is well that ends well as SS Nander De Sedas singled in a run in the second and then doubled in the walk-off game-winning run in the bottom of the 9th. The Seminole bullpen threw 8.2 scoreless innings keeping FSU's record for the season perfect at 11-0 and putting Coach Martin's all-time win record just two away from 2,000.

March 8, 2019: Two days later, ACC opponent VA. Tech came to town and would be the victim of another Seminole walk-off win. Cooper Swanson, Elijah Cabell, and Jonathan Foster hit homers for FSU in the first four innings, yet the two teams entered the 10th inning tied at 6-6. FSU's struggle intensified when the Hokies scored two in the top of the 10th. It was time for the Noles closer JC Flowers to show some heroics, but at the plate, not on the mound. Trailing 8-6, Flowers delivered a clutch three-run double in the 10th for the Seminoles third walk-off win of the season and second in as many games. Martin was now one win away from 2,000, which he would get two days later in a 5-3 win in the second game of a DH vs Va. Tech.

March 30. 2019: The Seminoles got a walk-off win for the 4th time of the season by beating Boston College, 4-3 at home. The Noles got off to a 3-0 lead. Tim Becker walked and advanced to second on a sac bunt by Mat Nelson. This set the stage for Mark Salvatore to slash a game-winning single thru the right side, scoring a sliding Becker at home plate. Four different players had now contributed walk-off wins in 11's final season.

June 9, 2019: It was 11's final walk-off win as the Seminoles Head Honcho, and it was for Seminole fans a thing of beauty. Game two of the Super Regional, in Baton Rouge, LA. By virtue of winning game one, FSU was the home team against LSU in this one. In that game, 11 had secured a 40-win season in all of his 40 years as head coach. Now he was hoping for a return trip to Omaha for the 17th time and 23rd for FSU. After regulation, the score was FSU 4 LSU 4. Same score after 11 innings. In the 12th inning, after a Salvatore single, he advanced to second on a wild pitch. Then Drew Mendoza ripped a two-strike pitch to right-center for the walk-off game-winner. Yes, FSU was going back to the College World Series one final time for 11. Mendoza said: "Unbelievable! I don't think anyone in this room, let alone this country, would have put us right now in Omaha. We are all blessed. It's been an incredible ride."

11: MAKING BASEBALL HISTORY

THE CAST OF CHARACTERS
(11's 608 Players)

#	First	Last	Pos	Home/School	Year	
20	Lanny	Abshier	OF	Belleview (Lake Weir)	1985	
24	Josh	Adeeb	OF	Jacksonville (Bolles)	1995	1997
12	Tyler	Ahearn	P	Jupiter (IMG Academies)	2018	2020
23	Reese	Albert	OF-P	Jupiter (Jupiter)	2018	2019
29	Bobby	Alexander	P	Baltimore, MD (Cardinal Gibbons)	1982	
1	Giovanny	Alfonzo	IF	Port Saint Lucie (Lincoln Park Academy)	2012	2014
1	Luis	Alicea	2B	Guaynabo, PR (Liceo International Castro)	1984	1985
1	Edwin	Alicea	2B	Guaynabo, PR (Roesler/Chipola JC)	1987	1988
12	Cody	Alling	P	Pensacola (Pensacola Catholic)	2012	2013
15	Roy	Alvarez	1B	West Palm Beach (Cardinal Newman/Palm Beach CC)	1980	
27	Mario	Amaral	C	Miami (Reagan-Doral)	2012	2013
7	Dennis	Anderson	IF	Jacksonville (Bishop Kenny)	2004	2005
20	Travis	Anderson	OF	Bristol (Liberty County/Chipola JC)	2006	2007
40	Jack	Anderson	P	Tampa (Jesuit)	2019	2020
38	Rhett	Aplin	P	Fleming Island (Fleming Island/Seminole State College of Fl)	2017	2018
13	Eric	Arce	1B-C-OF	Tampa (Lakeland)	2011	2012
16	Bob	Armstrong	1B	Dallas, TX (Tallahassee CC)	1992	1994
21	Bill	Ashford	C	Thiells, NY (North Rockland/Morris County CC)	1982	1983
32	Al	Ashmont	P	Winfield Park, NJ (Union Catholic Regional)	1985	1986
7	Brooks	Badeaux	SS	Scott, LA (Teurlings Catholic)	1995	1998
4	Roger	Bailey	P	Chattahoochee (Chattahoochee)	1991	1992
51	Nico	Baldor	IF	Tampa (Jesuit/Miami)	2019	2020
18	Pichi	Balet	3B	West Palm Beach (Forest Hill/Tallahassee CC)	2000	2001
30	Blake	Balkcom	OF	Chipley (Chipley/Chipola JC)	2003	2004
6	Rob	Bargas	3B	Sacramento, CA (Sacramento City CC)	1989	1990
1	Mark	Barineau	IF	Tallahassee (Godby)	1982	1983
27	Ryan	Barthelemy	1B-OF	Miami (Killian)	1999	2002
37	Tim	Becker	OF	Wellington (Palm Beach Central/Palm Beach State College)	2019	
44	Mike	Bell	P-1B	Sarasota (Riverview/Pasco-Hernando CC)	1994	1997
13	Robert	Benincasa	P	Tampa (Armwood)	2010	2011
20	Daniel	Bennett	P	Tallahassee (Leon/Tallahassee CC)	2010	2014
30	Scott	Bentley	OF	Aurora, CO (Overland)	1994	1996
4	John	Bentley	P	Tallahassee (North Florida Christian)	1997	1998
19	Michele	Bertoldi	C	Tallahassee (Florida/South Georgia JC)	1991	1992
18	Cole	Beverlin	P	Port Orange	2019	
45	Charlie	Beverly	P	Wise, VA	1981	
1	Allen	Bevis	2B	Tallahassee (Florida)	1989	1990
36	Boomer	Biegalski	P	Tallahassee (Chiles/College of Central Florida)	2015	
25	Grant	Bigilin	IF-OF	Fleming Island (Fleming Island)	2012	
14	Kyle	Bird	P	Orange Park (Clay)	2012	2013
	Bart	Birnbaum	C	Miami (Coral Park)	1980	1981
24	Barry	Blackwell	C	Summit, NJ (New Providence)	1985	1987
12	Garrett	Blanton	3B-OF	Tallahassee (Lincoln)	1989	1991
39	Tony	Blasucci	OF	Miramar (Miramar/Broward CC)	1983	
16	Taylor	Blatch	P	Stuart (Jensen Beach)	2015	2016

JIM CROSBY

#	First	Last	Pos	Home/School	Year	
26	Jon	Bolin	C	Panama City (Mosley/Gulf Coast JC)	1990	1991
24	Jimmy	Bonenberger	OF	Melbourne Beach (Central Catholic/Brevard CC)	1997	1999
45	Alex	Boston	OF	Bartow (Bartow)	2004	2005
12	Rafael	Bournigal	SS	Santo Domingo, DR (Canada JC)	1987	1988
27	Rafael	Bournigal	IF	Mulberry (Lakeland Christian/Belmont)	2018	2019
26	Scott	Boyd	3B	Pensacola (Washington/Jefferson Davis CC)	2001	2004
16	Jayce	Boyd	IF	Cantonment (Tate)	2010	2011
27	Mike	Brady	P	Jacksonville (Bolles)	1987	1990
37	Wil	Breton	OF-1B	Keystone Heights (Keystone Heights/Saint Johns River CC)	2012	2015
53	Jose	Brizuela	IF-P	Weston (Archbishop McCarthy)	2012	2014
45	Chris	Brock	OF	Altamonte Springs (Lyman)	1989	1991
17	Pete	Brown	P	Horseheads, NY (Horseheads)	1985	
29	Billy	Brown	OF	Fort Lauderdale (Saint Thomas Aquinas)	1996	1998
5	Jerrod	Brown	1B	Auburndale (Auburndale/Hillsborough CC)	2002	2003
36	Dillon	Brown	P	Lynn Haven (Mosley)	2016	2018
29	Barret	Browning	P	Jesup, GA (Wayne County/Chipola JC)	2005	2006
7	Parker	Brunelle	C	Snellville, GA (Wesleyan)	2008	2011
20	Calvin	Brutus	P	Hardee (South Florida CC)	2008	
30	Tommy	Bryant	3B	West Caldwell, NJ (James Caldwell)	1984	
28	Terrell	Buckley	OF	Pascagoula, MS (Pascagoula)	1991	1992
14	Tye	Buckley	OF-P	Tallahassee (Lincoln/Seminole CC)	2011	2014
1	Travis	Burge	P	Port Saint Joe (Port Saint Joe)	2006	2007
36	Kenny	Burkhead	P	Deltona (Trinity Christian Academy)	2013	2014
16	Thad	Busby	P	Pace (Pace)	1996	1997
28	Dylan	Busby	SS	Sarasota (Sarasota)	2015	2017
27	Brian	Busch	P	Boca Raton (West Boca Raton Community)	2009	2012
53	Bryan	Bussey	C	Weaverville, NC (North Buncombe/Walters State CC)	2016	2019
51	Steve	Butler	P-1B	Miami (Westminster Christian)	1995	1996
23	Mike	Buttery	OF	Tampa (Polk CC)	1994	1995
21	Rod	Byerly	P	Orlando (Oak Ridge/Brevard CC)	1987	1988
20	Clint	Byrd	OF	Miami (Hialeah-Miami Lakes)	1997	2001
31	Alec	Byrd	P	Miami Shores (Saint Thomas Aquinas)	2014	2017
19	Elijah	Cabell	OF	Winter Park (TNXL Academy)	2019	2020
5	Vince	Calandra	OF	Los Angeles, CA (El Camino/College of the Canyons)	1984	1985
44	Bryan	Campbell	P	Dunedin (Dunedin/Saint Petersburg JC)	1987	1988
29	Eddie	Cannon	P	Sebring (Sebring/South Florida CC)	2003	2005
38	Stephen	Cardullo	IF	Coral Springs (Saint Thomas Aquinas)	2007	2010
46	Drew	Carlton	P	Lakeland (Jenkins)	2015	2016
21	Alex	Carpenter	P	Satellite Beach (Central Catholic/Eastern Florida State College)	2017	2019
42	Sid	Cash	2B	Maitland (Lake Highland Prep)	1990	1991
13	Kevin	Cash	3B-SS	Tampa (Gaither)	1997	1999
44	Kris	Castellanos	P	Brandon (Newsome)	2009	2011
20	Kyle	Cavanaugh	1B	Winter Park (Trinity Prep/North Carolina State/Tallahassee CC)	2017	2018
39	Chris	Cawthon	OF	Decatur, GA (Avondale/Dekalb JC)	1981	1984
42	Michael	Cetta	P	Miami	2012	
30	Brian	Chambers	P	Tampa (Jefferson)	2004	2007
10	Tyler	Chambliss	P	Live Oak (Suwannee)	2004	2006
41	Lane	Chance	P	Tallahassee (Leon/Tallahassee CC)	1994	
20	Gibbs	Chapman	2B	Saint Cloud (Saint Cloud/Lake-Sumter CC)	2004	2005
10	Chris	Chavez	P	Pensacola (Washington)	1995	1999
19	Aaron	Cheesman	C	Sarasota (Sarasota)	2001	2005

11: MAKING BASEBALL HISTORY

#	First	Last	Pos	Home/School	Year	
21	Randy	Choate	P	San Antonio, TX (Winston Churchill)	1995	1997
20	Greg	Clayborne	OF	Jacksonville (Ed White/Florida CC)	1986	1988
45	Matt	Clements	C	Wallkill, NY (Wallkill Valley)	1988	
13	Charles	Cleveland	IF	Tampa (Tampa Catholic)	2005	2006
3	Hal	Cohen	OF	Augusta, GA	1982	1983
20	Chris	Cole	1B	Hernando (Hernando)	2001	
30	Robby	Coles	P	Crawfordville (Wakulla/Chipola JC)	2013	
9	Ty	Colston	OF	Sacramento CA (Cosumnes River JC/Sacramento City CC)	1989	1990
19	James	Colzie	OF	Miami (South Miami)	1994	
17	Mike	Compton	P	Branson, MO (Branson)	2012	2016
26	John	Cook	C	Elmira, NY (Elmira Free Academy)	1992	
27	Brian	Cox	OF	Tallahassee (Florida/Tallahassee CC)	1997	1998
34	Keith	Craig	C	Laurel Springs, NJ (Collingswood)	1980	1981
24	Wes	Crawford	P	Winter Haven (Winter Haven/Polk CC)	1996	1998
5	Buddy	Cribb	3B-1B	Myrtle Beach, SC (Myrtle Beach)	1988	1990
28	Casey	Cribb	C	Jacksonville (Providence/Jacksonville/Tallahassee CC)	2018	
49	Charlie	Cruz	P	Miami (North Miami)	1992	1995
42	Mike	Cullen	OF	Detroit, MI (Brother Rice/South Alabama)	1980	
44	Mark	Culp	P	Coral Springs (Coral Springs)	2003	
2	Ohmed	Danesh	OF	Orlando (Doctor Phillips)	2007	2010
42	Phil	Dannunzio	OF	Wantagh, NY (Wantagh)	1988	1989
1	Tyler	Daughtry	IF	Warner Robins, GA (Veterans)	2017	2018
18	Daniel	Davidson	P	Panama City (Mosley/Gulf Coast JC)	2002	2003
44	Bret	Davis	P	Vallejo, CA (Hogan/Sacramento City CC)	1988	
7	Tim	Davis	P	Bristol (Liberty County/Gulf Coast JC)	1991	1992
17	Josh	Davis	P	Pensacola (Pensacola Catholic)	1996	
6	Mike	Davis	P	Rocky Face, GA (Tallahassee CC)	1996	
9	Hunter	Davis	P	Wakulla (Wakulla/Florida CC)	2004	
24	Marcus	Davis	OF-1B	Cincinnati, OH (Princeton/Walters State CC)	2013	
13	Danny	De La Calle	C	Miami (Ferguson/Miami Dade CC)	2014	2015
2	Nander	De Sedas	IF	Panama City, Panama (Montverde Academy)	2019	2020
35	Nicholas	Debacker	P	Tampa (Plant)	2007	
10	Eric	Deddens	OF	Plantation (Plantation)	1983	1984
38	Alex	Deise	P	Saint Petersburg (Saint John's/Saint Petersburg JC)	2015	2016
3	Tony	Delmonico	IF	Knoxville, TN (Tennessee)	2008	
20	Don	DeLoach	SS	Tallahassee (Leon)	1978	1981
2	Josh	Delph	OF	Bartow (Bartow)	2012	2015
43	Timmy	Delph	OF	Bartow (Bartow)	2015	
21	Ben	DeLuzio	IF	Windermere (First Academy)	2014	2016
20	Greg	Dennis	3B	Chattanooga, TN (Notre Dame/McLennan CC)	1984	
3	Nick	Derr	IF	Lakewood Ranch (Sarasota)	2017	2018
29	Jordan	Desguin	IF	Newport Beach, CA (Newport Harbor)	2013	
26	Zach	Diaz	P	Lakeland (Santa Fe Catholic)	1996	1999
32	Matt	Diaz	OF	Lakeland (Santa Fe Catholic)	1998	1999
5	Danny	Diaz	C	Miami (Southridge)	2004	2006
29	Mike	DiBlasi	P	Clearwater (Countryside)	1997	2000
32	Matt	DiBlasi	P	Clearwater (Countryside)	2003	2006
27	Danny	Dichter	P	Hollywood (Hollywood Hills)	1993	
20	Spencer	Dickinson	OF	Tequesta (Benjamin)	2009	
19	Kevin	Dodge	P	Miami	1981	1983
31	John	Doolittle	C	Newnan, GA (Northgate)	2008	

JIM CROSBY

#	First	Last	Pos	Home/School	Year	
5	Danny	Dowell	C	Tampa (Plant/Pennsylvania)	1981	1983
39	J.D.	Drew	OF	Hahira, GA (Lowndes County)	1995	1997
4	Stephen	Drew	SS	Hahira, GA (Lowndes County)	2002	2004
39	Jay	Drivas	P	Winter Park (Lake Howell/Seminole CC)	1984	
42	Chip	Drobine	P	Miami	1986	
5	Shane	Drohan	P	Jupiter (Cardinal Newman)	2018	2020
14	Matt	Dunbar	P	Dunedin (Dunedin)	1987	1990
21	Marc	Dunbar	C	Crystal Beach (Dunedin)	1989	1992
13	Chris	Dunn	P	Brooksville	1986	
33	Andrew	Durden	OF	Port Saint Lucie (Port Saint Lucie/Indian River CC)	2010	
23	Taiwan	Easterling	P-OF	Hattiesburg, MS (Oak Grove)	2008	2011
16	D.J.	Echols	P	Pensacola (Washington/Alabama Southern CC)	2005	2006
49	Scott	Edwards	OF	Fort Myers (Fort Myers)	1989	1990
9	Jon	Egertson	P-3B	Thousand Oaks, CA (Thousand Oaks/Moorpark JC)	1987	
33	Brian	Ellington	P	Gainesville (Oak Hall)	2009	
9	Jack	Emerick	C	Waukegan, IL (Waukegan/Pensacola JC)	1979	1980
39	Roy	Eppley	OF	Jacksonville	1985	
32	Robert	Epstein	C-OF	Baltimore, MD (Pikesville)	1987	
13	Donny	Erickson	3B	Woodland Hills, CA (Kennedy/College of the Canyons)	1987	1988
28	Tyler	Everett	P	Tallahassee (Lincoln)	2008	2011
10	Matt	Fairel	P-OF	Winter Haven (Winter Haven)	2007	2008
1	Adam	Faurot	3B-SS	Blountstown (Blountstown/Chipola JC)	1995	1996
6	Frank	Fazzini	C	Belleville, NJ (Belleville)	1983	
15	Kenny	Felder	OF	Niceville (Niceville)	1990	1992
6	Bobby	Fernandes	P	Elk Grove, CA (Elk Grove/Sacramento City CC)	1991	
30	Carl	Ferraro	P	Tampa	1981	1982
12	Rick	Figueredo	3B	Tampa (Plant)	1980	1983
12	Bien	Figueroa	SS	Santo Domingo, DR (San Luis/Canada JC)	1985	1986
32	Gar	Finnvold	P	Boca Raton (Palm Beach CC)	1989	1990
49	Ken	Fischer	P	Lincoln, MA (Tabor Academy)	1978	1981
8	J.C.	Flowers	P-OF	Orange Park (Trinity Christian Academy)	2017	2019
5	Victor	Floyd	OF	Pensacola (Pensacola)	1988	
26	Taylor	Folsom	P	Doerun, GA (Tiftarea Academy)	2015	
36	Jonathan	Foster	C-1B	LaGrange, GA (Troup County/Auburn/Chattahoochee Valley CC)	2018	2019
	Leon	Fowler	OF	Fort Myers (Fort Myers)	1989	
7	Nick	Francis	IF	Tallahassee (Godby)	2005	
30	Ben	Francis	P	Panama City (Mosley/Gulf Coast JC)	2008	2009
22	Clem	Freeman	P	Lakeland (Manatee CC)	1981	
14	Mike	Freeman	C	Sarasota	1986	
1	Skylar	Frey	OF	Sarasota (Sarasota/Polk State College)	2018	
29	Mike	Fuentes	OF	Coral Gables (Coral Gables)	1978	1981
43	Ed	Fulton	C	Dry Fork, VA (Tunstall)	1985	1987
8	Mike	Futrell	OF-3B	Tallahassee (Lincoln)	1999	2002
22	John	Gagnon	OF-P	Lantana (Lake Worth/Palm Beach CC)	1979	1980
3	Dakota	Gaillard	IF	Jupiter (Jupiter)	2019	
12	Dave	Garrison	2B	Birmingham, AL (Huffman/Jefferson JC)	1984	
22	John	Gast	P	Longwood (Lake Brantley)	2008	2010
15	Evan	Geist	P	Roswell, GA (Marist School)	2011	2013
45	Steve	Gelmine	P	New Providence, NJ (New Providence)	1982	1985
7	Alan	Gentry	OF	Layton, UT (Layton)	1983	1984
18	Mark	Gildea	OF	Tampa (Middleton)	2005	2007

11: MAKING BASEBALL HISTORY

#	First	Last	Pos	Home/School	Year	
10	Brian	Gilliland	SS	Marianna (Chipola JC)	1989	1990
3	Sean	Gilmartin	P-OF	Moorpark, CA (Crespi Carmelite)	2009	2011
37	Chris	Ginn	P	Tallahassee (Lincoln)	1998	2001
6	Marc	Giordano	OF	Sunrise (Piper/Brevard CC)	1987	1988
9	Steve	Givens	OF	Tallahassee (Godby/George Wallace JC)	1982	1983
5	Bert	Givens	C-3B	Tallahassee (Chiles)	2012	
3	Devin	Gonzalez	IF	Jacksonville (Fletcher)	2007	
10	Justin	Gonzalez	IF	Miami (Columbus)	2010	2014
23	JJ	Gould	IF	Sarasota (Sarasota)	2013	
31	Conor	Grady	P	Tampa (Tampa Catholic)	2018	2020
1	Nick	Graganella	OF	Tallahassee (North Florida Christian/Tallahassee CC)	2014	2016
27	Caleb	Graham	P	Tampa (Gaither)	2006	2007
27	Jeff	Gray	P	Miami (Southridge)	1981	1984
43	Brad	Gregory	P	Sarasota (Manatee CC)	1989	1990
20	Danny	Griffin	SS	Valparaiso (Niceville)	1982	1985
39	John-Ford	Griffin	OF	Sarasota (Sarasota)	1999	2001
22	Pedro	Grifol	C	Miami (Columbus)	1989	1991
51	Reggie	Griggs	1B	West Palm Beach (Wellington)	1997	
42	Undra	Griggs	1B-OF	Palm Beach (Royal Palm Beach)	2004	
1	Brett	Groves	SS	Tampa (Bay Tech)	1998	2001
24	Dennis	Guinn	IF	Winter Haven (Winter Haven)	2005	2008
10	B.J.	Guzzone	OF	Jacksonville (Sandalwood/Florida CC)	1987	
7	Mark	Hallberg	SS	Barron, WI (Barron/Illinois-Chicago)	2007	
33	John	Halliday	1B	Clearwater (Clearwater/Pasco-Hernando CC)	1999	2000
14	Troy	Hamilton	IF	Royal Palm Beach (American Heritage-Delray Beach)	2019	
33	Chase	Haney	P	Winter Garden (Windermere Prep)	2016	2020
42	Dave	Hanselman	P	Tallahassee (Leon)	1984	
39	Danny	Harrell	P	Tallahassee	1986	
15	Todd	Harrell	P	Tallahassee (Leon/Gulf Coast JC)	1993	1994
31	Bryan	Harris	P	Peachtree City, GA (McIntosh)	1990	1993
23	Dean	Harrison	1B	Margate, NJ (Atlantic City)	1988	1990
2	Chris	Hart	C	Clearwater (Central Catholic)	1999	2003
33	Rick	Hatcher	P	Marianna (Marianna/George Wallace JC)	1979	1981
13	Tim	Hatcher	C	Marianna (Port Saint Joe/George Wallace JC)	1980	
18	Ken	Heath	C	Layton, UT (Layton)	1984	
18	Eric	Heath	OF-1B	Palmetto (Palmetto/Manatee CC)	1998	
17	Terry	Henderson	OF	Melbourne (Central Catholic/Brevard CC)	1997	1998
24	Matt	Henderson	IF	Chico, CA (Pleasant Valley/Santa Barbara CC)	2016	2017
24	Clint	Hendry	OF	Wauchula (Hardee)	1993	1994
22	Bryan	Henry	P-IF	Tallahassee (Florida/North Florida CC)	2005	2007
16	Jared	Herron	C	Orlando (Trinity Prep)	2017	2018
17	Chris	Hitt	P	Houston, TX (Jersey Village/Seminole CC)	1995	
12	Randy	Hodges	OF-3B	Ocala (Vanguard)	1992	1995
7	Daniel	Hodges	P	Hilliard (Bishop Kenny)	2000	2003
13	John	Holland	IF	Johns Creek, GA (Northview)	2012	2013
25	Mike	Holman	2B-SS	Jacksonville (Bolles)	1987	
15	Tyler	Holt	OF	Gainesville (Gainesville)	2008	2010
33	Bryant	Holtmann	P	New Baden, IL (Breese Central)	2012	2015
14	Tyler	Holton	P-OF	Tallahassee (Lincoln)	2016	2018
42	Bill	Howard	P	Fox Point, WI	1985	
28	Lee	Howard	C	Fleming Island (Fleming Island)	2012	2014

JIM CROSBY

#	First	Last	Pos	Home/School	Year	
39	Chuck	Howell	P	Tallahassee (Leon)	1994	1997
47	Ed	Howser	2B	West Palm Beach (Forest Hill/Palm Beach CC)	1980	1982
16	Jason	Hubbard	P	Jacksonville (Ed White)	1998	1999
44	Scott	Hudson	P	Ocilla, GA (Irwin County)	1997	1999
10	Ken	Huff	OF	Columbus, GA (Hardaway)	1978	1981
20	J.C.	Huguet	C	Miami (Coral Park/Miami Dade CC)	1999	
7	Cade	Hungate	IF-P	Abingdon, VA (Abingdon)	2019	2020
46	Gage	Hutchinson	P	Port Orange (Spruce Creek/Daytona State College)	2018	2019
25	Michael	Hyde	P	Tallahassee (Lincoln/Tallahassee CC)	2005	2007
43	Vince	Insogna	C	Fort Pierce (Fort Pierce Central)	1983	1984
42	William	Jackel	P	Kennesaw, GA (Kennesaw Mountain)	2005	
31	Kevin	Jackson	1B-OF	Pensacola (Tate)	2010	
22	Rhett	James	P	Pensacola (Escambia/Pensacola JC)	2003	2004
10	Link	Jarrett	SS	Tallahassee (Florida)	1991	1994
33	Trent	Jarvis	P	Destin (Fort Walton Beach)	2004	2008
9	Karl	Jernigan	IF	Milton (Milton)	1998	2001
8	Ryne	Jernigan	IF	Milton (Milton)	2005	
13	Jay	Johnson	C	Sanford	1979	1981
31	Barry	Johnson	P	Joliet, IL (Joliet Catholic Academy)	1988	1989
19	Jonathan	Johnson	P	Ocala (Forest)	1993	1995
32	Sherman	Johnson	IF	Tampa (Alonso)	2009	2012
51	Brandon	Johnson	P	Tampa (Alonso)	2011	2013
6	Cobi	Johnson	P	Holiday (J. W. Mitchell)	2015	2018
14	Jimmy	Jones	C	Langley, VA (Kecoughtan)	1982	1985
35	Hunter	Jones	P	Palm Beach Gardens (Dwyer)	2003	2005
13	Grady	Jordan	1B	Tallahassee (North Florida Christian/South Alabama)	1992	1993
35	Hayden	Jordan	P	Peachtree City, GA (Whitewater/Tallahassee CC)	2013	
19	Matt	Kane	C	Lake Worth (Palm Beach Central)	2008	2009
26	Danny	Kanell	P-3B	Fort Lauderdale (Westminster Academy)	1993	1994
19	Andrew	Karp	P	Winter Garden (West Orange)	2015	2018
	Bill	Keck	1B	Newark, OH (Newark)	1980	
43	Jay	Keeler	P	Miami (Palmetto/Miami Dade CC)	1980	1982
4	Clyde	Keller	3B-P	Carmichael, CA (Del Campo/Sacramento City CC)	1988	1989
43	Brian	Kelley	P	Ormond Beach (Seabreeze)	2005	2006
33	David	Kelly	P	Tallahassee (Leon/Tallahassee CC)	1998	
32	Hayden	Kelly	IF	Inverness (Citrus/Polk State College)	2015	2016
18	Keith	Kidd	OF	Richmond, KY (Madison Central/Eastern Kentucky)	1985	1987
16	Ricky	Kimball	P	Lithonia, GA (Redan)	1988	1991
5	Matthew	Kinney	P	Alpharetta, GA (Blessed Trinity Catholic/Belmont)	2016	
25	Jeremiah	Klosterman	C	Jacksonville (Bolles)	1996	1999
25	Brett	Knief	OF	Ramsey, NJ (Don Bosco Prep/North Carolina/Seminole State College/fl)	2013	2014
2	John	Kolb	P	Cedar Rapids, IA (John F. Kennedy)	1981	
23	Shaun	Kopczynski	C	Orlando (Bishop Moore)	1997	
30	Dru	Kosco	1B-OF	Youngstown, OH (Poland Seminary)	1984	1985
17	Steve	Kovensky	P	San Diego, CA (Poway/Palomar CC)	1986	1987
5	Brian	Kraft	SS	Gainesville (Oak Hall)	2000	
14	Kevin	Krietemeyer	IF	Collinsville, IL (Collinsville)	1993	
17	Clayton	Kwiatkowski	P	Tampa (Jesuit)	2017	2020
26	Mark	Lacy	1B	Clearwater	1981	1982
31	Marc	LaMacchia	P	Palm Harbor (East Lake)	2001	2003
29	Billy	Lawrence	P	Westville (Gulf Breeze/Pensacola JC)	1993	

11: MAKING BASEBALL HISTORY

#	First	Last	Pos	Home/School	Year	
2	Jeff A.	Ledbetter	P	Clearwater (Clearwater)	1982	1985
6	Jeff	Ledbetter	P-OF	Largo (Largo)	1979	1982
23	David	Ledbetter	P-1B	Largo (Largo)	1982	
6	Mike	Lee	P	Tallahassee (Florida/Chipola JC)	1986	
37	Brandon	Leibrandt	P	Alpharetta, GA (Marist)	2012	2014
47	Loren	Levy	C	Tallahassee (Florida)	1982	1984
7	Greg	Lewis	C	Basking Ridge, NJ	1982	
4	Richie	Lewis	P	Muncie, IN (Muncie)	1985	1987
7	Ronald	Lewis	OF	Jacksonville (Raines)	1987	1988
35	Jimmy	Lewis	P	Jacksonville (Terry Parker/Florida CC)	1991	
14	Joe	Licata	OF	Tampa	1981	
9	Tony	Liebsack	SS	Gardena, CA (Gardena/LA Harbor JC)	1991	1992
25	Doug	Little	P	North Palm Beach (North Shore)	1983	1986
29	LaWhit	Lizzmore	P	Jacksonville (Raines/Florida CC)	1991	1992
24	Kyle	Long	P-1B	Ivy,VA (Saint Anne's-Belfield Left school after Fall semester)	2009	
2	Mickey	Lopez	3B-2B	Miami (Westminster Christian)	1993	1995
29	Rafael	Lopez	C-IF	Wellington (Summit Christian/Boston College/Indian River CC)	2009	2011
33	Justin	Lord	P	Marianna (Marianna/Chipola JC)	2001	
44	Mike	Loynd	P	Short Hills, NJ (Millburn)	1983	1986
2	Jackson	Lueck	OF	Orlando (Orangewood Christian)	2016	2018
46	Matt	Lynch	P	Fort Pierce (John Carroll)	2000	2003
26	Kevin	Lynch	P-3B	Fort Pierce (John Carroll)	2002	2005
35	Keith	Lyttle	OF	Boca Raton (Boca Raton Academy/Central Florida)	1989	
6	Corben	Madden	P	Orlando (Boone)	2010	
18	Mike	Madonne	P	Oakland, NJ	1989	
3	Ryne	Malone	IF	Gainesville (P.K. Yonge)	2004	2006
37	Neil	Malpass	OF-P	Destin (Niceville/Okaloosa-Walton CC)	2006	2008
6	Brandon	Manasa	IF	Miami (Southridge)	2003	2005
9	Eric	Mangham	OF	Atlanta, GA (Feldwood)	1984	1986
13	Tom	Manley	OF	Sacramento, CA (Sacramento City CC)	1989	
12	JohnMarc	Tamayo	2B	Tampa (Jesuit)	1988	1990
23	T.R.	Marcinczyk	OF	Plainville, CT (Saint Thomas Aquinas)	1993	
23	Chris	Marconcini	IF-OF	Brentwood, TN (Battle Ground Academy/Duke)	2015	
35	Brent	Marsh	P	Tallahassee (Leon/Tallahassee CC/South Carolina)	2006	
26	Jimmy	Marshall	P	Tallahassee (Chiles)	2006	2009
4	Mike	Martin	C	Tallahassee (Maclay/Manatee CC)	1993	1995
26	Robby	Martin	OF	Tampa (Jefferson)	2019	2020
4	Lionel	Martinez	2B	Tampa (Tampa Catholic/Indian River CC)	1980	1981
30	Michael	Martinez	P	Miami (Columbus)	2008	
13	Eddy	Martinez-Esteve	3B	Miami (Westminster Christian)	2003	2004
19	Jose	Marzan	C	Bayamon, PR (Colegio San Ignacio)	1984	1987
23	David	Maus	P-OF	Tallahassee	1984	
15	Kyle	Maxie	C	Hattiesburg, MS (North Forrest)	2006	
25	Bret	Maxwell	C	Saint Petersburg (Northeast)	2015	
22	Henry	Mayfield	C	Tallahassee (Leon)	1996	1998
38	Ryan	McArdle	1B	Atlanta, GA (Tallahassee CC)	2006	
32	Blair	McCaleb	C	Marietta, GA (Lassiter/Pensacola JC)	2000	2002
22	Justin	McClain	1B	Cartersville, GA (Cartersville)	2000	
7	Chad	McClellan	3B-OF	Findlay, OH (Findlay)	1986	
35	Shawn	McCorkel	OF	Dothan, AL (Northview)	1997	1998
5	Kevin	McCray	1B	Tallahassee (Florida/South Florida)	1992	1993

JIM CROSBY

#	First	Last	Pos	Home/School	Year	
54	Jacobbi	McDaniel	1B	Madison (Madison County)	2010	
41	Jon	McDonald	P	Orlando (Edgewater)	1997	2000
31	Marshall	McDougall	2B	Valrico (Buchholz/Santa Fe CC)	1999	2000
25	Mike	McGee	P	Port Saint Lucie (Port Saint Lucie)	2008	2011
9	Stephen	McGee	C	Port Saint Lucie (Port Saint Lucie)	2010	2013
24	Mike	McLeod	P	Tallahassee (Godby)	1975	1977
20	Kyle	McMullen	P	Jupiter (Jupiter/Palm Beach State College)	2019	2020
18	John	McNeese	P	Columbia, MS (Columbia Academy)	1991	
29	Eric	McNitt	P	Mesick, MI (Mesick)	1985	
2	Tony	McQuade	OF	Gainesville (Buchholz)	2001	2003
33	Charles	McQuaig	C	Milledgeville, GA (John Milledge Academy)	1993	1994
23	Ryan	Mejia	OF	Tampa (Alonso)	2017	
31	Gary	Merians	P	Ocala (Ocala/Santa Fe CC)	2011	2012
45	Mike	Meschke	1B	Marietta, GA (Pope/North Florida CC)	2009	2010
44	Jared	Middleton	P	Lakeland (Jenkins)	2016	
25	Doug	Mientkiewicz	1B	Miami (Westminster Christian)	1993	1995
29	Tim	Miller	P	Williamsport, PA (Williamsport Area)	1994	
13	Justin	Miller	P	Quincy (Maclay)	2002	
40	Peter	Miller	P-IF	Lutz (Cambridge Christian)	2011	2014
18	Seth	Miller	OF	Southport (Mosley/Northwest Florida State Coll)	2011	2013
3	Darren	Miller	IF-C	Key West (Key West)	2015	2016
4	Bart	Mitchell	OF-2B	Tallahassee (Lincoln)	1982	1984
31	Orson	Mobley	1B	Miami (Palmetto)	1982	1983
32	Ladson	Montgomery	C	Saint Johns (Creekside/Alabama/Chipola JC)	2013	2014
49	Al	Moreya	P	Miami	1983	
13	Todd	Morgan	P	Church Road, VA (Dinwiddie)	1982	1984
35	Scooby	Morgan	P	Lake Placid (Taravella)	1993	1994
37	Jeremy	Morris	OF	Quincy (Robert F. Munroe)	1994	1997
51	Brett	Morris	P-1B	Valrico (Bloomingdale)	2006	
2	Taed	Moses	UTL	Valrico (Durant/South Florida CC)	2011	
30	Ty	Mueller	OF	Fort Walton Beach (Fort Walton Beach)	1989	1993
27	Matt	Mulroy	OF	Boca Raton (West Boca Raton Community/Palm Beach State College)	2014	
9	Ray	Navarro	IF	Miami (Florida Christian)	2009	
44	John	Nedeau	P	Cape Coral (North Fort Myers)	1990	1993
27	Steve	Nedeau	OF	Cape Coral (North Fort Myers/Tallahassee CC)	1994	1996
20	Tim	Nedin	P	Valencia, CA (College of the Canyons)	1989	
16	Stephen	Neill	P	Fort Pierce (John Carroll/Indian River CC)	1996	1997
63	Matheu	Nelson	C	Largo (Calvary Christian Academy)	2019	2020
22	Jason	Newlin	P	Tallahassee (Godby/Tallahassee CC)	2002	
22	Jerry	Nielsen	P	Fair Oaks, CA (Jesuit/Sacramento City CC)	1987	1988
29	Quincy	Nieporte	1B-C	Atlanta, GA (Saint Pius X Catholic/Tallahassee CC)	2015	2017
18	Jack	Niles	3B/SS	Key West (Key West/Seminole CC)	1993	1994
33	Randy	Niles	P	Key West (Key West)	1995	1997
35	Ben	Nobles	P	Alva (Riverdale/Tallahassee CC)	2010	
3	John	Nogowski	OF-1B-P	Tallahassee (North Florida Christian)	2012	2014
33	Connor	Nolan	P	Salem, NH (Salem/Saint John's River CC)	2011	2012
6	Sean	O'Brien	IF	Clearwater (Clearwater)	2011	
4	Stephen	Ochs	P	Marietta, GA (Lassiter)	2005	2007
9	Ruairi	O'Connor	UTL	River Forest, IL (Oak Park-River Forest)	2005	2009
16	Bo	O'Dell	P	Kissimmee (Osceola/Seminole CC)	2007	2009
6	Phil	Olson	P	Sarasota (Riverview)	1993	1995

11: MAKING BASEBALL HISTORY

#	First	Last	Pos	Home/School	Year	
6	Tommy	Oravetz	2B	Tallahassee (Chiles)	2006	2009
6	George	Otero	OF	Miami (Pace)	1997	1998
14	Jackson	Owens	IF	Lake Dallas, TX (Lake Dallas)	2015	
27	Joe	Pacetti	2B	Jacksonville (Bishop Kenny)	1985	
39	Gary	Painter	P	Bowling Green (Hardee/Polk CC)	1989	1990
30	Keith	Parenteau	P	North Palm Beach (Cardinal Newman/Palm Beach CC)	1980	
19	Brad	Parker	1B-3B	Tallahassee (Leon)	1988	1990
21	Geoff	Parker	P	Dade City (Zephyrhills)	2008	2010
43	Drew	Parrish	P-OF	Rockledge (Rockledge)	2017	2019
33	Kyle	Patrick	P	Apopka (Apopka)	2003	
17	Brant	Peacher	OF	Milton (Milton)	2004	2005
35	Brent	Pearson	P	Tallahassee (Florida/North Florida CC)	2001	
24	Eduardo	Perez	1B	Santurce, PR (Robinson)	1989	1991
43	Trent	Peterson	P	Tallahassee (Florida)	2001	2003
17	Mark	Peterson	P	Fort Pierce (Lincoln Park Academy)	2008	2009
13	Donovan	Petrey	OF	Arcadia (Port Charlotte)	2016	2017
44	Tim	Phillips	P	Tallahassee (Godby/George Wallace JC)	1980	1982
29	Chris	Pinder	P	Yorktown, VA	1984	
29	Chris	Pollack	P	Canoga Park, CA (El Camino/College of the Canyons)	1987	1988
29	Austin	Pollock	P	Tallahassee (Lincoln)	2018	2020
23	Nick	Polston	IF	Lake Wales (South Florida CC)	2008	
30	Ed	Porcelli	P	Clearwater (Wilton/South Florida)	1986	1987
16	Cory	Posey	C	Panama City (Mosley/Gulf Coast JC/McNeese State)	2000	
8	Buster	Posey	SS-P	Leesburg, GA (Lee County)	2006	2008
5	Jack	Posey	IF	Leesburg, GA (Lee County)	2008	2011
35	Jordan	Priddle	P	Tallahassee (Leon)	2012	
15	Jeff	Probst	2B-SS	Clearwater (Central Catholic)	2001	2002
31	Scott	Proctor	P	Stuart (Martin County)	1996	1998
1	Ryan	Proly	P	Clearwater (Central Catholic)	1997	
23	Frank	Radziwon	P	Palm Beach (Royal Palm Beach/Palm Beach CC)	2004	
35	Cal	Raleigh	C	Cullowhee, NC (Smoky Mountain)	2016	2018
25	Ronnie	Ramirez	P	Tampa (Jesuit)	2016	2018
21	Craig	Ramsey	C	Atlanta, GA (North Springs)	1977	1981
23	James	Ramsey	IF	Alpharetta, GA (Wesleyan)	2009	2012
9	Rocky	Rau	SS	LaGrange, TX (San Jacinto JC)	1989	1990
21	Bobby	Rauh	OF	Orlando (Edgewater)	2007	
20	Robby	Read	P	Tallahassee (Leon)	2000	2002
39	Derek	Reams	C	Tallahassee (Florida)	1993	
2	Bob	Reboin	SS-2B	Carmichael, CA (Sacramento City CC)	1989	1990
3	Jody	Reed	SS	Brandon (Brandon/Manatee CC)	1983	1984
17	Brandon	Reichart	OF	Tallahassee (Godby/Tallahassee CC/Mercer)	2006	2007
12	Brandon	Reitz	P	Ocala (Trinity Catholic)	2017	
46	Ray	Revak	P	Key West (Key West)	1984	1985
10	Dave	Rhino	OF	Atlanta, GA	1982	
5	D'Vontrey	Richardson	OF	Leesburg, GA (Lee County)	2007	2009
23	Tony	Richie	C	Jacksonville (Bishop Kenny)	2001	2003
9	Kevin	Richmond	SS-2B	Clearwater (Countryside)	2002	2003
33	Justin	Rigney	OF	Westport, CT (Staples)	1992	
13	Chris	Roberts	P-OF	Middleburg (Middleburg)	1990	1992
16	Clay	Robertson	P	Newport News, VA	1987	
18	Matt	Robinson	2B	Tallahassee (Godby/George Wallace JC)	1982	1983

JIM CROSBY

#	First	Last	Pos	Home/School	Year	
2	Kenny	Robinson	P	Akron, OH (Archbishop Hoban/Florida CC)	1991	
20	Dominic	Robinson	OF	Diamond Bar, CA (Diamond Bar)	2002	
2	Shane	Robinson	OF	Tampa (Jesuit)	2004	2006
25	Raul	Rodriguez	C	Miami (Florida Christian)	2004	
25	Nick	Rogers	OF	Ponte Vedra Beach (Bolles/Tallahassee CC)	2001	2002
16	Louis	Rojas	1B	Miami (Belen Jesuit Prep)	2004	
14	Shane	Roland	OF	Adel, GA (Cook County)	1996	
24	Eric	Roman	P	Orlando (Doctor Phillips)	1999	2002
17	Marc	Ronan	C	Tampa (Plant City)	1988	1990
2	Rocky	Roquet	OF	Anaheim, CA (Canyon)	2002	
40	Danny	Rosen	P	Miami (Miami Dade CC)	2007	
21	Chris	Ruckdeschel	OF	Davie (Saint Thomas Aquinas)	2019	2020
26	Mike	Rudi	1B	Baker, OR (Baker)	1987	1988
35	Jim	Rushworth	P	West Munroe, LA (Panola JC)	1992	
46	Jack	Rye	OF	Irvine, CA (Woodbridge)	2005	2008
42	Tom	Sailor	OF	Cinnaminson, NJ	1982	
12	Jeremy	Salazar	C	Lafayette, LA (Northside)	1995	1998
16	Mike	Salvatore	IF	Ewing, NJ (Ewing/Northwest Florida State Coll)	2018	2019
24	Alec	Sanchez	IF	Jacksonville (Providence)	2019	
2	Deion	Sanders	OF	Fort Myers (North Fort Myers)	1986	1988
26	Cole	Sands	P	Tallahassee (North Florida Christian)	2016	2018
25	Chase	Sanguinetti	IF	Tampa (Plant)	2019	
12	John	Sansone	IF	New Castle, PA (Neshannock)	2013	2016
15	Jerry	Santos	P	Miami (Columbus)	1988	1989
21	Mark	Sauls	P	Panama City (Bay)	2003	2006
8	Matt	Sauls	OF	Panama City (Bay/Gulf Coast JC)	2003	2004
10	Craig	Saxner	C	Miramar (Miramar)	1985	1986
30	Hunter	Scantling	P-1B	Jacksonville (Episcopal)	2009	2012
17	Joe	Schlim	P	Newport News, VA	1984	
15	Mike	Schmit	P-1B	Longwood (Lake Mary)	1987	
16	Mike	Schmitz	1B	Coconut Creek (Coconut Creek/Brevard CC)	1993	
17	Ed	Schneider	P	Cincinnati, OH (Oak Hills/Indian River CC)	1980	1981
21	Scott	Schroeffel	OF	Pittsburgh, PA (North Allegheny)	1993	1994
15	Brian	Schultz	P-OF	Lakeland (Lake Gibson)	2004	2005
32	Dave	Schumacher	P	Rochester, NY (Greece Athena)	1991	
13	Jonah	Scolaro	P-OF	Valrico (Durant)	2018	2020
22	Sam	Scott	IF	Stilwell, KS (Blue Valley/Cowley County CC)	1999	
36	Robby	Scott	P	Miami (Saint Thomas Aquinas/Broward CC)	2010	2011
29	Bryan	Senior	OF	Columbus, GA (Brookstone)	1995	1996
23	Nandy	Serrano	3B	Carolina, PR (Florida/Gulf Coast JC)	1991	1992
42	Buddy	Shaw	P	Hollywood, CA (Hollywood Hills)	1983	
7	Chad	Sheffer	2B	Dover (Bloomingdale)	1993	
25	Jamey	Shouppe	P	Chattahoochee	1981	1982
21	Dylan	Silva	P	Lake Worth (American Heritage-Delray Beach)	2013	2015
38	Adam	Simmons	P	Sebring (Sebring/South Florida CC)	2011	2012
51	Glen	Simon	P	Lake Worth (John I. Leonard)	2003	2005
26	Scott	Sitz	P	Jacksonville Beach (Fletcher)	2010	2013
39	Mike	Skoutelakis	OF	Fort Lauderdale (Saint Thomas Aquinas/Broward CC/Oklahoma State)	1987	
46	David	Smalley	P	Fort Lauderdale (Stranahan)	1980	1983
23	Mike	Smalley	P	Orlando (Bishop Moore)	1998	1989
10	Luke	Smierciak	P-OF	Gainesville (Gainesville)	2008	2009

11: MAKING BASEBALL HISTORY

#	First	Last	Pos	Home/School	Year	
43	Casey	Smit	IF	Tampa (Alonso/College of Central Florida)	2013	2014
26	Ken	Smith	P	Hollywood (South Broward/Miami Dade CC)	1979	1980
13	Kevin	Smith	P	Orlando (Boone/Miami)	1985	
15	Chris	Smith	OF-P	Wantagh, NY (Wantagh)	1999	2000
29	Richie	Smith	OF	Bristol (Liberty County/Chipola JC)	2001	2002
24	Derrick	Smith	OF	Vienna, GA (Dooly County)	2003	2004
19	Gage	Smith	P	Tallahassee (North Florida Christian)	2010	2014
35	Carter	Smith	C-IF	Fort Myers (Canterbury School/Florida South Western State Col)	2019	2020
34	Tom	Snyder	C-1B	Tampa	1982	
29	David	Sorokowski	P	Miami (Southridge)	1988	1989
5	Justin	Sorokowski	P-IF	Mechanicsville, VA (Lee-Davis)	2017	
15	Paul	Sorrento	OF-P	Peabody, MA (Saint John's Prep)	1984	1986
7	Bobby	Spano	IF	Naples (Barron Collier)	1999	2000
45	Josh	Spivey	OF-1B	Tampa (Wharton/Saint Leo)	2005	2007
20	Stephen	Spradling	OF	Boynton Beach (American Heritage Delray Beach/Broward CC)	2012	2013
2	Geoff	Sprague	1B	Tallahassee (Leon/Indian River CC)	1996	1997
42	Ron	Spyker	P	Clearwater (Pinellas Park/Manatee CC)	1987	
17	Jamie	Stafford	OF	Tallahassee (Leon)	1994	
36	Robby	Stahl	OF	Saint Petersburg Beach (Saint Petersburg Catholic/Tallahassee CC)	2009	2011
19	Matt	Stanford	P	North Fort Myers (North Fort Myers/Chipola JC)	1997	1998
46	Scott	Steinitz	P	North Palm Beach (North Shore/Edison CC)	1989	1990
42	Tommy	Stewart	OF	Largo (Carrollton/North Florida CC)	2002	
8	DJ	Stewart	OF	Yulee (Bolles)	2013	2015
32	Grant	Stewart	P	Paxton (Paxton)	2017	
13	Jason	Stidham	IF	Palm Bay (Melbourne)	2007	2009
45	Drew	Stilley	P	Jacksonville (Bishop Kenny)	2003	
30	Nick	Stocks	P	Tampa (Jesuit)	1997	1999
14	Ryan	Strauss	P-OF	Tampa (Bloomingdale)	2005	2008
5	Billy	Strode	P	Parkland (American Heritage Delray Beach/Indian River CC)	2013	2015
32	Mike	Stubbs	OF	Guaynabo, PR (Cupeyville)	1988	1989
7	Sean	Stuyverson	SS	Tallahassee (North Florida Christian)	2006	
9	Cooper	Swanson	IF	Fort Myers (Canterbury School)	2018	2020
32	Allen	Swindle	P	Clewiston (Clewiston/Indian River CC)	1980	1982
16	Alvin	Swoope	IF	Port Saint Lucie (Treasure Coast)	2013	
45	Steve	Taddeo	OF	Plantation (Saint Thomas Aquinas/Manatee CC)	1986	1987
43	Jeff	Tam	P	Melbourne (Eau Gallie/Palm Beach Atlantic College/Brevard CC)	1992	1993
15	Bruce	Tanner	C	New Castle, PA (Neshannock)	1981	1983
1	Stuart	Tapley	IF	Orlando (Boone)	2008	2011
18	George	Tebbetts	IF	Anna Maria (Manatee/Valencia CC)	1980	1981
14	Clint	Thigpen	OF	Lakeland (Lakeland)	1999	2000
39	Paul	Thomas	P	Pittsburgh, PA (North Hills)	1984	1987
23	Tony	Thomas	IF	Valrico (Bloomingdale)	2005	2007
19	Brady	Thomas	C	Anderson, SC (T.L. Hanna)	2006	2007
1	DiCarlo	Thompson	P	Tallahassee (Leon)	2004	
51	Scott	Thorson	P	Deltona (Pine Ridge)	2007	2008
39	Jeff	Tibbitts	P	Springboro, OH (Springboro)	1991	1992
16	Scott	Toole	2B-3B	Jacksonville (Bolles/Tallahassee CC)	2001	2002
43	Chris	Tramel	P	Daphne, AL (Southern Union CC)	1996	
8	Devon	Travis	IF	Wellington (Palm Beach Central)	2010	2012
34	Doug	Treadway	P	Tallahassee (Leon/Jackson State)	1983	1984
27	David	Trexler	P-OF	Lynn Haven (Mosley)	2010	2011

243

JIM CROSBY

#	First	Last	Pos	Home/School	Year	
49	Shawn	Troxel	C	Winter Park	1987	
15	Hank	Truluck	IF	Ocala (Forest)	2014	2017
31	Luke	Tucker	P	Niceville (Niceville/Okaloosa-Walton CC)	2006	2007
44	Robert	Tyree	P	Atlanta, GA (Dunwoody)	1996	
44	Pat	Underhill	P-OF	Coral Springs (Valencia CC)	1989	1990
27	Derek	Vail	P	Gainesville (Buchholz/Santa Fe CC)	2015	2017
27	Ryan	Valdes	OF	Odessa (Alonso)	2014	2015
15	C.J.	Van Eyk	P	Lutz (Steinbrenner)	2018	2020
21	Blair	Varnes	P	Pascagoula, MS (Pascagoula)	1998	2002
10	Darren	Vazquetelles	SS	Guaynabo, PR (Colegio Marista)	1988	
30	Antonio	Velez	P	Brandon (Brandon/Hillsborough CC)	2019	2020
20	Nick	Vickerson	IF	Tuscaloosa, AL (Hillcrest)	2008	2011
35	Ryan	Vigue	P	Merritt Island (Merritt Island)	2008	
27	Elih	Villanueva	P	Miami (Miami Dade CC)	2008	
28	Dean	Vinson	OF	Valdosta, GA (Valdosta)	1995	
18	Ed	Voyles	P	Atlanta, GA (Holy Innocent's Episcopal)	2014	2018
42	Jim	Voyles	P	Atlanta, GA (Holy Innocent's Episcopal)	2014	2017
10	Taylor	Walls	IF	Cordele, GA (Crisp County)	2015	2017
23	John	Wanish	P	Palm Harbor (Saint Petersburg JC)	1987	
9	Andy	Ward	P	Oviedo (Oviedo)	2014	2016
27	Danny	Wardell	1B-OF	Wesley Chapel (Zephyrhills/Pasco-Hernando CC)	2003	2005
23	Tyler	Warmoth	P	Orlando (Lake Brantley/Stetson)	2015	
17	John	Wasdin	P	Tallahassee (Godby)	1991	1993
44	Mack	Waugh	P	Naples (Barron Collier/Tallahassee CC)	2011	2012
2	Jim	Weaver	OF	Holmes Beach (Cardinal Mooney/Manatee CC)	1980	
22	Colby	Weaver	C	Warwick, NY (Warwick Valley)	1992	1994
7	Luke	Weaver	P	Deland (Deland)	2012	2014
27	McGuire	Weaver	IF	Tampa (Jesuit)	2019	
7	Steven	Wells	P-OF	Key West (Key West)	2015	2018
19	Ryan	West	OF	Tallahassee (Lincoln)	2000	
20	Gage	West	C	Tallahassee (Lincoln)	2014	2016
17	Chris	Whidden	P	Tallahassee (Leon)	1999	2003
13	Nick	Whidden	OF-P	Tallahassee (Leon)	1999	2001
32	Casey	Whitmer	P	Kilgore, TX (Kilgore)	2007	
39	Dick	Wiggins	P	Saint Petersburg (Lakewood/Valencia CC)	1979	1980
32	Paul	Wilson	P	Orlando (Boone)	1992	1994
44	Jameis	Winston	P-OF	Hueytown, AL (Hueytown)	2013	2015
25	John	Wolfer	P	West Palm Beach (Forest Hill/Miami Dade CC)	1979	1980
14	Austin	Wood	P	Niceville (Niceville)	2009	
18	Willie	Woods	C	Mukwonago, WI (Mukwonago)	1987	
15	Matt	Woodward	1B	Redmond, WA (Redmond)	1995	1998
2	Casey	Yarbrough	SS	Fort Myers (North Fort Myers/Edison CC)	1992	1992
8	Mike	Yastrzemski	OF	Highland Beach (Cardinal Gibbons)	1980	1983
38	Corey	Yawn	P	Seminole (Northside Christian)	2019	
31	David	Yocum	P	Miami (Columbus)	1994	1995
18	Tyson	Young	P	Palm City (South Fork)	2010	
19	Jose	Zabala	3B-SS	Miami (Columbus)	1995	1998
9	Scott	Zech	SS	Boca Raton (Boca Raton)	1994	1997
14	Bryan	Zech	2B	Wellington (Wellington)	2001	2004
35	Mike	Ziegler	P	Glen Burnie, MD (Old Mill/Tallahassee CC)	2000	
30	Will	Zirzow	P	Jacksonville (Bolles)	2014	2018
26	Tom	Zoeller	C	Shorewood, WI (Marquette)	1983	1986

11: MAKING BASEBALL HISTORY

608 Players Donned the Garnet and Gold and Played for #11 (1980-2019)

One of the areas of greatest consistency in Mike Martin's record-setting career has been his constant recognition of those who helped write the success story. Without fail, he would always give credit to the players, the assistant coaches, the administration, and the loyal Seminole fans. This is a comprehensive list of his players.

Next up is a list of the two-sport contributors who played for him while participating in another Seminole Sport, most of these played football in addition to baseball. There were even some who added a third sport---track.

Then a list of the talented assistant coaches who contributed to the Seminole success under 11 follows. These players and coaches are a varied and colorful collection of characters. What they have in common is a love of baseball and Florida State University.

All in the Family

Florida State athletes say that playing on a Seminole team is like being in a family. Every player and coach support each other. It extends to multiple sports in which players play for more than one Seminole team. An example is football and baseball, where 25 players shared talents in both sports.

SEMINOLE FOOTBALL PLAYERS WHO PLAYED BASEBALL

Player	Baseball	Football
Scott Bentley	1994	1993-96
Alex Boston	2004	2003-07
Billy Brown	1996	1995
Terrell Buckley	1990-91	1989-91
Thad Busby	1995	1993-97
James Colzie	1994	1993-96
Taiwan Easterling	2008-11	2007-10
Scott Edwards	1989-90	1989
Kenny Felder	1990-92	1989-91
Victor Floyd	1987	1984-88

JIM CROSBY

- Leon Fowler · 1989 · 1992-95
- Danny Kanell · 1993-94 · 1992-95
- Bill Keck · 1980 · 1977-79
- Jeff A. Ledbetter · 1982-85 · 1980-81
- Ronald Lewis · 1987-88 · 1986-89
- Eric Mangham · 1984-86 · 1983
- Shawn McCorkel · 1997-98 · 1996-98
- Jacobbi McDaniel · 2010 · 2009-13
- Orson Mobley · 1982-83 · 1981-82
- Jeremy Morris · 1994-97 · 1993
- Brad Prior · 1976-77 · 1974-76
- D'Vontrey Richardson · 2007-09 · 2006-08
- Dominic Robinson · 2002 · 2001-04
- Deion Sanders · 1986-88 · 1985-88
- Jameis Winston · 2013-15 · 2012-14

(Nolefan.org)

11: MAKING BASEBALL HISTORY

Heisman Trophy Winner Plays Baseball
Jameis Winston (2012-14)

- Hueytown, Alabama
- Baseball 92 GP, Football 27 GP
- Closer, DH, LF, RF
- Heisman Trophy Winning QB
- #1 pick in NFL by Tampa Bay

Background

"Jameis Winston grew up in Hueytown, Alabama, a small town located in the Metropolitan Birmingham area, 312 miles from Tallahassee, about a 5-hour drive. Founded in 1921 with a population of 66, it currently has 16,778 people. Winston was the star player on the Hueytown Golden Gophers in football and baseball. It was here that he learned the fundamentals of both sports that enabled him to succeed in college and professionally." (According to 11)

Jameis the Two-Sport Star

"Growing up, Jameis Winston dreamed of playing both football and baseball in the Pro ranks. Bo Jackson, from his home state of Alabama, who played for Auburn, did it. Bo became the only professional athlete to be named an All-Star in both baseball and football. Deion Sanders of Florida State did it. (See Neon Shines Bright) The Florida State star became the only player in history to play in a Major League game and an NFL game on the same day. If Deion "Prime Time" Sanders and Jackson of "Bo knows" fame could do it, why not Jameis? So, when Florida State football coach Jimbo Fisher came calling, he told Jameis that he could play baseball under legendary coach Mike Martin and Seminole football at the same time. The two coaches collaborated on the joint recruitment of Jameis, and he became a Seminole." (According to 11)

Mike Martin on Jameis Winston

"Jameis Winston is one of the finest young men I have ever met. I am very proud that he is a Florida State baseball player. He went through spring football. He needed to be there. That's what I have to understand. And number one, we have to realize who pulls the train at major universities. Football is extremely important, and we happen to have a young man who can play the outfield. He can pitch. He's a switch hitter. He can run, and he is a Heisman Trophy winner. He will tell you come January he wants to play baseball." (Interview with Eastbay on YouTube-Dec 13, 2013)

Jameis in Baseball

"Although he was an effective switch-hitting outfielder and occasional DH, Winston made his mark in the vital role of closer. Mixing an overpowering fastball with a deceptive slider as closer, he struck out 52 batters in 60 innings of relief work. In his appearances against rivals Miami and Florida, he didn't allow a run. He had a 2 for 3 game at the plate against the Gators on April 9, 2013, as the DH. In early May, Jameis raised his batting average to .306 with a 3-for-4 day while playing LF against North Carolina State." (According to 11)

Jameis in Football

"The accomplishments of Jameis Winston in his Heisman Trophy-winning career are the stuff of Seminole legends. His last-second TD pass to Kelvin Benjamin that beat Auburn, 34-31, for the National Championship in 2013 remains at the top of the best all-time Seminole plays. This earned him 14-different 1st team All-American Awards. After the 2014 season, he was selected as the Number One pick in the NFL draft by the Tampa Bay Bucs. He completed five seasons with the Bucs before being traded to the New Orleans Saints in 2020, where he became the starting QB upon the retirement of the legend-Drew Brees. Through 7 seasons, Jameis Winston has passed for 20,982 yards and 135 touchdowns "(Nolefan.org).

11: MAKING BASEBALL HISTORY

ASSISTANT COACHES UNDER MIKE MARTIN

33 Assistant Coaches Worked with #11 Over the Years

Chip Baker	1985-02	Pete Jenkins	2006-07
Mike Bell	2012-18	Greg Jones	1983
Jerrod Brown	2004-05	Jay Kearce	1993
Chris Cates	2013	Clyde Keller	2016-19
Lazer Collazo	1992	Frank Martello	1998
Rod Delmonico	1984-89, 2008	Mike Martin Jr.	1998-2019
David Fannin	1981-83	Matt Matulia	2011-12
Bill Fuller	1980	Kevin McCray	1994-95
Mike Futrell	2003-04	Joe McFarland	1982
Randy Gailey	1982-84	Jon Matter	1987
Rick Hatcher	1984	Mike McLeod	1982-89
Jeremy Haynes	2015	Jim Morris	1980-81
Keith Hendry	1981	Jack Niles	1996-97
Bryan Henry	2014	Brian Rhees.	1991-92
Tyler Holt	2019	Jamey Shouppe	1990-2011
Brian Hoop	2009-10	Steve Winterling	1986-91
Link Jarrett	2002-03		

(2019 FSU Media Guide)

THE COACHES
Dave Fannin Coach: 1981-83

Dave Fannin, a Tallahassee native, and Leon High alumnus, was derailed on his way to becoming an outstanding baseball player. A catcher with great potential in high school, Fannin suffered a career-ending knee injury. But that didn't dampen his love for baseball. He coached the Post 13 American Legion baseball team for six years, during which over 50 of his players went on to become collegiate baseball players.

So, Mike Martin didn't have to travel far to find an assistant coach in his second season at the helm when he hired Dave Fannin in 1981. He only had to go shopping at Publix Grocery store in Tallahassee.

Martin Hires Fannin

Fannin recalls: "I had been coaching American Legion baseball in Tallahassee, and we had 60 players go on to play college baseball in six years. So, I had an offer from legendary college coach Rudy Abbott at Jacksonville State. I walked over to Publix from my house and bumped into Coach Martin there. He asked me what I was doing, and I told him it looked like I was going to Jacksonville State to coach. He said: "Don't do that. Come coach with me at Florida State."

So that's how fate intervened and brought Fannin to FSU to coach hitters and catchers and head up recruiting. He was also in charge of charting opponent's defenses, scouting, and management of equipment.

Fannin on Martin

"He was real fiery and early on was more of a my-way-or-the-highway coach. But he was also a mentor to his upper-class players, like Mike Fuentes, Donny Deloach, and others, and depended on them to lead their teammates."

Martin's Impact on His Life

Fannin points out that Martin's hiring of him and his lasting friendship has had long-term implications for his life:

"It still opened doors for me after I left coaching. I was able to become

11: MAKING BASEBALL HISTORY

a part of the radio broadcasts with Rod (Meadows) and Jim (Crosby) and stay close to what was happening in Florida State baseball. It helped me in my life in the business world. (Being a local guy) that's where my association with Coach Martin and Florida State baseball had a big impact."

Mike McLeod
Coach: 1982-90
Player: 1975-77

Mike McLeod was one of the first players recruited (1975) by Mike Martin, then an assistant coach on Woody Woodward's staff. The Tallahassee Godby product was a hard-throwing right-handed pitcher who mixed an excellent curveball with a sinking fastball to keep batters off balance.

During his three years as a player at Florida State, McLeod had 28 appearances (18 as a starter). He won 11 games against three losses. He had a solid 2.99 era and struck out 86 batters in 126.1 innings on the mound. On March 19, 1977, he tossed a no-hitter vs. Olivet. It was the third no-hitter of his pitching career as he had two as a freshman at Middle Georgia Junior College (Cochran, GA) before Martin signed him for the Seminoles.

Always a student of the game, especially the pitching part of it, McLeod was drafted twice (Pirates in 1974 & Yankees in 1977). He played three seasons in the minors but seemed destined to coach. McLeod spent six seasons doing just that in professional baseball. Three summers as a pitching coach in the Yankees organization, two with Montreal and a season with the Twins. Therefore, he was well-prepared to step into the role of Seminole pitching coach when Martin approached him in 1982. He would remain in that position for eight years, leaving in September 1990 to become head coach at Tallahassee Community College.

McLeod on Martin

"I was fortunate enough to be around for 500 of 11's wins. He has had power teams; he has had speed teams. He has had great pitching. He just figures it out, what he's got and manages to win."

In 2020 McLeod notched his 30th season at Tallahassee Community College and recorded his 1,000th win. He says that he learned his competitiveness from Martin.

Martin's Fiery Approach Rubbed Off

"He gave me the love and the competitiveness. He would fight you tooth and nail to pitch pennies. We used to do that on the road a lot and play word games. He was always extremely competitive. He has a great sense of humor, great to be around, and obviously a great coach." (Quotes shared by the Tallahassee Democrat, May 8, 2018)

Randy Gailey
Bradenton, FL, Manatee CC
OF, FSU, 1971-73
Assistant Coach 1982-84

When Randy Gailey returned to Florida State as an assistant coach in 1982, replacing Jim Morris, who left to accept the Head Coaching position at Ga. Tech, Mike Martin said:

"We are happy that Randy has come home. He is a true Seminole, and he's excited about returning to FSU. Having a person like Randy join my staff is very good for the program. He brings with him a great knowledge of the game."

As the Seminole left-fielder, Gailey played in 66 games and batted .302 in 1972, the middle season of his three-year stint in Tallahassee. One of his most memorable games was going 3-for-4 with a homer and a couple of RBI against arch-rival Miami in a 3-game series in which each game was decided by a run. That was back in the days before FSU & Florida played each other in baseball.

After graduating from Florida State, he served as head baseball coach and assistant football coach of Fernandina Beach High School. He was named Coach of the Year in 1976 & 1977 in baseball. He also had a hand in developing future Seminole QB Rick Stockstill.

As assistant coach at Florida State, Gailey was charged with coaching the pitchers, serving as hitting instructor, and overseeing various administrative duties.

11: MAKING BASEBALL HISTORY

Rod Delmonico
Coach: 1984-89, 2008

It says something about a program when they can add a former National Coach of the Year, two-time SEC Coach of the Year, and Tennessee Baseball Coach of the Year to the staff. That's what Mike Martin was able to do in 2008 when he welcomed back Rod Delmonico as an assistant.

Delmonico, who worked for Florida State from 1984-89, was a part of the staff that helped Coach Martin win 334 games, rank in the top 15 each year, and go to the College World Series in three of the six seasons, including a national runner-up in 1986. He left to become the University of Tennessee head coach in 1990, where he won 699 games in 18 seasons.

Delmonico came back as a volunteer coach to lend his overall coaching knowledge to the program but also to enjoy watching his son Tony perform as the team's starting shortstop. Tony performed very well, playing in 66 games, batting .374 in 254 at-bats with an OBP of .455 and slugging .559. He was drafted by the Los Angeles Dodgers.

In the spring of 2010, Coach Martin told Unconquered Magazine he remembered the night that he stood outside the delivery room in the Tallahassee Hospital and congratulated Rod on the birth of his baby son, Tony.

Delmonico on Mike Martin

"I think Mike Martin is one of the most underrated coaches we've had in the history of the game, and it's because he hasn't won a national championship."

In the year (2008) Delmonico returned to FSU they went back to the College World Series for the first time in seven seasons.

Steve Winterling
Coach: 1986-91

Jacksonville native Steve Winterling served as Mike Martin's assistant for six seasons. He handled a variety of responsibilities over this time period in which the Seminoles appeared in six Regionals and made four World

Series visits. In Winterling's first season (1986), the Noles made it all the way to the National Championship game. During his time on the Florida State staff, the Seminoles won 78% of their games, chalking up 334 wins against 96 losses.

At various times Winterling coached the outfielders, was first base coach, joined 11 in the dugout to keep players prepared and organized, oversaw the grounds crew to keep the playing field in shape, and worked the highly successful Mike Martin Summer baseball Camps. In addition, he was charged with overseeing the academic progress of the baseball student-athletes.

Following his Florida State career, Winterling coached baseball in Florida at Temple Terrace, then started the baseball program at Pasco-Hernando Community College (PHSC). His career coaching record shows 705 wins and 601 losses. He stepped down as head coach after the 2018 season after 40 years of coaching but remained at PHSC as athletic director.

Jamey Shouppe
Chattahoochee, FL
Player: 1981-82
Assistant Coach: 1990-11

Jamey Shouppe was a LHP for two seasons for the Seminoles. He appeared in 60 games, won 10, lost 4, saved 10. In 126.1 innings, he walked just 49 and struck out 122 while recording a 3.78 ERA. He was drafted by the Houston Astros in the 8th round of the 1982 MLB Draft.

Shouppe's pitching coach at Florida State was Mike McLeod. The two have remained friends over the years, with several of McLeod's TCC players moving on to play for Shouppe at Florida A&M.

Shouppe returned to FSU in 1990 as an assistant, remaining on Coach Martin's staff for 21 years. He took over the role of recruiting coordinator, then in 1992 added the role of pitching coach. Under his leadership as head recruiter, the Seminoles had a top 25 class every season, including six top-five and 13 top 10 classes. Baseball America ranked the 1992 recruiting class #1. Shouppe recruited 24 First Team All Americans. 152 of FSU's players have received All-American honors.

Under his tutelage as pitching coach, Florida State had 58 pitchers drafted. Sean Gilmartin (2009) and Blair Varnes (1999) were named National Rookie of the Year.

In 2013 Jamey Shouppe was named head coach at Florida A&M, where he won 159 games before the coronavirus pandemic shortened the 2020 season to 15 games.

The Palm Ball Artist
Clyde Keller
Player: 1988-89
Assistant Coach: 2016-2019

- Fair Oaks, California
- 41 app; 207.2 ip 23-5 W-L, 203 Ks
- Palm ball artist, pitching coach

Keller played for Martin in the '80s, then returned as a volunteer coach in 2016-18. He was promoted to full-time pitching coach for 2019 to replace the departed Mike Bell, now head coach at Pittsburgh

He was a valuable player because he pitched as well as played in the field. At various times he could be seen at 2B, 3B, LF, CF RF & DH. As a pitcher, he won 23 games against only 5 losses while striking out 203 batters in 207 innings. What made him so effective on the mound was a pitch that hardly any pitchers have in their arsenal---the palm ball. It is very difficult to control and even tougher to hit.

The Keller Palm Ball

"I have always really thrown the palm ball. It was taught to me by my dad. It is a hard pitch to grasp. Honestly, I have tried to teach people. But the only two people who got it were my two sons. It is probably because I work with them on it all the time. Other people get frustrated with it and quit."

As a hitter, Keller had a .312 avg. in 101games. He was the leadoff hitter and 2nd baseman in 11's 500th win on February 5, 1989, vs Arizona State. In the 8-3-win, Keller went 2-for-3 with 2 RBI, 2 walks, and scored a run. The Seminoles trailed 3-2 entering the 8th inning but put the game away with a 6-run inning.

Is 11 Different Than He was When You Played for Him?

"I think from the strategy standpoint everything is the same. He has always taught what he has taught, and it has been the same. Very successful doing it.

The thing I think that is different is that he was more on the intense side. He was very intense back then, and now he realizes the way he engages the players is very key."

Coach Martin Still Teaching

"It is absolutely amazing. He is teaching every single practice, every single game. It is what he does. I think that the best way to describe 11 is as a teacher of baseball."

His Personal Impact On Your life

"Tremendous. He is just a great person in general, but we all know he is a superb, excellent coach. Baseball kinda crosses over into life quite a bit. You can really tell that with 11, he is a great (role) model for every one of the student-athletes coming through here."

Mike Bell
Assistant Coach: 2012-18
Player: 1994-95

Mike Bell, from Sarasota, FL, was a LHP who also played first base and DH after transferring from Pasco-Hernando CC, where he set a school record with a .372 batting average. At Florida, State Bell appeared in 26 games, pitching in 137.2 innings. He won 14 games and struck out 120 batters. His ERA was 3.01, and he held opposing batters to a .273 average. Bell helped Florida State reach the College World Series in both his seasons.

In 2012 Bell returned to Florida State as pitching coach and to assist in recruiting. Prior to his return, he was an assistant at the University of Tennessee, where he helped the Vols reach the 2005 CWS. He then spent four years as the Oklahoma pitching coach. Prior to his return to Florida State, he helped recruit and develop 22 pitchers who were selected in the Major League Baseball draft.

Bell on Martin
(As Told to the Tallahassee Democrat-April 10, 2019)

"... as players the things you do in a practice setting and the way that he would talk to you, coach you and teach you he would talk the game. He would tell you in this adverse situation, this is what we're looking to do, and this is how we're going to do it, and you're doing it in a practice situation. The next thing you know, come springtime, you're two weeks into the season, and you're in that same situation and dang sure if it isn't just how he described, just the way it was supposed to be. Two pitches later, you're out of the inning, and you're thinking this is what he prepared us for."

In 2019 Mike Bell left Florida State to become head baseball coach at the University of Pittsburgh.

Jack Niles (1993-97)

- Key West, FL, 1993-94, 3B;
- 111 gp, 233 ab, .266 avg, .361 slg
- 1995-97 asst. coach

Jack Niles was a versatile player who found a home at third base after playing shortstop and second base in his first season. The Key West native transferred from Seminole Community College, where he was an All-Mid Conference selection after hitting .359. At Florida State, Niles became a steady player appearing in 111 games over his two seasons in Tallahassee.

A personable team player, Niles batted .266 with 62 hits and 42 RBIs. In his first game against the Florida Gators, he went two for three with a homer and scored two runs.

In 1995 Niles joined the Seminole coaching staff as a volunteer assistant coach while he finished his undergraduate degree in finance. He worked with the Seminole outfielders for three seasons.

JIM CROSBY

MARTINISM #18
11's Winning Philosophy

In the 1992 Seminole Baseball Media Guide, Mike Martin shared his thoughts on why his teams were able to win so many games. That was 12 years into his career as FSU's head coach. This philosophy would hold true for the rest of his career, spanning 28 additional years:

"I just feel that if you go out, work as hard as you can, put everything in God's hands, and accept everything that comes your way, good and bad, good things are going to happen."

CJ Van Eyk (2018-2020)

CJ Van Eyk from Lutz, FL, won 18 games with a 3.21 ERA and 225 strikeouts in 176.2 innings pitched. After the 2020 season was shortened by the coronavirus pandemic, he was chosen by the Toronto Blue Jays with the 42nd pick in the MLB Draft. He expressed on Twitter what being a Seminole and playing for Mike Martin meant to him:

"From the moment I was given the opportunity to play at Florida State University, I knew it would be one of the best decisions of my life, and it proved to be nothing but that! The Animals of Sections B, FSU's tradition and winning atmosphere are second to none in college baseball.

"Nothing I know of yet will compare to the feeling of lacing them up every day with a group of guys that were truly family. Our laughs, dog-piles, and struggles turned teammates into life-long brothers that I am forever indebted to. Thank you for the memories we shared in Garnet and Gold.

"Thank you as well to my unbelievable coaches and staff members I had the pleasure of playing with over 3 years. The program and myself would be where they are today without men like them doing all the right things.

"To 11, it was truly an honor to play for a living legend like yourself. It was always about US and what was best for the Team. You encouraged us to be Christians, students, and then the best athletes we could be, whether it was on the diamond or the golf course.

"Thank you to Florida State University and the community for the best 3 years of my life."

11: Making Baseball History

The Stars Speak

John Bentley (1997-2001)
- Tallahassee, FL- North Florida Christian HS
- Pitcher
- 43 App; 13-3 w-l; 143 ip; 3.34 era

Seminole Dream
"As soon as I knew I was pretty decent at baseball, that's when playing for Florida State turned into my dream. My first time talking with 11 was when they had Little League Day at Howser, and we got to run out on the field to the position we wanted to play. Then later, I got to talk to 11 as a recruit, and that was amazing."

Signing Day
"It was at my school North Florida Christian. It was kind of a bad look to me (now) I had this button-down shirt and khakis. They were really cool back in the '80s. I had a couple of other guys signing with smaller schools, but it was kinda neat that I was getting to go to Florida State."

Came to FSU to Play, What Stood Out about Coach Martin
"Still to this day, I remember that 11 was the most organized and had the most efficiently run practices. Anyone learning to coach baseball should watch 11's practices. Every drill was timed, and we would do 10 minutes of them, but we would not move on until we did them right, even if it meant going off schedule.

But he was very structured. The practices were perfectly timed out. He had this little piece of paper he kept in his hat. At times, he would take his hat off and pull out that piece of paper if he wasn't sure where he was in the schedule."

11 Beyond Baseball
"The other thing that stands out to me was his faith. His faith in Jesus Christ. That was an even bigger impact on me than baseball. One time when he was sitting on one end of the bench in a game, we were losing to Cal State Fullerton. When something happened, a player at the other end of the bench said: 'Jesus Christ' out loud and in a derogatory tone.

We saw 11 move his head down, look around over all the people on the bench, put his glasses kind of down at the tip of his nose, and said: 'You better be praying."

"There is a lot he wouldn't have said anything about, but not that one."

Moving into a Starting Role

"You know this is going to sound weird. I have never been somebody who is arrogant at all. I knew when I came in that FSU had a strong staff with Jon McDonald & Nick Stocks, who could throw much harder than I did. But I knew I could pitch. My idol growing up was Greg Maddux, and that's how I pitched. I was in the upper 80's, never in the '90s, but I had a hard sinker, good slider, a good changeup, and I didn't walk people. I came in relief in some big games against Florida, Miami, and Arizona State. I did well. I was ready to be a starting pitcher.

Bentley's First Start

"In a spring tournament game against St. Bonaventure, we were beating them bad. I think I had 10 strikeouts" (he also gave up 0runs, 1 hit, and had no walks). That earned him some midweek starts (Mercer & Jacksonville). Weekend starts would come later.

I got a start against Duke in the ACC tournament and went the full 9 innings. I threw 146 pitches. In the 8th inning, 11 asked me if I was feeling all right. I said, 'I am OK, don't take me out. I feel better than I did in the first inning.'

"On paper, you might not think I should have been pitching. But I really thought I could go out there and do what some other people couldn't ---just not let the moment overwhelm you."

Almost a No-hitter Changed the Headlines

On February 17, 1998, John Bentley tossed a one-hitter against Charleston Southern. It was a great performance as FSU won 16-0. Bentley recalls: "I had a no-hitter going into the 9th but ended up with a one-hitter. So, the next night Chris Chavez, who was my roommate, threw a no-hitter and stole my thunder. I had a nice article written about me—hometown boy throws a one-hitter—then Chris stole my thunder." (The Noles won that one 13-0.)

Final Martin/Bentley

"A midweek game in Jacksonville after a rough weekend series. During the week, we would practice bunt situations with runners on first and second, and the 3rd baseman would have to read whether to stay on third and let the pitcher take it or charge in to get the ball.

It had rained, and it was hot and humid. JU lays down a bunt with runners on first and second, just like we had practiced. I ran over to do exactly what I was supposed to do, but my feet slipped, and I fell down. Now the bases are loaded. 11 comes out to the mound and looks perplexed. He looks at the ground like what happened? I said: 'I don't know. I fell down. So, 11 says, 'JB, Seminoles don't fall down.'"

John Bentley won 13 and lost only 3 games. He pitched 143 innings giving up just 53 hits, and had a 3.34 ERA. He was a pitching coach's dream in that he only walked 32 batters.

Scooby Morgan (1993-96)

- Coral Springs, FL Taravella HS
- P: 76 g; 25-9 W-L; 271 IP; DH: 64 g; .311avg; 13 hr; .635 slg
- Nat. Collegiate Writers Assoc All-American

How Scooby Got to FSU

"I was taking pitching lessons from Lazer Collazo, Miami pitching coach who was recruiting me for the Canes. My sister Pamela Morgan won a national championship as a cheerleader for Miami football. Collazo left Miami to be the Seminole pitching coach. So, I ended up going to a Florida State baseball camp and had a really good week. Coach Martin invited me up to his office and asked me if I would like to play baseball for Florida State. I committed to FSU, and my sister transferred to FSU as well and went to law school."

Acquiring a Name

"My name is actually Steven Morgan, but when I was born, my one-year older brother had a hard time saying, Steven. It always came out Scooby. So, it stayed at that, and everyone has called me Scooby since then."

Florida State's Impact on My life

"I was only 17 when I entered FSU. So, I was a little immature as a freshman and as a sophomore. I couldn't even get into a nightclub. As a senior, it became real who I was as a person. I learned to be a man by being myself and being alone. You add the coaching aspect to that (and I gained maturity.)

I always wanted to be a leader, and I showed that throughout my career. But back in my freshman year, I wanted to be my own person as a player and a teenager as well. I was an idiot."

Scooby's Versatility

"I was the Chris Roberts (two-way player) of the '90s. Did good as a hitter, but that wasn't discovered until my senior year." (JD Drew led the team with 21 homers, but Scooby and Jeremy Morris tied for second most with 13.) I didn't really get a shot until my senior year." (in 64 games, Scooby slashed .306/.420/.639.

Playing Under 11

"11 took every moment seriously. Baseball was more of a business at that time but, I didn't learn that right away. Baseball was just fun, fun like it had always been as a kid. When I realized I would have a chance to play professional baseball and make something of myself, I tried to do that. Under 11, baseball was strictly business.

"You had to make a name for yourself because we had some dominant players at that time. We played for the winningest coach of all time."

Favorite Memories

"I guess being on the road. When Florida State was on the road, we traveled better than anybody. I played lowball (Class A) in the minors, and we traveled by bus. At Florida State, we traveled by plane. We stayed in the best places. Traveling, to me, was exciting.

"We went to Hawaii. Jack Niles and I talk about that and having our pictures taken in front of the Big Kahuna with Charlie Cruz, Chuck Howell, Jonathan Johnson, and Jose Zabala."

Travel After FSU

"I used to own a travel program called The Tomahawks Baseball Academy. Our travel ball team wore Garnet and Gold. All of our uniforms were just like Florida State uniforms. We even had the Sunday golds. We had the Grays and the Whites. We had five different hats. My twin boys Tyler and Peyton (now 14), were on the team. One was the catcher, and the other played third base. They play baseball 6-days a week and my daughter, Reese, goes to dance four days a week." It's a full life!

Some of Scooby's Best Games

When Scooby's senior year rolled around, he had developed into a complete player, starting 18 games as a pitcher with a 12-3 record. He went six or more innings 12 times. His 13 home runs as batter included a 2-homer 4-RBI game vs Virginia. He had multiple RBI games 9 times.

Scooby Morgan played in three of Mike Martin's 17 College World Series visits during his career as a Seminole. Florida State was glad he decided to become a Seminole after originally being tutored by the Miami Hurricane pitching coach.

MARTINISM #19

Changing Times on the Mound

"We used to have one or two that throw over 90 and think--- 'Yeah!' Now we've got seven guys that throw 90 plus. It's an arms race going on. It's a spectacle, but it's good for the fans." (Mike Martin, as told to AP at the 2019 CWS)

Martin and the Major Leagues

Over the course of his 40-year coaching career at Florida State, Mike Martin has an impressive record of players being selected in the Major League Baseball Draft. 242 of his players have been drafted. 19 of those went in the first round of the MLB draft:

1st Rounders (19)

- Jeff Ledbetter — 1B-OF — Boston Red Sox — 1982
- Luis Alicea — 2B — St. Louis Cardinals — 1986
- Eduardo Perez — 1B — California Angels — 1991
- Chris Roberts — P-OF — New York Mets — 1992
- Kenny Felder — OF — Milwaukee Brewers — 1992
- John Wasdin — P — Oakland Athletics — 1993
- Paul Wilson — P — New York Mets — 1994
- Jonathan Johnson — P — Texas Rangers — 1995
- David Yocum — P — L. A, Dodgers — 1995
- JD. Drew — OF — Phils/Cards — 1997/98
- Nick Stocks — P — St. Louis Cards — 1999
- John Ford-Griffin — OF — New York Yankees — 2001
- Stephen Drew — SS — Arizona Dbacks — 2004
- Buster Posey — C — San Fran. Giants — 2008
- Sean Gilmartin — P — Atlanta Braves — 2011
- James Ramsey — OF — St. Louis Cards — 2012
- Luke Weaver — P — St. Louis Cards — 2014
- DJ Stewart — OF — Baltimore Orioles — 2015
- Matheu Nelson — C — Cincinnati — 2021

11: MAKING BASEBALL HISTORY

Major League Success Story

27 of Martin's Seminoles Played in the Big Leagues for 5 or More Years

Player	# of Years	Teams
Randy Choate	15	Yankees, Dbacks, Marlins, Dodgers, Cardinals
JD Drew	14	Cardinals, Braves, Dodgers, Red Sox
Eduardo Perez	13	Angels, Reds, Cardinals, Rays, Indians, Mariners
Luis Alicea	13	Cardinals, Red Sox, Angels, Rangers, Royals
Stephen Drew	12	Dbacks, A's, Red Sox, Yankees, Nationals
Doug Mientkiewicz	12	Twins, Red Sox, Mets, Royals, Pirates, Dodgers
John Wasdin	12	A's, Red Sox, Rockies, Orioles, Blue Jays, Rangers, Pirates
Matt Diaz	11	Rays, Royals, Braves, Pirates, Marlins
Buster Posey	12*	Giants
Jody Reed	11	Red Sox, Dodgers, Brewers, Padres. Tigers
Paul Sorrento	11	Twins, Indians, Mariners, Rays
Deion Sanders	9**	Yankees, Braves, Reds, Giants
Shane Robinson	9	Cardinals, Twins, Angels, Yankees.
Kevin Cash	8***	Blue Jays, Rays, Red Sox, Yankees, Astros
Rafael Bournigal	8	Dodgers, A's, Mariners
Scott Proctor	8	Yankees, Dodgers, Braves
Paul Wilson	7	Mets, Rays, Reds
Richie Lewis	7	Orioles, Marlins, Tigers, A's, Reds
Rafael Lopez	7	Cubs, Reds, Padres
Chris Brock	6	Braves, Giants, Phillies, Orioles
Jeff Tam	6	Mets, Indians, A's, Blue Jays
Jonathan Johnson	6	Rangers, Padres, Astros
Devon Travis	6	Blue Jays
Jim Weaver	5	Tigers, Mariners, Giants
Sean Gilmartin	5	Mets, Orioles
Luke Weaver	5*	Cardinals, Dbacks
Robby Scott	5*	Red Sox

*Still Active.
**Sanders also played 14 yrs. In NFL
***Cash in his 8th season as Rays Mgr.

JIM CROSBY

The Stars Speak

Bryan Henry (2005-07)

- Tallahassee, Florida High
- North Florida CC, Madison, FL
- P-IF; 32-9 w-l; 2.60 era 1st Team All-American

Ever a Doubt as to Where Bryan Henry Would Play Baseball?

"Never a doubt. I grew up at Florida State and with my dad (Jim Henry, Tallahassee Democrat) covering them as a writer, I was able to spend countless hours at baseball games and meet the players growing up. I told 11 when I was 12 years old that I was going to be a Seminole. Clemson did make a little run, but there was never a doubt I would end up at FSU."

Memories of Watching the Seminoles Play as a Kid

"My earliest memories were of Brooks Badeaux. He was my favorite player. I remember being in elementary school, and it was a reading day. The players came to read to us, and Brooks was one of them. He was who I wanted to be (like). I wanted to play shortstop and then was when I knew for sure I wanted to go to Florida State."

Earliest Impressions of 11

"I did go to the camps, so I knew a little about his personality. But there was still this nervousness he created—the intimidation factor. I wanted to impress him."

Henry Got There and Played for the Guy Who Would Win the Most Games Ever

"That was nothing short of amazing. I learned more in my first fall at FSU than I learned in all of my 18 or 19 years before. The knowledge of the game that 11 had. Every aspect of it that he passed down. I remember being soaking wet getting ready for what I thought was the middle of practice, and we were just getting ready to start practice. Every practice was like that.

We worked our tails off, and 11 was right there with us. Pushing us. That's why Florida State has been so successful."

11: MAKING BASEBALL HISTORY

First pitching performance-April 6, 2005-Hawaii-Hilo

"We were in between games of a double-header in Hawaii. We played something like 9 games in 8 days, so we were short of pitching. Our starter for the 2nd game came up with an injury, so I remember 11 saying to 'get loose.' I was kinda looking around like, who? So, I went down and got ready and really enjoyed it." (Henry went 5 innings, gave up just three hits, no runs in the 9-1 win)

Did You Expect to Pitch or Play the Infield?

"Out of high school, I got drafted as a pitcher in 2004 and went to North Florida Community College (Madison, FL) but practiced with the infielders. I was shocked when the first game, I ended up playing 3rd base and batting cleanup. Then at Florida State in my first year (2005-Soph year), 11 had told me I could do both but called me in before Christmas break and said they had good pitching depth and wanted to use me at 3rd base. (Henry ended up pitching in 17 games and playing 3rd base in 35 in 2005)

Most Memorable Games

"Will never forget my first start in Howser against the Gators (April 19, 2005). Going deep in the game (7.1 ip, 2 earned runs, 5ks for the win). Matt DiBlasi came in to get a big out, keep the lead, and Howser went crazy.

Then, the regional game against Auburn (June 4, 2005). Got off to a rocky start, got straightened out, and threw a complete game. And my whole senior year was a blast."

11's Impact

"Being a Christian man, he never pushed us in that direction. He just led by example in that area. He always kept baseball in perspective, saying: 'Baseball is what we do, but it is not who we are.'" (Henry never had an ERA above 2.90, A control pitcher who only walked 75 batters in 322 innings. ACC pitcher of the year (' 06). 9 years in minors. Now pitching coach at Florida A&M for Jamey Shouppe, his pitching coach at FSU.)

Charlie Cruz (1992-95)

- North Miami HS
- 75 App.; 11-6 w-l; 2.73 era; 208 ip; 231 ks
- Pitched in 3 CWS; Drafted by the Braves

Cruz Comes to Florida State

"I attended the Seminole select baseball camp in 1990. I had some good outings, and that is the first time I set eyes on 11. I was just striking out everybody; I had a good curveball. I saw 11 come riding in on his golf cart to watch me throw a few innings. Later, I went to see them play in Miami. I went up to say hi to pitching Coach Jamey Shouppe. He asked me how it was going. I was 10-0 at the time. The next day Jamey offered me a scholarship."

Martin's Impact

"When I came to Florida State, I was very young, just 17 years old, and had never lived away. Some of the things 11 was teaching were discipline and hard work. I loved that we did everything in practice that made it seem like a real game. 11 pushed you hard. It didn't matter if it was 100 degrees out there; he was out there working with you, making sure every player. Was giving 110%."

How Cruz improved at Florida State

"When I came to Florida State, I was pretty much a two-pitch pitcher—curveball and fastball. I remember 11 saying if you do not have a changeup, you will not pitch at Florida State. I was like, 'whoa, I'd better learn to throw a changeup.' It actually became one of my best pitches. What I heard was one of the things the Braves loved about me was my changeup like a Tom Glavine type. With Jamey Shouppe helping me, I could throw it at any time in the count. That pitch changed my career."

Cruz shows up against Rivals
(March 11, 1995)

"One of my favorite games. I still have it on video. I don't know how many times I have shown it to my kids. I was actually coming off a knee injury. Nothing like pitching against the Gators in Gainesville. Jonathan Johnson and David Yocum got wins over the Gators at home, and I started in Gainesville." (Cruz shut out Florida for 8 innings on seven hits and struck out 8 in a 7-0 win). In the CWS that year, Cruz was involved in another memorable rivalry game. This time against the Hurricanes. Fellow Miamian David Yocum started and only lasted one-third of an inning while giving up 4 runs. Cruz explains: "I came in the first inning; then we had an hour-and-a-half rain delay. But there was no way they were gonna get me out of that game." Cruz pitched 8.2 shutout innings, striking out 6 in a losing effort, 4-2. Afterward, Coach Martin said: "The Cruz-er came in and pitched marvelously."

11's Influence

"He always stressed the importance of the education part. He demanded that you respect the game, stay disciplined and do things the right way off the field."

That extends to the present as Cruz has two sons, Gabriel and Jacob, at Florida State. His daughter Kaitlin is a senior in high school.

Charlie Cruz had a 5-year minor league career for the Atlanta Braves before deciding that with Greg Maddux, Tom Glavin, John Smoltz, Steve Avery, and Greg McMichael, there might not be an opening on the MLB roster anytime soon. He retired after 5-years with a 21-15 record, 167 games, 351 innings, and 335 Ks.

From the Field to the Press Box

Rod Meadows (Radio-1980-89)

- University of North Dakota
- FSU baseball & Durham Bulls play-by-play
- VP, Sales & Marketing for Minor League Baseball, 23 years

Rod Meadows was responsible for FSU baseball broadcasts getting on radio when he became General Manager of WTNT radio in 1980. He broadcast Seminole baseball for nine years and was joined in the booth by Dave Fannin, former assistant coach, and Jim Crosby, former TV sports anchor on WECA, the ABC affiliate: Looking back, in 2019, here are some of his memories of 11.

A Class Act

"Back then, we held the post-game up in the radio booth, and no matter how tough the loss was, he used to come up to the press box after the games and did a live interview on the air. He always faced it head on. I always admired him for that reason. A lot of coaches would duck that and send an assistant or not come even. He never missed one. I am very happy for him setting the record for most wins."

Not Just a Coach, A Psychologist Too:

"I remember we were playing in Miami at Mark Light Stadium, where FSU had experienced some frustrating losses. We were in a car going over to the stadium for the first game of a three-game series. Coach Martin was talking to Jeff Ledbetter about what to expect from the hostile crowd and how brutal they could be. He explained that FSU would get a bunch of grief and how they (fans) would be nasty and hostile. He talked to Jeff about not letting that bother him. I was so impressed by the way he got Jeff ready to play. I always thought Coach Martin was a great baseball coach, but he was also a psychologist that day."

Lee Bowen (1990-2004)

Lee Bowen joined the Seminole radio broadcasts as the new Voice of Seminole baseball in 1990. Bowen served in that role for 15 years until his untimely death in 2004. Bowen called over 1,000 games and was largely responsible for the local radio affiliate contracting to broadcast the entire schedule of baseball games every year.

Lee and broadcast partner Jim Crosby took the broadcasts to new levels of popularity with such features as "Home Run Inning," "Pre & Postgame one-on-one Interviews with Coach Martin," and from-the-dugout live interviews with the "Stars of the Game."

Bowen's knowledge of the game, especially the NCAA rule book, was unsurpassed. He had a talent for capturing the excitement of Seminole baseball and putting it on the airwaves.

Lee also served as the broadcast coordinator for football and men's basketball on FSU's radio network. Prior to his arrival at Florida State, Bowen called play-by-play for the Burlington (NC) Indians of the Appalachian League.

11: MAKING BASEBALL HISTORY

After Lee's passing, Mike Martin took time to express his personal feelings and speak for the Seminole Baseball Nation, "I don't know of anybody who had more of a passion for Florida State baseball than Lee Bowen," said FSU head coach Mike Martin. "When you lose an outstanding junior or a senior to the draft, you know one day you can replace them. You can't replace Lee Bowen. Our thoughts and prayers go out to his family."

In 2005 the broadcast booth at Dick Howser Stadium was named after Bowen.

The Lee Bowen Radio Booth

For 15 years, Lee Bowen served as the voice of the Florida State Seminoles. From Marshall McDougall's record-setting six home run game at Maryland to numerous NCAA postseason appearances, Lee Bowen was Seminole baseball.

Bowen called the action for over 1,000 Florida State baseball games over his 15-year career, including 26 from the College World Series. He was behind the microphone for more than 100 Seminole NCAA postseason games.

He was a one-man show on the road, calling the action from as far away as Hawaii and California. At home, Bowen teamed with longtime partner Jim Crosby as the many fans sitting at Dick Howser Stadium would listen in as they watched the ballgames. Bowen traveled with the team to the College World Series in Omaha eight times, including the 1999 CWS in which Florida State defeated Stanford in extra innings to advance to the national championship game.

Over his last five years, Bowen was joined in the radio booth by his wife, Adrienne. The two were married on June 27, 1999, and Adrienne would often accompany her husband on Seminole baseball road trips.

Bowen, who was instrumental in getting all Florida State baseball games on the radio, also served as the broadcast coordinator for football and men's basketball on FSU's radio network. He began his career as a statistician on the network after he came to Tallahassee from the Burlington Indians of the Appalachian League, where he called play-by-play for the rookie league team.

11: MAKING BASEBALL HISTORY

Jim Crosby (1981-2004)

In 1981 Jim Crosby moved from TV at the local ABC affiliate (WECA) as sports anchor to radio to become news and sports director at WNLS AM and WTNT FM radio. GM Rod Meadows hired Jim to join the baseball broadcast team with him and Dave Fannin. He would occupy this position for the next 23 years working with Lee Bowen starting in 1990.

Crosby had also served as sideline announcer for Seminole football, one of the first college sports broadcasts to have such a position. Jim was the play-by-play announcer on the first-ever women's basketball telecast in Tallahassee when WFSU TV produced the live telecast of the FSU women vs Memphis State.

In 1980, in his role as TV sports anchor, Crosby asked the newly hired baseball coach Mike Martin to appear live as a guest on sports in the 5:30 evening news. 11 almost gave him a heart attack as he got to the station just moments ahead of Crosby's Live Sports Segment. Martin had gotten stuck behind a house that was being moved on the road to the station.

Crosby served as color commentator on the first two live telecasts of Seminole football road games. He and the late Tom Mees (1949-96), who had preceded him at WECA before leaving for the new sports giant ESPN TV, broadcast the FSU-Miami (9-27-80) and the FSU-Nebraska (10-4-80) games back-to-back from South Florida and Lincoln Nebraska. The historic upset at Nebraska is still available to be seen on YouTube.

In 2021, Jim Crosby, who started out in Quincy as DJ and Sports Director in 1976, began his 45th year of covering Seminole Sports.

Steve Melewski (2005-06)

Steve Melewski joined the Seminole Network in 2005 as baseball play-by-play announcer. He brought a wealth of sportscasting experience with him. He was working as the broadcaster of the Aberdeen Iron Birds of the New York-Penn League, the class A affiliate of the Baltimore Orioles. He called all 76 of their games. Prior to that, he was the number two announcer with the AAA Richmond Braves.

Next, Melewski's relationship with the MLB Baltimore Orioles included four years as pre-and post-game call-in host of Orioles Talk on the team's flagship station WBAL.

Melewski said: "I am thrilled to be joining one of college baseball's best programs ever. Florida State baseball is like the big leagues, everything from a great winning tradition to incredible facilities. Coach Martin has built an amazing program, and I am honored to become a part of it."

Melewski added: "The fans have become used to Lee Bowen's first-rate broadcast and enthusiasm for FSU baseball. I will work very hard to continue that and honor what he meant to the FSU program.

FSU Senior Athletic Director Charlie Carr said: "It's great to have a genuine baseball enthusiast as part of our program. Steve is a baseball fan and a lifetime follower of the game. He has big shoes to fill, but we have hired the best man for the job."

Melewski left FSU after two seasons to cover the Orioles on MASN-The Mid-Atlantic Sports Network.

Eric Luallen (2007-2021)

In 2020 Eric Luallen began his 14th season as the play-by-play announcer for Seminole baseball on Radio. After Steve Melewski left to work with the Baltimore Orioles, Luallen teamed with longtime Seminole broadcaster Tom Block for seven seasons before Block left to work on television and a variety of other responsibilities within the University. In the seven years since Block's departure, Luallen has been the sole announcer of Seminole baseball on radio.

Before working in radio, Luallen was a valuable member of the Seminole football offensive line under legendary Head Coach Bobby Bowden. He was called on to play all five OL positions during his gridiron career.

Luallen spent nine years hosting WNLS' pre-game coverage of FSU football games, and from 1997-2002 he hosted an afternoon drive-talk show on WNLS. During that time, the Tampa native has done play-by-play on select FSU men's and women's basketball games and was the broadcaster for the Tallahassee Thunder of the AF2. Luallen also has experience working in television as he hosted the Mike Gillespie show for five years.

Luallen on Broadcasting FSU Baseball

"As an FSU alumnus, a huge baseball fan, and someone who has known the members of the coaching staff at Florida State for a number of years,

11: MAKING BASEBALL HISTORY

I am very excited about the opportunity to work with Seminole baseball" said Luallen. "As a broadcaster, I am very thankful to be getting this opportunity." (Seminoles.com January 30, 2007)

FSU BASEBALL ON TELEVISION
Tom Block (1995-2021)

When it comes to Seminole Sports, Tom Block has done a little of everything. The Fort Lauderdale native has been associated with Seminole IMG Sports Network, ACC Network Extra, ESPN Networks, Sun Sports, and other responsibilities. He has been a play-by-play announcer, sideline reporter, and post-game locker room reporter. He has worked on live telecasts of FSU football, baseball, and Women's basketball.

In 2007 he joined with Erick Luallen to broadcast the Seminole baseball games on radio, a position he held for 7 seasons. When hired for that position, he told Seminoles.com:

"The opportunity to call FSU baseball games is a dream come true," said Block. "I have the utmost respect and admiration for Coach (Mike) Martin and his staff and players and what they've been able to accomplish over the years. The chance to follow in the footsteps of Lee Bowen, Jim Crosby, Steve Melewski, and the others who have announced FSU games is truly a privilege." (Seminoles.com January 30, 2007)

The television aspect of Block's career began as sports anchor for Tallahassee's WTXL-ABC 27 from 1993-98.

Block took on dual duties with Seminole baseball by joining Gene Deckerhoff and Keith Jones in televising the games on weekends on SUN Sports Network five years (2007-11) while also broadcasting the games on radio. Additionally, Tom Block was hired by Florida State University in 2018 as Vice President for Advancement Relations.

GENE DECKERHOFF (1979-2021)
FSU Hall of Fame 2002

Perhaps the most well-known name and certainly one of the most well-liked ones in Seminole Sports is that of Gene Deckerhoff. The personable Jacksonville native has been the play-by-play voice of Seminole football since 1979, FSU basketball since 1974, and FSU baseball on TV for Sunshine Network later SUN Sports for 10 years. In 1989 Gene also became the p-b-p guy for the NFL Tampa Bay Bucs, a post he has now held for 32 years.

11: MAKING BASEBALL HISTORY

In 2002 Gene was elected into the FSU Hall of Fame. He has also been elected into the Florida Hall of Fame.

Deckerhoff Elected to the FSU Hall of Fame in 2002

Gene Deckerhoff is the Voice of the Seminoles, and there is no one else like him. Fans look forward to hearing Gene's play-by-play every Saturday, and even if they're sitting in the stands, you will see most with their headsets tuned into Gene.

For over 40 years, Deckerhoff has been hosting coaches' shows and serving as the on-air talent for the Tribe. In 1989, he added the Tampa Bay Buccaneers to his weekend schedule and served as the play-by-play announcer for AFL teams, the Tampa Bay Storm and the Orlando Predators.

Deckerhoff is a nine-time winner of the Florida Sportscaster of the Year Award, an 18-time winner of the best play-by-play announcer for college and pro ball, and in 2000, was inducted into the Florida Sports Hall of Fame. Gene also received an ADDY award for the best regional TV promo for "The Bobby Bowden Show" in 1986, and in 1991 won a silver medal award from the American Advertising Association.

Gene has been married to the lovely Ann Deckerhoff for over 37 years, and they have three sons, Emerson, Dennis, and Eric, and six grandchildren. In the off-season, Gene enjoys traveling with his family, woodworking, photography, and cooking. *nolefan.org

JIM CROSBY

A FINAL MARTINISM #20

What more appropriate way to wrap up Mike Martin's career and all of the Martinisms of this colorful coach than with his oft-quoted explanation for all the crazy things that happened.

That's Baseball!

11: MAKING BASEBALL HISTORY

NEXT UP FOR THE NOLES

FOR IMMEDIATE RELEASE: FLORIDA STATE BASEBALL

Mike Martin, Jr. Named FSU Baseball's Ninth Head Coach

Longtime Seminole assistant will take the reins after 25 years as a Seminole player and coach

TALLAHASSEE, Fla. – Longtime Florida State assistant coach Mike Martin, Jr. has been named the ninth head baseball coach in FSU history. Florida State Director of Athletics David Coburn made the announcement Friday, elevating Martin to the head role that his father held for 40 years before him. Martin becomes the first new head baseball coach the Seminoles have hired since 1980.

"I have every confidence Mike Martin Jr. will carry on the winning tradition of Florida State University baseball," said FSU President John Thrasher. "For more than two decades as an assistant coach, he has shown he is a talented recruiter, passionate competitor, and respected mentor to our student-athletes. While Mike Martin Jr. brings his own strengths and style of coaching to the program, his values, integrity, and love for this university will carry on the proud legacy of his father."

"I want to thank President John Thrasher and Director of Athletics David Coburn for entrusting me with this special program," said Martin. "I'm very honored and humbled to be able to lead Florida State. It's been a privilege to serve at this great University for the past 22 years, and I'm excited to extend FSU's 70-year history of success moving forward."

Martin has spent all 22 years as an assistant coach at his alma mater, focusing on hitting and recruiting. The former All-American catcher for the Seminoles has compiled eight straight Top 10 recruiting classes, while his offenses have a combined .300 batting average since 1998. Florida State has made the postseason and won at least 40 games every year under Martin, with eight College World Series appearances, 17 NCAA super regionals, and six Atlantic Coast Conference titles.

"After serving under one of the all-time greats, we will combine much of what was learned from him with our new staff's style and ideas in our pursuit of championships," added Martin.

Martin has coached 16 Major Leaguers, 16 freshmen All-Americans, 21 first-team All-Americans, and 41 student-athletes who have earned first, second or third-team All-America accolades. In all, 77 Seminoles have earned All-ACC honors, and 65 hitters have been selected in the Major League Baseball draft during that stretch. Martin has coached four Seminole hitters that captured National Player of the Year honors—Shane Robinson, Tony Thomas, Buster Posey, and James Ramsey.

Prior to joining Florida State's staff, Martin was FSU's starting catcher from 1993-95, leading FSU to the College World Series in 1994 and 1995. He was drafted out of college by San Diego in the ninth round in 1995. Before coming to Florida State, Martin played high school ball at the Maclay School in Tallahassee and at Manatee Community College in 1992.

"We are very excited to have Mike Martin, Jr. leading our baseball program into the future," said Coburn. "His commitment to, passion for, and experience with the Seminole program is second to none. "His plan for the next era of Seminole baseball is impressive. He knows what he wants to do and how he wants to do it. After traveling with this team for the last three and a half weeks, I have come away very impressed with his relationships with the players, his attention to detail, and his understanding of the great game of college baseball."

11: MAKING BASEBALL HISTORY

MIKE MARTIN IMMORTALIZED

NCBWA Coach of the Year Award Named for Mike Martin

The coach whose favorite four words in the English language are "see you in Omaha" now will be honored annually in that baseball-rich city with the National Collegiate Baseball Writers Association Mike Martin Coach of the Year Award starting in 2020 for the top NCAA Division I baseball coach.

The NCBWA board of directors voted unanimously to name the annual award after the winningest head coach in NCAA Division I baseball history after Martin retired at Florida State in 2019 with a 2,029-736-4 mark over 40 seasons in leading the FSU program from 1980-2019.

"We could not think of any other coach historically to associate a name for this annual award besides coach Mike Martin," said NCBWA executive director Bo Carter. "He has meant so much to college baseball as it has continued year-by-year to gain additional national popularity."

Martin guided the Seminoles to at least 40 wins for all 40 seasons – a feat accomplished by no other college head coach in any sport – and took FSU to the NCAA World Series 17 times during his tenure.

He was National Coach of the Year in both 2012 and 2019 by Baseball America and is a member of both the ABCA Hall of Fame and the College Baseball Hall of Fame. As head coach at Florida State, he won 20 regular-season conference titles in the Metro and Atlantic Coast Conferences and was conference coach of the year 13 times in those two circuits.

More importantly, Martin was noted for being a class act coach with disciplined and dedicated student-athletes and one of the great humorists in the game. He received a standing ovation from the media at his final news conference at the NCAA World Series in Omaha last June.

The famed Florida State player, assistant coach under Woody Woodward, and the immortal Dick Howser expressed delight when he was notified that the NCBWA was naming the award after his diamond legacy.

"When I heard about it," he said with a smile, "I was simply flabbergasted. It is such an honor to have my name associated with this award, and it is a tribute to all the players and coaches who worked with me at Florida State."

Martin took the Seminoles to NCAA runner-up finishes in the World Series in both 1986 and '99 and set another national record by making every NCAA tournament from 1980-2019 with the Seminoles. Many felt he did one of his best coaching jobs in '19 as the Noles upset their way through the Athens, Georgia., NCAA Regional over host Georgia and then swept heavily-favored LSU in the NCAA Baton Rouge Super Regional.

The personable coach is one of the most well-known clinicians in the country and also helped prolong FSU's record skein of 42 consecutive tourney appearances (began in 1978 when he was an assistant coach under Woodward) in the NCAA Championships.

In April 2005, Dick Howser Stadium was retitled Mike Martin Field at Dick Howser Stadium as the Seminoles legend was in the midst of his 26th season at the helm. On May 5, 2018, Martin passed the late coaching legend Augie Garrido (1,975 victories from 1969-2016) as the winningest head coach in NCAA Division I annals. (www.batsandblogsbka.wordpress.com/02/13/2020)

MIKE MARTIN INDUCTED INTO COLLEGE BASEBALL HALL OF FAME
November 2, 2019

Baton Rouge, Louisiana: College baseball greats came together on a Saturday night to celebrate and honor eight new inductees into the National College Baseball Hall of Fame and the 2019 College Baseball Foundation award winners.

Mike Martin, who was named the 2019 College Coach of the Year, was inducted at a banquet along with seven other inductees. His Hall of Fame inscription says:

Mike Martin – Florida State / 1980-2019

- Finished his coaching career with a record of 2,029-736-4, the only coach in college baseball history with 2,000 wins.
- 17 of his teams advanced to the Super Regionals in 21 years since the format was established
- 17 of his teams advanced to the College World Series
- His teams won at least 40 games and made the NCAA Tournament in all 40 seasons as head coach
- NJCAA All-American player at Wingate (North Carolina)
- Starred in center field for the 1965 Seminoles College World Series team
- Served as an assistant coach at FSU from 1975-1979 under coaches Woody Woodward and Dick Howser

In 2005, the field at Dick Howser Stadium was named in his honor. At the presentation, Martin said: "It's certainly something I'll always remember," Martin said of his induction and the Night of Champions event. "I'm so pleased to be around people that are strictly baseball. It's fun to talk to guys like Andre Dawson. It's just fun to be a part of a fraternity, and you could say family because that's what we are as baseball people."

Other members of the 2019 Class included: Andrew Dawson (Florida A&M), Wally Hood (Southern California), Mark Kotsay (Cal State Fullerton), Billy Wagner (Ferrum), Dave Chalk (Texas), Lloyd Simmons (Seminole State coach), Dennis Poppe (NCAA Director Championships).

JIM CROSBY

UNSUNG HEROES

It would be very difficult, no, make that impossible, to recognize everyone who has contributed to the success of the book: *11: Making Baseball History*. Countless players, coaches, sports information staff, writers, family, and friends have combined to make this a special book. After all, there is only one coach who has contributed so much to the game of college baseball while influencing—make that changing—so many lives in such a unique and positive fashion.

Upfront, my sincere and warm appreciation goes to Mike Martin. 11 was always gracious, cooperative, and understanding of not only what it took to do his job but how to help others in the media and authors do theirs. His friendship is a treasure.

Likewise, Coach Martin's family members are due a debt of gratitude, starting with his wonderful wife, Carol. She's one of a kind. Also, Mike Martin Jr.—thank you, Meat. And 11's daughters Mary Beth and Melanie.

Chip Baker, aka The Big Shooter, deserves special recognition. If you want to know anything about FSU baseball, he's the man. Universally liked, he is always approachable and unfailingly pleasant to talk with.

While talking about family, I must try to find the right words to thank my wife, The Lovely Susette. She influences everything I do. She is the love of my life. Always supportive and a great sounding board. Not afraid to tell me when something I've written can be better.

I'm grateful to my son Clint and Daughter-in-law Holly for their support and to granddaughters Quinn, the softball star who has brought us so much joy, and Ellee, the amazing singer/dancer who lives with us and brightens our lives every day,

My stepson Austin is one of the all-time great supporters of Seminole Sports and once threw out the first pitch at a Seminole game.

My brother Bob is not only my greatest friend but his love of Seminole sports, knowledge of baseball, and his 29 years of teaching English proved to be a valuable source of information. Sister-in-law Mikki is the best at spotting the little things that need to be corrected to improve the writing and is always ready to help. Also, great supporters are their daughter, former Seminole bat girl Lindy and Andy, a great player at Oglethorpe, and a knowledgeable baseball coach.

11: MAKING BASEBALL HISTORY

On this journey, I had great support from my friends Terry and Linda Cole, whose support of Seminole Sports as well as my sports writing is unparalleled. Our other mates who are always ready to help are Herb and Carol McRae, Carlos and Betty Henley, Jerry and Janice Wise, as well as Bill Fuqua, Barbara Powell, and JoAnn Etheridge.

Former FSU Alumni Association President Jim Melton is a good friend who has shared countless valuable bits of information from his vast knowledge of FSU history that helped pull this story together.

Many hours and fruitful discussions about writing and life have been shared with my longtime friend and fellow author, Jim Croushorn, who helped me immensely by sharing publishing ideas and information.

My friend Gerry Gilmer has always been a source of encouragement with his wise suggestions and belief that this whole thing would work out.

In the faith community, Pastor Betsy Ouellete-Zierden has always been a great encourager and special friend who had confidence in my work. She has been there for us in downtimes and to celebrate the good times, too. Likewise, prayer warrior Cathy Harrell has been faithful to keep my work uplifted.

Reverend Bob Tindale is a valued source and strong supporter. Bishop Ken Carter provided strength for the journey and is an avid baseball fan. A group of District Superintendents who believed in my work made it easier. Thanks to Tony Fernandez, Bob Gibbs, and Durwood Foshee.

My heartfelt thanks to Rev. Clint Purvis, the team chaplain for Seminoles sports. He has a way of lifting you up and always making you feel better.

I certainly want to thank all the Seminole players who made themselves available for one-on-one conversations to share experiences they had with 11 and FSU baseball. Special thanks go to Ryan Barthelemy and Jeremy Salazar for tracking down needed contact info and sharing it.

My apologies go out to those players who gave their all for the Seminole success story that I was unable to recognize individually in print. With 608 players, that became an impossibility. Please know that your contribution was important and helped make this story possible.

Florida State President John Thrasher has been a great advocate for this work which was also influenced by the late Presidents T. K. Wetherell and Bernie Sliger. Athletic Directors Dave Hart, Hootie Ingram, Bob Goin, Stan Wilcox, current AD David Coburn, and former Assistant AD Charlie Carr were also valued, supporters. The late John Bridgers was also a great help.

JIM CROSBY

The Florida State Sports information department made my writing life easier and more enjoyable over the years. These professionals have elevated Seminole sports to such elite levels that I would be remiss if I didn't publicly recognize this. I wish there was enough space to say more about each person, but I hope these mentions will suffice.

Over the years, Mark Carlson, Wayne Hogan, Rob Wilson, and Elliott Finebloom have directed many talented people who provided great support. Among these were, in no particular order, because they are all great: Bob Thomas, Chuck Walsh, Steve Stone, Dan Pearson, Lisa Morton, Joey Ferolito, Donna Turner, Jeff Purinton, Michael Morrell, Jason Leturmy, Bob Burda, and Nick Gandy.

I owe a big debt of gratitude to current FSU Baseball SID Steven McCartney, who provided great service to this book in many ways, especially lining up interviews and providing photos. You are a great one, Steven!

Always on the scene and willing to help were photographers Ryals Lee, Jr., Mike Olivares, Ross Obley, and in the press box the always dependable scoreboard operator and baseball aficionado, Pat Campbell.

Having the friendship and support of the Sports World's best cameraman, Tigger Gray, is a joy. Tigger and I go all the way back to our TV days at the local ABC affiliate WECA, now WTXL. Boy, were there some stories that unfolded there in the early days!

My good friend Woody Pelt, one of the all-time great PA announcers and an extremely popular radio personality, has provided a great example of professionalism and friendship.

Preston Scott is one of the top radio talk hosts in the country and a longtime friend.

And Jeff Cameron is just a special guy and one of the best-ever sports talk hosts whose friendship over the years, and our many conversations have meant a lot.

In addition, radio General Managers Mark Halverson, Dave Lowe, Mark Leopold, and Jack Lenz kept the radio ship righted over the years and were great supporters of my sports reporting and sales. Thanks to TV News director Jack Sinks for hiring me at WECA (now) WTXL.

My teammates at WECA-TV, the ABC affiliate, Mary Anne Loughlin, John Joyce, Beth Campbell, Jerry Brown, Al Willis, and the late Tom Mees were super to work with as we all tried to make local television coverage informative and entertaining.

11: MAKING BASEBALL HISTORY

My friends at Unconquered Magazine have graciously afforded me opportunities to expand my coverage of Seminole Sports. Thanks go to editor Derril Beech, my longtime friend and great supporter of my work.

Jerry Kutz of The Osceola Newspaper is a special friend who has played a key role in my development as a writer and provided opportunities for me to advance in the world of sports journalism. Bob Ferrante is a solid, dependable writer who is always helpful. Thanks also to Daniel Mitchell, who helped me get my feet on the ground in the early days at The Osceola.

WTNT Radio GM and sportscaster Rod Meadows was super to work with, and we shared lots of good times on the Seminole baseball broadcasts, especially those in Omaha at the College World Series. Dave Fannin added a lot to those game broadcasts and is still a great friend.

Two managers in radio who were great supporters of my broadcasting the baseball games and were instrumental in helping tell the Seminole Baseball and Mike Martin Story are Judy Bailey and Belinda Bininger. They are great friends who were a major help in my job.

My work on this book over the years has been aided by a number of exceptional sportswriters. Chief among these are a parade of talented writers for the Tallahassee Democrat that includes the late Steve Ellis (I still miss you, Steve-O).

Great sportswriters who helped and influenced me are John Nogowski, who raised a heckuva ballplayer in son "Nogo" now an MLB player with the Pirates, Bob Cohn, George Maselli, David Whitley, David Lee Simmons, Wayne McGahee III, and Curt Weiler.

Others include Corey Clark; I love every one of his articles. He is a former Democrat writer who is now with Warchant.com.

Likewise, Warchant's Ira Schoffel has a unique understanding of what makes sports programs tick.

Gene Williams, the founder of WarChant.com, is a good friend. He is an example of the value of commitment to a novel idea and what sticking to it and working hard can accomplish. His internet product is a must for true Seminole fans.

Mike Bianchi of the Orlando Sentinel is one of a kind—a special writer and keen observer of the sports world who has an ingenious way of describing it.

Gary Smits of the Florida Times Union also provided a great example of how to cover Seminole sports.

Roger Sockman was always a steady, dependable professional and great friend in the press box.

Two writers who left an indelible imprint on my Seminole psyche and are still missed are the late Gerald "Perk" Ensley, one of the kindest, most decent individuals in the business, and Bill McGrotha, who was always dedicated to quality Seminole Sports coverage.

Special attention is directed to current Democrat Sports Editor Jim Henry, one of the most creative in the business. He is a true visionary with a fondness for Seminole Sports history. Jim is also the father of a great Seminole pitcher and young man of character, Bryan Henry (see Bryan's "Stars Speak" section in this book).

I would be remiss if I didn't include longtime AP writer Brent Kallestead in my list of thank yous. Always well-informed and willing to share thoughts about the Seminoles.

Kerry Dunning is one of the best sports reporters in the business. She and I go way back in time covering all Seminole sports. Her friendship is a treasure.

I would also like to thank Tallahassee Magazine's owner Brian Rowland and former Capitol Outlook newspaper owners Walter and Jeraldine Smith for those writing opportunities in the early years that laid the foundation for today's success.

FSU Hall of Fame Member Judge James Joanos has been a valued source of inspiration and information concerning Seminole Sports.

A very important contributor to this book is my friend Ron Wallace, FSU pass-rusher par excellent. Always ready to help, Ron provided my contact with Tim Taylor and Burkhart Books.

And last but definitely not least is a true Seminole Hall of Fame member Bob Perrone the creator and preserver of every bit of Seminole Sports History on his marvelous internet site: www.Nolefan.org. I cannot say enough good things about him. Without his great work, this book could not have been written. A thousand thanks to Bob and my friend Andrew Brady for his assistance in the task of recording and helping preserve valuable Seminole information.

Well, that was an exhaustive list. If you made it all the way through, thank you! Obviously, this book was a work of love which I hope achieved its purpose in preserving the history, not only of the all-time best college baseball coach but of one who always took the high road and elevated FSU baseball to unequaled heights.

That could only have been accomplished by the one they call "11"— Mike Martin.

ABBREVIATIONS

AB	At-Bat
ACC	Atlantic Coast Conference
AFCA	American Football Coaches Association
AL	American League
ASU	Arizona State University
AVG	Average
BB	Base on Balls/Walk
BSU	Black Student Union
C	Catcher
CBWA	College Baseball Writers Association
CF	Centerfield
CL	Class
CWS	College World Series
DH	Designated Hitter
FB	Football
FIU	Florida International University
GP	Games Pitched
HBP	Hit by Pitch
HGT	Height
HR	Home Runs
IP	Innings Pitched
JSU	Jacksonville State University
K	Strikeout
LF	Leftfield
LHP	Left-handed Pitcher
MLB	Major League Baseball
MVP	Most Valuable Player
NAIA	National Association of Intercollegiate Athletics
NFL	National Football League
NL	National League
NO	New Orleans
OBP	On Base Percentage
P	Pitcher
PJC	Pensacola Junior College
POS	Position
RBI	Runs Batted In
RF	Rightfield
RHP	Right-handed Pitcher
RPI	Runs Per Inning
SB	Stolen Base
SC	South Carolina
SLG%	Slugging Percentage
SS	Shortstop
WGT	Weight
WS	World Series
YSU	Youngstown State University

SOURCES

These are some of the sources for which the author is grateful were available. Others are referenced within the book.

- The Tallahassee Democrat
- www.Nolefan.org
- Unconquered Magazine
- The Orlando Sentinel
- www.Seminoles.com
- The Osceola
- www.warchant.com
- Sports Spectrum Magazine
- Florida Times Union
- wikipedia.com

ABOUT THE AUTHOR

Jim Crosby is a well-known sportswriter and media personality who has covered Florida State University sports for 45 years. He has worked in radio and television and written for newspapers and magazines on a local and national level.

His credits include 23 years as color analyst/play-by-play broadcaster of Seminole baseball games on radio that include Seminole trips to the College World Series. He has also written articles on Seminole baseball, football, basketball, and golf. He is the author of five books in addition to *11: Making Baseball History*.

His weekly devotions have been viewed in over 100 countries and can be accessed at www.writeman.com. Jim lives in Tallahassee, FL, with his wife Susette and granddaughter Ellee. He enjoys reading, writing, and reading about writing.

Check out Jim's other books available at Amazon.com:

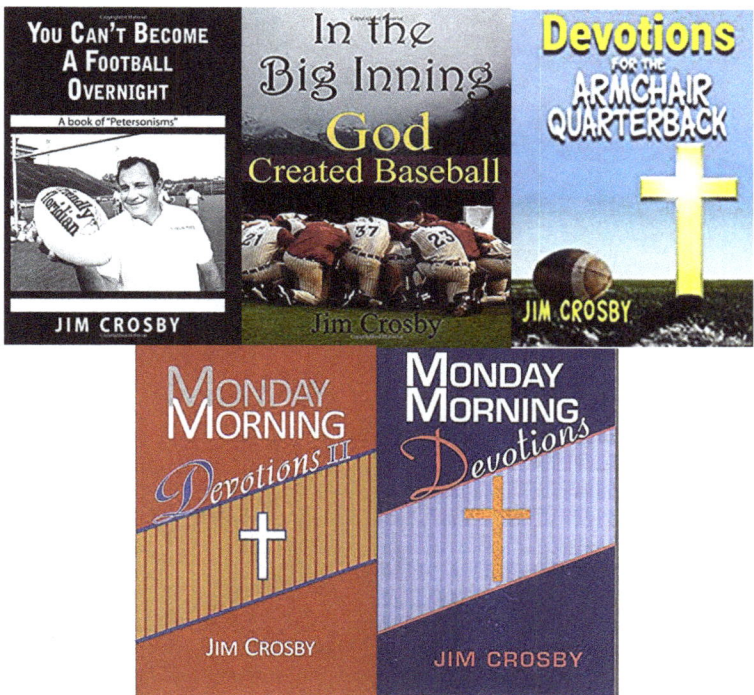

CPSIA information can be obtained
at www.ICGtesting.com
Printed in the USA
LVHW080717090622
720760LV00003B/51